Camarades

turquoise

3

Teacher's Book

Gwen Berwick
with IT opportunities by
Pam Haezewindt

Camarades 3 – Turquoise

Components of course:
Pupil's Book
Teacher's Resource File
Teacher's Book
Cassettes (5)

Edited by Michael Spencer, 50 Whinmoor Crescent, Leeds, LS14 1EW
Typeset by AMR, Stocks Barn, Minchens Lane, Bramley, Hants., RG26 5BH

The authors and publishers would like to thank the following:
Caroline Woods and Steve Crossland for writing the Assessment sections
Pam Haezewindt for writing the IT sections

First published 1997

97 98 99 00 01 / 10 9 8 7 6 5 4 3 2 1

A catalogue record for this book is available from the British Library

ISBN 0 7487 2352 8

Mary Glasgow Publications
An imprint of Stanley Thornes (Publishers) Ltd
Ellenborough House
Wellington Street
CHELTENHAM
GL50 1YW

CONTENTS

Introduction:

    General   3

    Presentation sheets   6

    Assessment   9

    IT opportunities   11

Unité 1   13

Unité 2   31

Epreuve 1   48

Unité 3   52

Unité 4   69

Epreuve 2   87

Unité 5   91

Unité 6   113

Epreuve 3   135

Epreuve Finale   139

INTRODUCTION

Camarades is a four-stage course designed to motivate your pupils and help them to achieve success in learning French.

By stage three, pupils' differing abilities and rates of progression are such that there is a real need to work from different materials. **Camarades 3** has been carefully planned and written at two levels: **Turquoise,** for pupils of middle to higher ability, and **Orange,** for less able pupils.

These two sets of materials, with differing content, scope and approaches, take into account different pupils' abilities and attitudes, in order to meet their needs more effectively. However, the books are structured in close parallel. This ensures that all pupils are given the opportunity to work on every topic and allows for comparisons and movement between sets.

Camarades 3 addresses the following National Curriculum levels (England and Wales):

Turquoise: levels 3–8

Orange: levels 1–5

While **Camarades 3 Turquoise** carries through features and methodology from **Camarades 1** and **2**, it has been written for use by pupils who have begun learning French with any course. It aims to ensure that, by the end of the book, pupils have built up a firm and thorough foundation as a solid grounding for subsequent examination courses. As such, it is also an ideal course for pupils entering at Year 9 from a middle school.

Content and approach

Camarades 3 Turquoise aims to motivate and support pupils as they learn:

- the storyline, following six teenage friends from the same street, engages pupils' interest
- activities are interesting and enjoyable
- the topics, situations and issues dealt with are of interest and relevance to young people
- the course sets realistic goals
- hints and strategies provide support, to ensure that these goals are achieved.

Components

Pupil's Book

- The Pupil's Book contains 6 units, each focusing on one of the six friends.
- Each Spread, or *Objectif,* is self-contained. Most are used to teach and practise new language. Some are devoted to grammar explanation and practice, while others provide reading material.
- The *Atelier* spread at the end of each unit draws together aspects of work from that unit, in the form of a project. Pupils have the opportunity to use the new language creatively, often working in pairs or groups.
- New grammar is taught and practised within the units and is also summarised in a reference section at the back of the book.
- There are French-English/English-French vocabulary lists and a summary of useful classroom language.

Teacher's Resource File

- Photocopiable worksheets provide supplementary material for consolidation and extension.

- Bilingual vocabulary sheets summarise key vocabulary, spread by spread. They can be used in a number of ways. Pupils can copy from them or stick them into their exercise book, whole or cut into sections. They can be used for reference, to help pupils as they work on a spread, or as backup later on. They are valuable in helping pupils to learn and revise vocabulary.

- Differentiated 'single skill' worksheets give practice in listening, speaking, reading and writing at two levels (◆ and ♣).

- The *Que sais-tu?* sheets sample some of the work of the unit, helping you and your pupils to gauge what they have learned.

- Other worksheets provide consolidation of key grammar, revision of work from **Camarades 1** and **2** as well as **Camarades 3**, and grids to support listening activities in the Pupil's Book.

- Four assessment sections are provided for use at intervals throughout the course. See the Assessment Introduction below for more details.

Cassettes

- The five C90 audio cassettes may be copied for use within your school or for pupils' individual work at home. For ease of use, cassettes 1–3 have one unit on each side, while cassettes 4 and 5 accompany the worksheet and assessment material.

- Tapescripts are provided in the Teacher's Book, within the notes for each spread.

Teacher's Book

- As well as outlining the methodology and approach of the course, the Teacher's Book provides one page of detailed teaching notes and suggestions for each teaching spread in the Pupil's Book.

- To help you plan your work, each unit begins with:

  - an overview of the unit content, listing the vocabulary, grammar and strategies covered in each spread;

  - notes and tapescripts for the worksheets;

  - suggestions for ways in which IT can be used to support and enhance the work of the course.

Apart from in the assessment materials, specific National Curriculum levels are not indicated for each activity. NC documents stress that a picture of a pupil's performance should be built up across a range of work, and in a variety of contexts, rather than by assessing individual pieces of work. They underline the importance of the teacher's professional judgement regarding the level at which a pupil is operating. Specific guidelines regarding levels can be found in the Assessment Introduction below.

Methodology

It is a fundamental principle of **Camarades** that real and thorough learning should take place. **Camarades** has been carefully designed and written so that pupils are led and supported through an active learning process, and not left to 'absorb' new language.

- New language is introduced in context, for example through a photo story. Visual material for the OHP is also provided, and additional suggestions are made in the Teacher's Book.

- Pupils go on to work with the language in controlled situations, practising using it correctly and successfully, orally and in writing. Although controlled, this practice always involves thought and focuses on meaning.

- Grammar and structures are explained and practised.

- Thus prepared, pupils move on to productive and open-ended tasks. These challenge pupils to take ownership of the language they have learned, using it imaginatively, or to talk about their own situation and opinions.

Differentiation

Some worksheets and at least one activity per spread are differentiated: activities marked ◆ are more straightforward, while those marked ♣ stretch the more able. Further opportunities for differentiation are suggested in the Teacher's Book. Differentiation is achieved in a variety of ways, as appropriate to the activity: by input, by support, by complexity of task, by length of task and by outcome.

Many pupils will find that, while they are better suited to the ◆ activities in some cases, they can successfully attempt the ♣ activities in others. They should be encouraged to experiment in this way.

Skills and strategies

Stratégie boxes in the Pupil's Book give specific tips and advice, to help pupils develop transferable skills in listening, speaking, reading, writing and use of the dictionary. They thus enhance pupils' autonomy and confidence as language learners and users.

There is also guidance and practice relating to common problems of French pronunciation.

Grammar

Particular attention is paid to thorough teaching and practice of grammar. By the end of the book, pupils will have revised and extended a range of key grammar points, in preparation for beginning an exam course.

Grammaire boxes on the spreads invite pupils to examine grammatical patterns as they arise and direct them to special *Grammaire* spreads, where the point is outlined and practised. The activities are grouped together on one spread for ease of reference and flexibility of use. Pupils can work on them all at once, or one or two at a time, to avoid overload and to give repeated reinforcement. Additional practice is given on Grammar worksheets.

Recycling and revision

Key language from this book and previous stages is deliberately recycled throughout the book. It arises in different contexts, so as to encourage transfer of language from one situation to another.

Revision of specific topics is carried out on two worksheets per unit and in every second unit in the Pupil's Book. Language is re-presented before being practised, so that pupils genuinely have the chance to re-learn it – they are not simply being tested.

Homework

At least one worksheet per unit is completely free-standing and can be used by pupils working alone, either for homework, or in class when the teacher is absent. Many of the activities in the Pupil's Book are also suitable for homework, in particular the *A toi!* activities.

Presentation sheets

A set of Presentation sheets is provided in the Resource File. These can be used to present and practise new language in a number of ways. They can be used as whole sheets or cut up into individual pictures and labels. Here are some suggestions:

- Show the pictures on the OHP and model the pronunciation for pupils to imitate. Then say the words or phrases at random. Pupils have to tell you the number of the picture which corresponds.

- Go on to reverse the above game: you give the number; the pupils say the words. After playing these games together as a class, pupils can go on to play in pairs.

- Play *Répétez si c'est vrai*. Point to a picture and say a word or phrase. Pupils only repeat what you say if it really does apply to the picture indicated.

- Display the pictures, with the words or phrases next to them. Match up four or five wrongly, on purpose. Pupils race to identify the mistakes.

- Having introduced the language, get pupils to come out and match up the words or phrases with the correct pictures.

- Play 'Kim's Game'. Let pupils look at a selection of pictures on the OHP for 30 seconds. They try to memorise them. You turn the projector light off, and pupils have to say or write down as many as they can remember.

- Let pupils look at a selection of pictures on the OHP for 30 seconds. Then turn it off or cover it up and remove one or two pictures. Display the remaining ones again: can pupils identify which are missing?

- Put two or three pictures at a time onto the OHP and hold over them a large sheet of paper in which you have made a small hole. Move the paper around so that parts of the pictures are visible. How quickly can pupils identify them?

- Put the words on the OHP back to front. Can pupils decipher the mirror writing?

- Put two or three pictures on the OHP, superimposed over each other. Pupils have to try to recognise which pictures are shown.

The pictures and words can also be copied onto card or paper and given to pupils to work with in pairs or small groups. For example, they can race to match up the words and pictures, or play snap or pelmanism.

Presentation sheets

Sheet 1 (top): Unit 1 A

1 sortir
2 me coucher
3 choisir mes propres vêtements
4 faire mes devoirs
5 garder mon petit frère
6 ranger ma chambre

Sheet 1 (bottom): Unit 1 C

1 je me réveille
2 je me lève
3 je me lave
4 je me détends
5 je me couche
6 on se dispute

Sheet 2: Unit 1 B

1 je regarde la télé
2 je sors
3 je vais au collège
4 j'écoute de la musique
5 je reste à la maison
6 je mange
7 je vais en ville
8 je fais des promenades
9 avec mes amis
10 avec ma famille
11 seul(e)

Sheet 3: Unit 1 I

1 ma chambre
2 la campagne
3 le parc
4 le club des jeunes
5 l'école
6 le centre commercial
7 le centre-ville
8 le centre sportif
9 le gymnase
10 le cinéma
11 McDonald's

Sheet 4: Unit 1 J

1 une chaîne hi-fi
2 un instrument de musique
3 des posters de mon groupe préféré
4 une plante
5 des fleurs
6 un trophée
7 un jogging
8 des baskets
9 des outils
10 un bloc à dessins
11 une calculatrice
12 des jeux-vidéo

Sheet 5: Unit 2 B

1 j'ai invité mes copains
2 j'ai dansé avec mon petit ami/ma petite amie
3 j'ai bavardé avec tout le monde
4 j'ai mangé des chips
5 j'ai mangé de la pizza
6 j'ai bu du coca
7 j'ai bu du jus de fruit
8 j'ai bu de la limonade
9 j'ai pris des photos
10 j'ai fait le ménage
11 j'ai préparé des sandwichs

Sheet 6: Unit 2 C

1 on a fait du patin à roulettes
   on a été à la patinoire
2 on a été au cinéma
   on a regardé un film
3 on a parlé de sport
4 on a joué aux cartes
5 on a écouté un concert à la radio
6 on a regardé un documentaire à la télé
7 on a été au centre commercial
   smiley face (☺)
   unhappy face (☹)

Sheet 7: Unit 2 I

1 il y a un défilé
2 il y a un feu d'artifice
3 on fait des jeux
4 on se déguise

5 on chante
6 on danse
7 on décore la maison
8 on fait un repas spécial
9 on prépare des plats spéciaux
10 on invite des amis
11 on envoie des cartes à ses amis
12 on offre des cadeaux à sa famille

Sheet 8: Unit 3 C

le bar
le café-bar
la grande salle
les toilettes
les vestiaires
le kiosque des souvenirs
au premier étage
au rez-de-chaussée
au sous-sol

Sheet 9: Unit 3 E

1 l'hôtel de ville
2 le vieux quartier
3 le centre commercial
4 le jardin public
5 le château
6 le port
7 le port de plaisance
8 la cathédrale
9 la place
10 la zone industrielle
11 les rues piétonnes
12 l'église

Sheet 10: Unit 3 F

1 un tabac
2 un parc
3 un hôpital
4 un supermarché / un hypermarché
5 un marché
6 une banque
7 une poste
8 une épicerie
9 une boulangerie-pâtisserie
10 une boucherie
11 une charcuterie
12 une pharmacie

Sheet 11: Unit 3 I (1)

1 faire des promenades
2 faire des randonnées
3 faire des randonnées à cheval
4 faire du vélo tout terrain (VTT)
5 faire des pique-niques
6 faire des barbecues
7 faire de la natation
8 faire de la voile
9 faire du canoë-kayak
10 faire du ski alpin
11 faire du ski de fond
12 faire du patin à glace

Sheet 12 (top): Unit 3 I (2)

1 faire un bonhomme de neige
2 faire une bataille de boules de neige
3 aller à la pêche
4 aller au lac

Sheet 12 (bottom): Unit 3 J

1 il fait beau
2 il fait mauvais
3 il fait chaud
4 il fait froid
5 il fait du soleil
6 il fait du brouillard
7 il fait du vent
8 il pleut
9 il neige

Sheet 13: Unit 4 A

1 Elle vole dans des magasins.
2 Elle fume des cigarettes.
3 Elle boit de l'alcool.
4 Elle est violente.
5 Elle est souvent absente.
6 Elle ne fait pas ses devoirs.
7 Elle quittera l'école sans diplôme.
8 Elle perdra ses amis.
9 Elle aura des problèmes avec la police.
10 Elle aura des problèmes au collège.
11 Elle aura des problèmes aux examens.
12 Elle aura des problèmes de santé.

Sheet 14: Unit 5 A and B (1)

picture of body for labels on Sheet 15 to be stuck on

Sheet 15: Unit 5 A and B (2)

le corps

le bras

l'estomac

le pied

l'œil

la tête

la main

l'oreille

la bouche

la jambe

les dents

J'ai mal à la tête.

J'ai mal à la gorge.

J'ai mal à la main.

J'ai mal à la bouche.

J'ai mal à la jambe.

J'ai mal à l'estomac.

J'ai mal au dos.

J'ai mal au genou.

J'ai mal à l'œil.

J'ai mal aux yeux.

J'ai mal aux dents.

J'ai mal à l'oreille.

J'ai mal aux oreilles.

J'ai mal au bras.

J'ai mal aux bras.

J'ai mal au pied.

J'ai mal aux pieds.

Sheet 16: Unit 5 C (1)

1   le chou

2   le chou-fleur

3   la salade

4   les bananes

5   les orange

6   les pommes

7   les tomates

8   les pommes de terre

9   le pain

10 le riz

11 les pâtes

12 les céréales

Sheet 17: Unit 5 C (2)

1   le bœuf

2   le jambon

3   le poisson

4   le poulet

5   la viande

6   les haricots secs

7   les œufs

8   le beurre

9   le fromage

10 le yaourt

Sheet 18: Unit 5 C (3)

1   les frites

2   les chips

3   les biscuits

4   les bonbons

5   les gâteaux

6   la confiture

7   le coca

8   le jus de fruits

9   la limonade

Sheet 19: Unit 5 G (1)

1   le rugby

2   le cricket

3   le basket

4   le volley

5   le badminton

6   le tennis de table

7   le cyclisme

8   le vélo tout terrain (VTT)

9   le patin à roulettes

10 le patin à glace

11 le karting

12 le skate-board

Sheet 20: Unit 5 G (2)

1   le tir à l'arc

2   le jogging

3   l'aérobic

4   le judo

5   le ski

6   la gymnastique

7   l'athlétisme

8   l'équitation

9   l'escalade

10 la voile

11 la planche à voile

12 la pêche

Sheet 21: Unit 5 I

1   une carte

2   un pique-nique

3   une trousse de secours

4   de l'argent

5   un K-way

6   des lunettes de soleil

7   un appareil-photo

8   un couteau suisse

9   des Kleenex

10 une lampe de poche

Sheet 22: Unit 6 C (1)

1   J'aime me détendre devant la télé.

2   Je fais du théâtre.

3   Je fais de la danse.

4   Je fais de la musique.

5   Je fais de la peinture.

6   Je collectionne les badges.

7   Je collectionne les timbres.

8   Je collectionne les autocollants.

9   J'aime bricoler.

Sheet 23: Unit 6 C (2)

1   Je chante dans une chorale.

2   Je joue dans l'orchestre scolaire.

3   Je suis membre d'un groupe de rock.

4   J'apprends à jouer d'un instrument de musique.

5   J'aime jouer sur mon ordinateur.

6   J'aime écrire des programmes.

7   Je m'intéresse à la nature.

8   Je fais des randonnées.

9   Je ne fais pas grand-chose.

Sheet 24: Unit 6 I

1   Je vais partir en vacances.

2   Je vais rester à la maison.

3   Je vais travailler.

4   Je vais sortir avec mes ami(e)s.

5	Je vais aller à la plage.	8	Je vais faire du camping.	11	Je vais aller au bord de la mer.
6	Je vais aller chez mes cousins.	9	Je vais partir avec ma famille.	12	Je vais aller en colonie de vacances.
7	Je vais faire un stage de voile.	10	Je vais louer une caravane.		

Assessment

Assessment Tests in the four skills of Listening, Reading, Speaking and Writing occur after Units 2, 4 and 6. In addition, there is a Final Assessment test.

All the tests are photocopiable and can be found in the Teacher's Resource File on the following pages:

Epreuve 1 (Units 1–2): pp 107–117
Epreuve 2 (Units 3–4): pp 118–128
Epreuve 3 (Units 5–6): pp 129–138
Epreuve Finale (Units 1–6): pp 139–152

The tests are based on the material covered in the book for the units to which they apply. The final test is based on the material in all six units. Although care has been taken to ensure that vocabulary and grammar arising in the tests closely match material in the units, there are instances when other lexical items may occur. This will almost always concern items that have been covered in **Camarades 1** and **2** and which may not have been specifically revised in **Camarades 3**. It has also been borne in mind that pupils following **Camarades 3** may not have used the preceding two books of the course. The authors have assumed, however, that certain structures and topics (such as numbers, weather, phrases to express likes and dislikes etc.) will have been taught during the first years of language learning whatever the course followed.

Within each test, some tasks are common to both **Camarades 3 Orange** and **Camarades 3 Turquoise**. This will enable comparisons to be made between the progress of individuals in different teaching groups. It will also be a motivating factor to pupils in a lower ability set, following **Camarades 3 Orange**, to know that part of their test is also being taken by those in the more able group following **Camarades 3 Turquoise**. In each test, the exercises gradually become more difficult, within the range of levels targeted. Each test has been written to provide pupils with the opportunity to display characteristics of performance across a range of contexts and through a variety of activities which feature in the National Curriculum level descriptions. There is an element of mixed-skill testing, although in each case only one skill is focused on for the purposes of the assessments. Although there is some variation, the general pattern in the first three assessments is as follows:

- **Camarades 3 Orange**: Four exercises, of which the first two are exclusive to this level and the second two also feature in **Camarades 3 Turquoise**.
- **Camarades 3 Turquoise**: Four exercises, of which the first two are the same as three and four in **Camarades 3 Orange** and the second two are exclusive to this level.

For the Final Assessment, a similar structure of 'overlap' has been used, except that each test has five exercises, of which three are common to both levels.

Levels of Attainment

The tests have been designed to encompass Levels 1 to 5 for **Camarades 3 Orange** and Levels 2 to 6 for **Camarades 3 Turquoise**. The higher levels are not tested until the later assessments. In the Final Assessment for **Camarades 3 Turquoise**, however, the last exercises are designed to give pupils the opportunity to show performance at Levels 7 or 8.

It is important to bear in mind that the tests in the assessments are simply representative of performance at a particular level of attainment. A pupil's overall level for any of the four skills cannot be judged on the basis of a single exercise or indeed on two or three exercises. Each teacher will make judgement on the basis of a number of exercises, tests and observations of each pupil's performance in class and homework throughout the Key Stage. The Assessment Tests can be used along with the other exercises in the book and your own assessments and observations to confirm or reinforce judgements of pupils' levels of attainment.

End of Key Stage 3 Assessment

At some stage towards the end of Year 9, teachers in England and Wales are required to assess and report on each pupil in the four skill areas. Each department will devise its own methods of doing this, but in most cases it is assumed that tests targeting particular levels, such as those produced by SCAA, will be used (though always remembering the caveat explained above of basing level assessments on a range of different tests and observations).

The Final Assessment can of course be used for this purpose. It is recognised, however, that classes may not have finished **Camarades 3** at the stage of the year when level assessment has to be carried out. For this reason, the Final Assessment is based on material up to Unit 6 Spread D only. The tests at the end of Unit 4 (*Epreuve 2*) can, of course, be used for Key Stage 3 assessments, but it must be remembered that these do not represent examples of performance above Level 6. It may be best for a department to select certain items from each of the Assessment Tests in order to formulate the material for Key Stage 3 assessment. Departments will no doubt use several sources for their tests, but it is hoped that the **Camarades 3** Assessment Tests will provide a useful additional source of material.

Points to note

The following points may be worth considering on a departmental basis in order to achieve consistency:

- **Listening:** You will need to decide on the length of timing of the pauses. It may be felt appropriate to lengthen the pauses to allow pupils adequate time in which to write the answers. All spoken material has been recorded twice. Recordings should not be repeated further. As in all skill areas, the rubrics should not be translated into English for the pupils; it is expected that teachers will have familiarised pupils with rubrics of the type used in the tests. Pupils should be taught the importance of paying careful attention to the examples given at the start of each exercise.

- **Dictionaries:** You may or may not allow pupils to use dictionaries. Unless otherwise stated in the Teacher's Notes, it is suggested that pupils have access to dictionaries in Reading and Writing tests and in preparation time for Speaking Tests. It is suggested that dictionaries should **not**, however, be permitted in the Listening Tests.

- **Speaking:** Each department or teacher will need to decide on the most appropriate way to use the Speaking Assessments, e.g. by interviewing individual pupils or observing them working in pairs. With more able pupils, it will be possible to omit tests designed to elicit performance at lower levels. This again may be the desired approach in other skill areas, but do not overlook the motivation provided in allowing pupils to perform with excellence in easy tasks. The Speaking Tests have been devised so that a variety of activities can usefully be tackled whilst allowing the teacher to circulate if necessary. For pupils working in pairs, two activities are given. Preparation time for such tests could be either at home or in class.

- **Timing of the tests:** Although the tests have been designed to take place after particular units of work have been covered the timing can be varied. The time allowed to complete a test is up to each teacher and can be varied.

- **Marking for comprehension:** Unless otherwise stated in the marking schemes (e.g. in some of the Writing Tests at higher levels) pupils' written French should be assessed for communication and not for accuracy. This applies to all skill areas. You should take the standpoint of the 'sympathetic French reader or listener' with no knowledge of English. Where answers in French are required they are not acceptable in English – although there are cases where the use of an English word would be recognisable to a French person because it is a cognate. The marking schemes, however, do give guidance in terms of utterances produced and a system of bonus marks can be used which enables communication/accuracy and the amount of teacher help needed to be assessed. For the more advanced writing exercises, criteria are given to assess pupils' French in bands.

- **Recording the outcomes:** You should judge progress and attainment against the level descriptions and according to the guidelines in the marking schemes. Each department should adopt its own methods for recording progress through the levels for individual pupils. A notional total of 25 marks per test per skill (30 for the Final Assessment) has however been retained, although not referred to directly in the marking schemes. This reflects the equal weightings of the four skills across the tests.

IT Opportunities

Information Technology is another resource for a language teacher to exploit. Its 'appropriate' use is referred to in the National Curriculum for Modern Foreign Languages and there are references made in the opportunities listed in the Programme of Study Part 1. It is intended that IT is used to support, enhance and extend language learning. Language learning can also provide a context in which pupils consolidate and develop their IT competence as well as their language competence. (In each unit, an * beside an IT activity denotes that this is one in which pupils' IT competence is likely to be further consolidated and developed.)

IT opportunities are listed at the beginning of each unit. In this way, a teacher using **Camarades 3** can see at a glance what sort of preparations need to be made, e.g. booking IT rooms, obtaining software etc. There is also a reminder symbol 🖥 in the summary box at the top of the pages of teaching notes for the spreads that have IT opportunities.

The activities

It is intended that the activities listed for each unit of work will either support an existing activity or extend it and, in some cases, extend the opportunities provided by a spread. Some of the activities make use of the cassette recordings for stimulus and the tapescripts for content. The activities are not exhaustive but intended to be 'starters' and teachers will no doubt add more of their own and adapt those suggested. They have been written to make use of existing software in schools: the word-processor, database, multimedia software and, where possible, access to the Internet. Many schools also have a text manipulating program. This is a program which allows text to be written and then manipulated in a variety of ways, e.g. reordering lines of text, filling in gaps, predicting the next word in a sentence and a 'storyboard' option which allows text to be uncovered gradually. Whilst many of the activities suggested are on a small scale, some are more comprehensive and will require planning in some detail and support from the IT co-ordinator.

Pupil entitlement

It is not intended that all activities will be used but that **all** pupils at some time during their work with **Camarades 3** will have the opportunity to use IT to support their learning, to draft and redraft text and to present their work appropriately for a specified audience. Whereas one class might have access to a suite of computers during their work with Unit 1, another might not have access until their work with Unit 3. Some activities lend themselves to the use of a computer in the classroom or use by groups of pupils working more independently. Again, some groups might work on activities in one unit and others in another. Some pupils will have access to a computer at home and use where appropriate should be encouraged. Your school may also have the facility to loan out portable computers to students which could be a useful resource for modern language homework from time to time.

Differentiaton

It is possible to differentiate activities in a number of ways using IT. In some of the activities suggested there is overt differentiation using ♣ and ♦. In others the following can be borne in mind:

- when a text manipulator is used, it is usually possible to preview the text before doing an activity. This may be supportive for some learners but unnecessary for others;

- text files written by the teacher can be of different lengths and difficulty depending on pupils' abilities;

- freer writing and presentation tasks will be open-ended to allow different levels of achievement;

- a sequence of activities on a theme ranging from practice through text manipulation to adapting model files to free writing can enable pupils to develop their skills at their own pace.

Practicalities

In activities listed in each unit, teachers are frequently required to write and save files for pupils to work on. A backup of these files should always be kept in case pupils should overwrite them.

Pupils should be reminded that when they edit a 'teacher file' in any way, they must save it under a different name in order to preserve the master file for others to use.

It is very useful to ensure that French dictionaries are available and consulted when pupils are working with IT, particularly if a French spell checker and thesaurus are unavailable.

A note about the Internet …

There are a wealth of French language resources available on the Internet and there are included a few activities which might be useful to support a unit. A URL is the Internet site address descriptor – the uniform resource locator. It is best to use search tools (engines) to search for sites unless they are already known, and using French language search tools speeds up the search. There are a number of these of which *Nomade, Lokace* and *Yahoo français* are known to be efficient. You can find and save these by typing into any search engine which is cited on your Internet browser.

… and E-mail

Whilst activities using electronic mail are not suggested explicitly for units, many of the themes would provide good subjects for joint curriculum 'projects' where a school has an electronic link with a French-speaking school. For example, in Unit 6 Spread A *Tu as un petit job?*, with its themes of part-time jobs and pocket money, would provide a useful basis for seeking and giving information and making comparisons. Likewise in Unit 5 Spread C with *La santé dans l'assiette*.

Useful address

There are a number of publications addressing different areas of using IT and the Internet in Modern Foreign Languages available from:

National Council for Educational Technology (NCET)
Milburn Hill Road
Science Park, Coventry
CV4 7JJ
Tel: 01203 416994
Fax: 01203 411418

They are also at their Internet web site:
http://www.ncet.org.uk

CAMARADES 3 (TURQUOISE) OVERVIEW – UNITE 1 – MA FAMILLE ET MOI   National Curriculum Areas of Experience: A, B, C

	Topics/objectives	Key language	Grammar	Skills and strategies	PoS coverage
A	**Les disputes en famille** Reasons for arguments with parents	*me coucher tard, pendant, ranger, sortir, garder, choisir; propres, c'est raisonnable, ce n'est pas juste, je peux, ne peux pas, veux, dois, j'aimerais mieux, vêtements, la semaine, petit frère, petite sœur, devoirs*			1 a b h 2 a h 3 d
B	**Famille, amis ou solitude?** Saying what you do alone/ with family/with friends	*souvent, parfois, écouter de la musique, aller au collège, faire des promenades, aller en ville, rester à la maison, manger ensemble, seul, mes amis, sortir, regarder la télé, avec* (and family members)	Present tense: focus on *je, on*	Writing: being careful with verb endings ♣ using useful phrases	1 a f i 2 a m n 3 f g
C	**Une journée typique: calme ou chaos?** Talking about a typical day	*se réveiller, se lever, se laver, se détendre, se coucher, rentrer* (and other reflexives, receptively) time, activities from spread B	Reflexive verbs: focus on singular		1 a c 2 a i k n 3 f
D	**Grammaire**		Present tense (revise -er verbs) Reflexives		3 f c
E	**La bande d'Olivier** Talking about your friends	*sportif(-ve), cool, dingue, marrant(-e), meilleur(-e), vraiment, s'babiller, s'amuser, raconter, blagues, ami, sympa, ensemble*		Dictionary: checking the feminine form of adjectives	1 a c i 2 c 3 d e f
F	**Infos: familles, bandes et tribus** Reading for interest			Dictionary: finding embedded phrases (use of ~); selecting correct meaning for context	1 a g i 2 j 3 d e 4 a
G	**Tu parles avec qui?** Saying who you talk to about different things	*parler, problèmes, ambitions, projets, grands-parents, grand-père, grand-mère, se confier, s'entendre avec, petit ami, sport, école, musique, copain, copine* (and family members)	Known verbs 1st and 3rd person Some negatives	Dictionary: finding reflexive verbs	1 c f i j 2 d n 3 d f
H	**Grammaire**		-ir -re verbs (new) Negatives		1 i 2 b 3 d f g
I	**Mon endroit préféré** Talking about places you like, which are important to you	*centre commercial, centre sportif, centre-ville, club des jeunes, gymnase, bof, ennuyeux, matchs, voir, endroit préféré, chambre, parc, campagne, stade, être seul, regarder, amis, faire, sport*	2nd verb infinitives		1 a c 2 a 3 f
J	**Ta chambre et ta personnalité** Talking about what you have or don't have in your bedroom	*baskets, jogging, chaîne hi-fi, plante, fleur, trophée, jeux vidéo, groupe, calculatrice, bloc à dessins, instrument de musique, outils, CD, cassettes, radio, animal, poster, ballon, raquette, ordinateur, préféré, je n'ai pas de*	*je n'ai pas de* (revised)	Listening: attention to detail (negatives) Speaking: giving an exposé	1 a h 2 a c e 3 a f
K	**Qui t'énerve?** Talking about who gets on your nerves and why	*lire, magazines, aîné, cadet, x m'énerve, devrait, pourrait, prendre, écouter, jouer, s'entendre, vêtements, CD, stylos, ordinateur, juste* (and recycled descriptions from Spread E, family members)	Present tense (3rd person) *lire; prendre*	Pronunciation: softened c and g	1 a h 2 f e 3 g
L	**Atelier** Writing profiles/Finding reasonable solutions to arguments				1 a b i j 2 n o 3 f g

Pupil's Book Introduction

This page introduces the six friends who feature in **Camarades 3**. Read through the profile cards with the class. Then read them in random order, omitting the name in each case. The pupils have to identify the person.

As well as introducing the characters, this revises basic questions.

1 – *Bonjour. Où habites-tu?*
  – *J'habite 13, rue du Paradis, à Rouen.*
  – *Et comment t'appelles-tu?*
  – *Je m'appelle Marc.*
2 – *Quel âge as-tu?*
  – *J'ai 16 ans.*
  – *Et tu habites où?*
  – *J'habite au numéro 4, rue du Paradis.*
3 – *Bonjour. Tu as des frères ou des sœurs?*
  – *Oui, j'ai deux frères, qui s'appellent Lucien et Paul.*
  – *Et tu t'appelles comment?*
  – *Je m'appelle Isabelle.*
4 – *Bonjour. Tu as quel âge?*
  – *J'ai quatorze ans.*
  – *Tu as des frères ou des sœurs?*
  – *Oui, j'ai un demi-frère et une demi-sœur.*
5 – *Qu'est-ce que tu aimes faire?*
  – *J'aime faire du sport. Je joue au volleyball. C'est super! J'aime la musique aussi.*
  – *Est-ce que tu as des frères ou des sœurs?*
  – *Oui, j'ai deux sœurs.*
  – *Elles ont quel âge?*
  – *Alors, Nejma a 18 ans, et Rania a 5 ans.*
6 – *Tu as quel âge?*
  – *Moi, j'ai 14 ans.*
  – *Tu as des frères ou des sœurs?*
  – *Oui, j'ai une sœur, qui a 6 ans.*

  – *Elle s'appelle comment?*
  – *Elle s'appelle Bénédicte. Elle est stupide! J'ai un frère, aussi, il s'appelle Jérémie.*
7 – *Qu'est-ce que tu aimes faire?*
  – *Euh, ça dépend. J'aime regarder la télé. Et parfois, je vais à la pêche.*
  – *Est-ce que tu as des frères ou des sœurs?*
  – *Non, je suis enfant unique.*
8 – *Qu'est-ce que tu aimes faire, le week-end?*
  – *J'aime aller au cinéma. J'adore les films!*
9 – *Et toi, qu'est-ce que tu aimes faire?*
  – *Euh, ça dépend. J'aime écouter de la musique. J'aime aller en ville avec mes copains.*
10 – *Tu as quel âge?*
  – *J'ai 14 ans.*
  – *Qu'est-ce que tu aimes faire? Tu as des passions?*
  – *Oui, j'adore la musique. Je fais de la danse aussi. De la danse moderne. C'est génial!*
11 – *Quel âge as-tu?*
  – *J'ai 14 ans.*
  – *Tu as des frères ou des sœurs?*
  – *Oui. J'ai une sœur, qui s'appelle Julie. Elle a dix-neuf ans.*
12 – *Qu'est-ce que tu aimes faire?*
  – *J'aime regarder les matchs de football et de basketball, et j'aime faire du sport, aussi.*

Unité 1 — Ma famille et moi

Worksheets

Recommended use of the worksheets (in some cases they can be used later, as revision):

Spread	Worksheet	Spread	Worksheet	Spread	Worksheet	Spread	Worksheet
A	7 and 8	D		G	17	J	5 and 6, 12
B	17	E		H	11	K	9 and 10
C	3 and 4, 14, 16, 17	F		I		L	

Feuille 1 and 2 Vocabulaire
These sheets provide a bilingual list of key language, spread by spread.

Feuille 3 On écoute ◆
If you prefer pupils not to write on the sheet, they could draw the clocks in their books and note the letters of the pictures in the correct order.

La chambre de mon frère, Lucien, est à côté de ma chambre. Normalement, pendant la semaine, il se réveille à sept heures.
Moi, je me lève à sept heures et demie, mais Lucien se lève à sept heures et quart – pour choisir ses vêtements! Il est très vaniteux!
Moi, je vais au collège toute seule. Mon frère va au lycée avec ses copines. Il en a beaucoup. Ils y vont normalement à huit heures vingt-cinq.
Après l'école, Lucien va souvent chez un copain ou une copine, et il rentre à six heures moins le quart.

Il fait toujours ses devoirs quand il rentre. Hm!
Moi, je les fais au collège, le matin!
Le soir, il veut sortir avec ses copains, mais il doit
souvent garder notre petit frère, Paul, qui a huit
ans. Il déteste ça, il trouve ça ennuyeux. Mais
parfois, il y a un bon film à huit heures et demie.
Le soir, Lucien se lave encore une fois! Oh là là! Il
passe des heures dans la salle de bains! C'est
ridicule!
Pendant la semaine, Lucien doit se coucher à dix
heures moins le quart, mais il aimerait bien se
coucher plus tard. Normalement, il se dispute avec
nos parents.
Au lit, Lucien aime lire ou écouter de la musique.
Quand il fait ça, ça m'énerve! J'entends la
musique de ma chambre. Ce n'est pas juste!
Souvent, il écoute la musique jusqu'à minuit!

Feuille 4 On écoute ♣

1   *Pierre se réveille normalement à sept heures et*
   quart, et se lève à sept heures et demie. Il prend
   son petit déjeuner et va au collège avec ses
   copains. Les cours commencent à huit heures et
   demie. A midi, il mange des sandwichs. Pierre
   rentre du collège à cinq heures moins le quart.
   Il fait ses devoirs, puis il regarde la télé. Il se
   couche à neuf heures et demie.

2   *Natacha se lève à six heures vingt tous les jours,*
   et va à la piscine. Elle fait de la natation
   pendant une heure. Elle adore ça! Elle
   commence son travail à des heures différentes.
   Ça dépend du travail. Elle se maquille et se
   coiffe pendant une heure! Quand elle travaille,
   Natacha ne prend pas de déjeuner. Si elle ne
   travaille pas, elle aime aller au café, prendre
   une salade et de l'eau minérale. Le soir, elle ne
   sort pas beaucoup. Elle lit des magazines, ou
   elle regarde la télé. Elle se couche à dix heures
   et demie.

3   *En général, Mireille se réveille à sept heures. Elle*
   écoute la radio au lit pendant une demi-heure,
   puis elle se lève. Après le petit déjeuner en
   famille, elle va au collège. A midi, elle mange à
   la cantine du collège. Les cours finissent à seize
   heures trente. Mireille fait ses courses au
   supermarché, puis elle rentre à la maison. Elle
   prépare le dîner. Le soir, elle travaille un peu.
   Parfois, elle sort avec des amis. Ils vont au
   cinéma ou au café. Elle se couche normalement
   à 11 heures et quart.

4   *Antoine se lève très tôt: à quatre heures moins*
   vingt. Il prend très vite son petit déjeuner, puis il
   va au travail. Il y a beaucoup de travail, parce
   que le magasin ouvre à huit heures moins le
   quart. Jeanne, la femme d'Antoine, travaille
   dans le magasin. Après le travail, Antoine se
   détend. Il va au café et prend un sandwich et
   une bière. L'après-midi, Antoine va à la piscine.
   Il aime bien la natation. A cinq heures, il va en
   voiture au collège pour chercher sa fille. Le soir,
   Antoine se couche tôt, à neuf heures moins
   vingt.

5   *François se lève assez tard: vers dix heures*
   moins le quart. Le matin, il lit le journal et
   parfois, il va en ville. A deux heures de l'après-
   midi, il va au café. De deux heures jusqu'à
   onze heures du soir, c'est le chaos! François
   aime son travail, mais c'est souvent le stresse
   quand il y a beaucoup de clients. Il finit son
   travail à onze heures du soir et il rentre à la
   maison. Pour se détendre un peu, il écoute de
   la musique. Il se couche à minuit ou, parfois, à
   une heure du matin.

Feuille 5 On parle ♦

Feuille 6 On parle ♣

Feuille 7 On lit ♦ (free-standing)
Pupils could also say which person is most like them.

Feuille 8 On lit ♣ (free-standing)
Pupils could go on to write their own answer to the question.

Feuille 9 On écrit ♦ (free-standing)

Feuille 10 On écrit ♣ (free-standing)

Feuille 11 Grammaire (free-standing)

Feuille 12 En plus (free-standing)
Pupils could go on to make their own crosswords/ anagrams/*trouve l'intrus* puzzles for their partner.

Feuille 13 Que sais-tu?

1   *Ma meilleur amie s'appelle Thérèse. Elle est*
   vraiment dingue! Elle raconte toujours des
   blagues très marrantes! On s'amuse très bien
   ensemble.

2   *Je vais souvent au stade avec mon frère, Gilles.*
   On regarde des matchs de foot ensemble. Mais
   parfois, il m'énerve un peu. Il veut toujours
   prendre mes vêtements.

3   *Moi, je suis fille unique. J'habite avec mes*
   parents. Ils sont très raisonnables. On ne se
   dispute pas. On sort souvent en famille. Par
   exemple, on fait des promenades, on va au
   cinéma ou au centre sportif. C'est génial.

4   *Moi, je me dispute toujours avec mes parents,*
   parce que j'aimerais me coucher plus tard. En
   plus, ils lisent mes lettres. Ça, ce n'est pas juste!

5   *Mon demi-frère est sympa. Il s'appelle Kévin. Je*
   sors parfois avec lui et ses copains le samedi
   soir. Mais, en général, je sors plus avec mes
   copines. Moi, j'adore le sport et Kévin déteste ça.

6   *J'ai un copain qui s'appelle Louis. Il est très*
   marrant, et on s'amuse assez bien ensemble. Je
   vais au club des jeunes avec lui, et on parle de
   sport ensemble. Mais, parfois, il n'est pas très
   gentil.

7   *J'ai de la chance, parce que je me confie à ma*
   mère. Je peux lui parler de tous mes problèmes
   et mes projets. Ma mère, c'est ma meilleure
   amie!

8   *Moi, mon père m'énerve beaucoup! Il parle*
   toujours du collège, de mes devoirs, de mes
   ambitions. Moi, je ne veux pas parler de ça avec
   lui. Je préfère parler avec des copains de mon
   âge. Mon père ne comprend pas!

Feuille 14 Révision 1: time (free-standing)
Pupils could cut out the table at the top and stick it into their exercise books. For more practice of 'time', pupils draw circles. You say a time, and they draw in the hands of the clock and the relevant numbers. They can also play this in pairs.

Feuille 15 Révision 2: where you live
(free-standing)

Feuille 16 Dictionnaire (free-standing)

Feuille 17 Grille
Support for Spread B Exercise 3; Spread C Exercise 4; Spread G Exercise 3a.

Feuille 18 Réponses
This provides answers for the Unit 1 worksheets.

IT Opportunities

B5 **Spread B Exercise 5**
To help pupils to write their responses, first prepare a description for a text manipulator with line jumbler and storyboard options using a mixture of the activities given in the Pupil's Book plus one or two more. Pupils in pairs then practise putting the sentences of the description back in order and then gradually disclose the text in the storyboard option, predicting the words and phrases. Next they write their own response using the text manipulation exercise as a model. If a word-processor is available, they could transfer into this to draft their response and then, after discussion with a partner, redraft their text for accuracy.

C2 **Spread C Exercise 2**
Word-process the sentences from Exercise 2 and save in a file for pupils to work on. Without their books, pupils listen a second time to the cassette for Exercise 1 and then edit the sentences as required. They check it with the Pupil's Book.

C4/5 **Spread C Exercises 4 and 5**
In order for pupils to practise the questions they would need to conduct an interview about daily routine and to be more familiar with questions ready to listen to the three interviews, write a selection of questions in time order into a text manipulator with line jumbler. The pupils' task is to put the questions in order of the daily routine. This could also be done using a word-processor: write the list of questions out of order and save the file. Pupils must then reorder the questions using 'cut/copy and paste'. This takes the exercise further in that they could later answer each question themselves or interview a partner, make notes and insert the answers after each question. The partner can then check for accuracy.

F1 **Spread F Exercise 1**
If there is access to the Internet, pupils (a small group of pupils, perhaps) could search for a passage in French (using a French search engine) on their favourite animal, print it out and make up some True/False questions or match up phrases for other pupils to do.

G3 **Spread G Exercise 3**
* Using the table drawing facilities on the word-processing package, pupils compose and complete the table in Exercise 3. They print it out and use it to pose questions to a partner and then report back to the class (*Peter parle de l'école avec son frère. Il parle de ... etc.*). The class listen and fill in information on their grids in order to make judgements about results. (Health warning: this type of *sondage* activity is more suitable for classes of small numbers and can pose problems for large classes! Alternatively, pupils could work in groups of six or eight.)

L3 **Spread L Exercise 3**
* This could provide an appropriate activity using a desk top publisher to produce a poster. Pupils plan the profile of a famous person, perhaps using information from magazines such as *Salut!,* according to the parameters set down in the exercise, and design and create a poster, printing out for display.

A Les disputes en famille

pp 2–3

Objectives
Reasons for arguments with parents

Resources
Presentation sheet 1 (top)
Cassette for Exercises 1 and 2

Key language
me coucher tard, pendant, ranger, sortir, garder, choisir, propres, c'est raisonnable, ce n'est pas juste, je peux, ne peux pas, veux, dois, j'aimerais mieux, vêtements, la semaine, petit frère, petite sœur, devoirs

Ways in
Presentation sheet 1 (top) summarises key language. You can use it to present the language before working on the Pupil's Book, and for practice and consolidation during work on the spread.

See page 6 for a number of suggestions for ways of using the Presentation sheets for introducing and practising key language.

The photo stories throughout the book are recorded on the cassette. Play them as pupils follow in their books. Transcripts are not given here, as the recordings are identical to the speech bubbles in the Pupil's Book.

The five other quotes are also recorded on the cassette. Each person is asked the question: *Tu te disputes avec tes parents?*

Answers
1 *Olivier*   2 *Sébastien*   3 *Coralie*
4 *Séverine*   5 *Hamed*   6 *Gaëlle*

After reading the photo story and the quotes, ask pupils whether they agree with Olivier, Hamed and Gaëlle's comments (*«C'est ridicule»; «Ce n'est pas juste!»*).

You could also encourage pupils to work out how to describe other problems, using language they already know, e.g. *je dois aider à la maison.*

Answers
1c 2a 3e 4d 5b 6f

> 1 – *Tu te disputes avec tes parents?*
>   – *Oui, parfois.*
>   – *Pour quelles raisons?*
>   – *Ben, le vendredi soir, je dois garder ma petite sœur. Ce n'est pas juste!*
> 2 – *Tu te disputes avec tes parents?*
>   – *Oui, quand je veux regarder la télé! Mon père dit que je dois faire mes devoirs avant.*
> 3 – *Tu te disputes avec tes parents?*
>   – *Oui, souvent.*
>   – *Pour quelles raisons?*
>   – *Normalement, c'est parce que je veux sortir avec mes copains. Je ne peux pas sortir pendant la semaine. C'est ridicule!*

> 4 – *Moi, ma mère achète mes vêtements. Mais elle choisit des vêtements horribles! C'est ridicule! Je veux acheter mes propres vêtements!*
> 5 – *Moi, je me dispute toujours avec ma mère.*
>   – *Ah bon, à quel sujet?*
>   – *Elle dit toujours que je dois ranger ma chambre. Et je déteste ça!*
> 6 – *Moi, je me dispute toujours avec mes parents.*
>   – *Ah bon, pourquoi?*
>   – *C'est parce que je dois aller au lit à dix heures, même le week-end. Je trouve que ce n'est pas juste. J'aimerais mieux me coucher plus tard!*

♣ Pupils could try to outdo each other as to who has strictest parents, inventing the details, e.g.
A *Je dois ranger ma chambre.*
B *Moi, je dois ranger le salon.*
A *Moi, je ne peux pas …*

Answers
♦ a, c

♣ Pupils have to draw conclusions. Here and elsewhere, encourage pupils to have a go at ♣ level activities. Pupils who usually work on ♦ level tasks should be encouraged to give ♣ activities a try if they can.

♦ Pupils can look at Exercise 1 (1– 6) and *Les situations* in Exercise 3, for models.
♣ Pupils are encouraged to add comments and opinions.

Differentiated extended reading on this topic can be found on *Feuilles* 7 and 8.

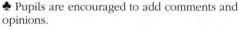

B Famille, amis ou solitude?

pp 4–5

Objectives
Saying what you do alone/with family/with friends

Resources
Presentation sheet 2
Cassette for Exercises 1 and 2

Key language
souvent, parfois, écouter de la musique, aller au collège, faire des promenades, aller en ville, rester à la maison, *manger ensemble, seul, mes amis, sortir, regarder la télé, avec* (and family members)

Grammar
Present tense: focus on *je, on*

Strategies
Writing: being careful with verb endings
♣ using useful phrases

Ways in
Use Presentation sheet 2, cut up, to introduce and practise the key language. Make three different combinations of activities and people with the words, and get a pupil to come out to the front and select the correct pictures. That pupil now does the same thing, and another volunteer comes out to arrange the pictures, and so on. Later, for revision or consolidation, pupils could arrange the pictures and ask their classmates to invent a sentence to match.

1

Answers

Damien; Marie et Paul

2

Answers
1 c (S)   **2** b (A)   **3** d (F)   **4** e (A)   **5** a (S)
6 d (S)   **7** e (F)   **8** c (F)

> 1   – *Tu fais souvent des promenades?*
>   – *Oui, je fais des promenades à la campagne.*
>   – *Avec qui?*
>   – *Normalement, je fais des promenades seule.*
> 2   – *Tu écoutes souvent de la musique?*
>   – *Oui, j'adore la musique. J'écoute des CD dans ma chambre.*
>   – *Avec qui?*
>   – *Ben, avec mes amis.*
> 3   – *Tu manges avec qui, le soir?*
>   – *Normalement, chez moi, on mange en famille.*
> 4   – *Tu vas souvent en ville?*
>   – *Oui. Parfois, je vais en ville avec mes amis.*
> 5   – *Tu regardes la télé avec qui, le soir?*
>   – *Je regarde la télé seule. J'ai ma propre télé dans ma chambre.*
> 6   – *Tu manges avec ta famille, le soir?*
>   – *Non, on ne mange pas ensemble. Normalement, je me fais un sandwich. Je mange seul.*
> 7   – *Tu vas en ville avec qui?*
>   – *Ça dépend. Parfois, je vais en ville avec ma mère et ma demi-sœur. On va dans les magasins de vêtements.*
> 8   – *Tu aimes faire des promenades?*
>   – *Oui, je fais souvent des promenades, j'aime bien ça.*
>   – *Tu fais ça avec qui?*
>   – *En général, avec mon père, mon frère et mon demi-frère.*

During whole-class oral reinforcement work, it would be useful to focus particularly on *je/tu sors/il/elle sort*, since pupils often fail to recognise the verb when it arises in this form rather than the infinitive. For example, ask pupils questions such as: *Tu sors avec qui? Tu sors le samedi soir, normalement? Tu sors à quelle heure?*

The question *Tu manges avec qui?* could lead to interesting cultural comparisons, especially after or in preparation for exchange. Many teenagers in this country eat on their own, at different times from other members of their family, while the French tend to spend longer at the dinner table, eating together as a family.

3

A grid is available for pupils to fill in (*Feuille 17*). As an alternative, you could ask pupils to note in English the actual activities, instead of putting a tick.

As a reminder, get pupils to find in the texts other words for *ami(e)* (i.e. *copain/copine*). Can they say which is which?

You could also ask *vrai/faux* questions, e.g. *Eric sort avec ses amis pendant la semaine?*

Answers

	avec famille	avec ami(s)	seul(e)
Sarah	✔	✔	✔
Agnès	✔	✔	✔
Julien	✔	✔	
Eric	✔		

This would be an appropriate time to look at the Grammar section on page 8, which revises present tense -er verbs.

4

After this activity, pairs could could team up. Each person then talks about their partner to the other pair (using 3rd person verbs).

5

♣ Discuss the phrases your pupils have found, and ensure they know how to use them.

Unité

I

Ma famille et moi

C Une journée typique: calme ou chaos?

pp 6–7

Objectives
Talking about a typical day

Resources
Presentation sheet 1 (bottom)
Cassette for Exercises 1 and 4

Key language
se réveiller, se lever, se laver, se détendre, se coucher, rentrer (and other reflexives, receptively), time, activities from Spread B

Grammar
Reflexive verbs: focus on singular

Ways in
Before starting on this spread, it would be a good idea to work on *Feuille 14*, which revises asking and telling the time.

Use Presentation sheet 1 (bottom) to introduce and practise the key language.

1

In the photo story, Olivier mentions that his lessons finish at midday on Wednesdays. Take this opportunity to remind pupils about this system, which operates in many French schools: pupils go to school on Wednesday and Saturday mornings and have the afternoon of those days off. Point out also that this is becoming less common than it used to be, with many schools favouring a full week-end off.

2

Answers
1 F *Olivier se lève à 7h30.* **2** V **3** V **4** V
5 F *Olivier va au lit à 21h30.*

You could exploit the photo story further in the following ways:
- More *vrai/faux* statements, e.g.
  Le matin, c'est très calme chez Olivier.
  Olivier est plus jeune que sa sœur.
- Read out captions at random, with mistakes. The pupils have to spot and correct them.
- Pupils read out the story in groups: one person is the narrator, and others take the parts.

3

Answers
3a **a** *je me couche* **b** *je me réveille*
  c *je me détends* **d** *je me lave* **e** *je me lève*
3b **b e d c a** or **b e d c d a** or **b e c d a**

This would be a good time to work on the *Grammaire* page on reflexive verbs (page 9).

4

An answer grid is available on *Feuille 17*.

Answers
1 7h15 7h45 8h30 5h00/17h00 7h00/19h00
  10h30/22h30
2 7h30 7h30 8h15 6h00/18h00 7h30/19h30
  11h30/23h30
3 7h45 8h00 8h15 5h00/17h00 6h30/18h30
  9h00/21h00

COUNTER

1 – *Cédric, tu te réveilles à quelle heure, normalement?*
 – *Eh bien, je me réveille à sept heures quinze.*
 – *Et tu te lèves immédiatement?*
 – *Ben … non. Je reste au lit, et j'écoute la radio. Je me lève à sept heures quarante-cinq.*
 – *Je prends mon petit déjeuner, puis je vais au collège.*
 – *A quelle heure?*
 – *A huit heures et demie.*
 – *A quelle heure est-ce que tu rentres du collège?*
 – *Normalement, je rentre à cinq heures et demie.*
 – *Et qu'est-ce que tu fais quand tu rentres?*
 – *Je fais mes devoirs. On mange en famille à sept heures.*
 – *Et le soir?*
 – *Je regarde la télé ou je sors avec des amis. Normalement, je me couche à dix heures et demie.*

2 – *Madame Petit, vous vous réveillez à quelle heure pendant la semaine?*
 – *Normalement, je me réveille à sept heures et demie.*
 – *Et vous vous levez immédiatement?*
 – *Eh oui, je me lève à sept heures et demie. Tout le monde se dispute le matin, chez moi. Tout le monde est en retard. Moi, je me dépêche pour aller au travail.*
 – *Vous allez au travail à quelle heure?*
 – *Normalement, je vais au travail à huit heures et quart.*
 – *Et vous rentrez à la maison à quelle heure?*
 – *Ça dépend. Je rentre souvent à six heures du soir, puis je dois préparer le dîner pour la famille. C'est difficile …*
 – *Vous mangez à quelle heure?*
 – *Nous mangeons à sept heures et demie.*
 – *Et le soir?*
 – *Oh, le soir, je fais du travail, je range le salon …*
 – *Vous ne vous détendez pas?*
 – *Ben, non! Je n'ai pas le temps!*
 – *Vous vous couchez à quelle heure?*
 – *Je me couche à onze heures et demie.*

3 – *Coralie, tu te réveilles à quelle heure, normalement?*
 – *Eh bien, je me réveille à sept heures quarante-cinq.*
 – *Et tu te lèves à quelle heure?*

> – *Je me lève à huit heures.*
> – *Je me lave très vite, je prends mon petit déjeuner, puis je vais au collège.*
> – *A quelle heure?*
> – *A huit heures et quart.*
> – *A huit heures et quart?!*
> – *Oui, je me dépêche pour prendre le bus!*
> – *A quelle heure est-ce que tu rentres du collège?*
> – *Normalement, je rentre à cinq heures.*
> – *Et qu'est-ce que tu fais quand tu rentres?*
> – *Ordinairement, je me dispute avec ma mère, parce que je dois faire mes devoirs!*
> – *Vous mangez à quelle heure, chez vous?*
> – *On mange à six heures et demie.*
> – *Vous mangez ensemble?*
> – *Non!*
> – *Et le soir?*
> – *J'écoute de la musique. Et souvent, je me dispute avec mes parents, parce que je ne peux pas sortir avec mes amies.*
> – *Tu te couches à quelle heure?*
> – *Je me couche à neuf heures. Ce n'est pas juste!*

Brainstorm questions together as a class before pupils go on to use them in pairs.

♣ Pupils are encouraged to use reflexives in the third person.

Feuilles 3 and *4* provide some listening work on this theme.

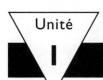
Ma famille et moi

D Grammaire   pp 8–9

Grammar

Le présent (the present tense) (-er)

Les verbes réfléchis (reflexive verbs)

Le présent

The present tense of -er verbs is revised from
Camarades 2. Before looking at this page, encourage
pupils to try to remember the conjugation pattern, or
parts of it, if they can.

The focus on the infinitive form at the start helps to
make clear the link between the -er category and the
conjugated forms. This is particularly important in
dictionary work.

Discuss with your pupils the reason for the extra 'e' in
mangeons (i.e. to soften the 'g'). More work on
softened 'e' and 'g' is done in Spread K.

Remind pupils of the different uses of *on*, which are
summarised in the table. Give examples of sentences
using *on*. Pupils have to say what the most
appropriate English equivalent would be in each case.
E.g.
– Le samedi, je sors avec mes amis. On va au cinéma.
– En France, on mange ensemble, le soir.
– Chez moi, on mange à six heures.
– On va au parc aujourd'hui?
– On parle français à Quebec, au Canada.

Your pupils might also benefit from extra practice in
matching nouns with the correct verb form. Say or
write up some sentences, asking pupils to replace the
person with *il, elle, ils* or *elles*. For example:
Ma mère s'appelle Evelyn.
Mon père s'appelle Donald.
Mes parents habitent à Edimbourg.
Ma sœur a vingt ans.
Mon frère aime le foot.

Point out that this applies to all nouns, not just
people, and include appropriate examples, e.g.
Mon chat est noir.
Ma souris habite dans une cage.
Mes poissons s'appellent Tic et Toc.

2

Answer
1 *regardez*   2 *regardons*   3 *regardes*   4 *regarde*
5 *regarde*   6 *regarde*   7 *regardent*

3

Pupils play the game using the present tense.

Verbes réfléchis

Point out that these verbs often refer to things which
you do to yourself, e.g. wash yourself, enjoy yourself,
dress yourself.

4

Answer
1 *te*   2 *me*   3 *se*   4 *vous*   5 *nous*   6 *se*

5

Pupils write out the full correct sentences.

For extra practice, to highlight the reflexive particle,
pupils could write out the whole conjugation of a
verb on paper. They write the words in large letters,
then cut out rectangles with the individual words.
je   me   lève
tu   te   lèves (etc.)

After shuffling their pieces of paper, they race to lay
them all out as complete phrases. This could be done
as a speed game against a partner.

Pupils could also play the game from Exercise 3, this
time using reflexive verbs.

Ma famille et moi

E La bande d'Olivier   pp 10–11

Objectives
Talking about your friends

Resources
Cassette for Exercises 1 and 4

Key language
sportif(-ve), cool, dingue, marrant(-e), gentil(-le), meilleur(-e), vraiment, s'habiller, s'amuser, raconter, blagues, ami, sympa, ensemble

Strategies
Dictionary: checking the feminine form of adjectives

From this spread onwards, dictionary skills are highlighted in *Stratégie* boxes in the Pupil's Book. In preparation for this, *Feuille 16* reminds pupils of basic principles and provides some practice activities.

Ways in
This spread focuses on character, using adjectives to describe personality, but also verb phrases – what a person does. You may wish to revise physical descriptions here as well. These could then be included in the productive tasks on page 11.

1 Pupils should be able to match up the French and English adjectives, based on the photos and the rest of the descriptions of Olivier's friends.

2 Adjectival endings are revised in more detail in Unit 3.

Your pupils might be able to tell you other adjectives they know, where the feminine form is the same as the masculine (because the masculine already ends in an *-e* or is invariable), e.g. *super, chouette, stupide, marron, calme, moderne.*

3 For further practice of descriptions, pupils write out a list of the characteristics of a friend in order of priority for them, or in two lists: *important/pas important.*

You could also ask them to describe famous people or characters in TV programmes, e.g.
Lennox Lewis est sportif. Il est très cool, aussi …

4a It is best to check pupils' answers to part **a** before they go on to describe the other two pictures in part **b**.

Answers
1 photo c   **2** photo b

4b Before pupils write their descriptions, you could go through the descriptions in part **a** with the class, discussing which phrases could be used and how some of them could be adapted.

4c

Photo A
Marie-Claire est vraiment dingue! Elle fait des choses ridicules! En plus, elle est marrante. Elle raconte toujours des blagues. On s'amuse très bien ensemble.

Photo D
Mon amie Céleste est très, très cool. Elle porte toujours des lunettes de soleil, et elle s'habille en jean noir.

5 As homework, pupils could write the description of someone in the class. You then have to identify the person when you mark the book.

6 As an extra game, pupils could write descriptions of their partner and themself. This could be in the form of a list of adjectives or in complete sentences. You could give individual pupils help with particular words they need. The pupils then compare notes with their partner. Does their description of themself correspond to the way their partner sees them? Are there any surprises?

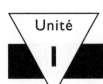

F Infos: familles, bandes et tribus

pp 12–13

Objectives
Reading for interest

Strategies
Dictionary: finding embedded phrases (use of ~);
selecting correct meaning for context

In this unit, pupils use French to talk about their own lives and attitudes. On this spread, the article on gorillas and sea horses gives them the experience of learning about the wider world through the medium of French. Opportunities like this can add a new and motivating dimension to pupils' view of French as a subject.

Encourage pupils to use the dictionary as necessary. However, here and elsewhere in the Pupil's Book, unknown words are listed in the *Vocabulaire* section at the back of the book, in case a dictionary is not available.

1 Answers
1 F   2 V   3 V   4 F

You could exploit the article further in the following ways:
- by asking questions, e.g.
  Est-ce que les gorilles sont violents, en général?
  Que mangent-ils?
  Chez l'hippocampe, qui pond les œufs – le mâle ou la femelle? (You will have to gloss *pond*.)
  Où développent les bébés?
  Il y a combien de bébés, en géneral?
- by asking pupils to find equivalent words or phrases in the articles, e.g.
  un groupe (une tribu)
  en général (normalement)
  père (papa)
  garde (prend soin de)

2 Answers
1 C   2 A   3 D   4 B

As an extra activity, pupils could extract information from this page, handwriting it neatly or word-processing it, and make it into a wall display.

♣ Some of your more able pupils might enjoy carrying out further research for interesting facts (e.g. other animals where the male plays a large rôle), and presenting it in French, orally or in writing.

3

Stratégies: invite pupils to suggest why many dictionaries use the ~ symbol (to save space).

◆ You could give extra help to less able pupils, by listing the topics in English. Pupils say which point in the text deals with each one:
- people with just one special friend;
- people with boyfriends/girlfriends;
- people with at least seven friends in their class;
- people with friends of with a foreign background;
- people who don't have any friends at school.

Before your pupils listen to the tape, get them to go through the list of numbers, saying each one aloud. This helps them prepare to listen and recognise the numbers as they come up on the tape.

COUNTER

Voici les résultats du sondage sur les amis:
43% des adolescents français ont au moins sept amis de classe. (53% à l'âge de 11 ans, contre seulement 29% à l'âge de 18 ans.)
4% des 16–18 ans n'ont aucun ami à l'école.
41% des jeunes français ont au moins une ami d'origine étrangère.
L'ami(e) unique concerne 8% des filles mais seulement 4% des garçons.
1% des collégiens et lycéens forment un couple.

As an extra activity, pupils could design and carry out a similar survey in the class.

G Tu parles avec qui?   pp 14–15

Objectives
Saying who you talk to about different things

Resources
Cassette for Exercises 1 and 2

Key language
parler, problèmes, ambitions, projets, grands-parents, grand-père, grand-mère, se confier, s'entendre avec, petit ami, sport, école, musique, copain, copine (and family members)

Grammar
Opportunities to practise using known verbs
Describing activities in 1st and 3rd person
Some negatives

Strategies
Dictionary: finding reflexive verbs

1

Ways in
Pupils listen to the text and follow it in their book. Can they work out the meaning of *se confier* from the context, and its resemblance to an English word?

Ask further questions on the texts, such as:
Qui est Nic?
Qui est Elsa?
Olivier s'entend bien avec qui?
Olivier se confie avec qui?

Look at the *Stratégie* box together. The class could play a speed game to practise looking up reflexive verbs. Write up reflexive verbs, one at a time, e.g.
je m'excuse
ils se battent
nous nous inquiétons
il s'étonne
vous vous reposez
ça se passe
elles se rapprochent

They race to be the first person to find each one in the dictionary.

If appropriate for your class, you could also highlight and work on *avec elle/lui/eux*.

2

Answers
1f   2f   3g   4g   5f   6g   7f

> **1 Elise**
> *Je parle de mes problèmes avec mon petit ami. Il est très gentil.*
> **2 Sophie**
> *Je parle de sport avec mon père. Nous nous intéressons tous les deux à la gymnastique et au football. On va aux matchs ensemble.*
> **3 Olivier**
> *Je déteste l'école. Je ne parle pas de ça! C'est ennuyeux!*
> **4 Sébastien**
> *Je parle de mes problèmes avec mon grand-père. Il est vraiment sympa. Il m'écoute, mais il n'est pas trop strict. Je m'entends bien avec lui.*
> **5 Catherine**
> *Je ne parle pas de mes ambitions. Pour moi, mes ambitions sont personnelles.*

> **6 Jean-Luc**
> *Je parle de musique avec mes copains. On va aux concerts ensemble.*
> **7 Sara**
> *Normalement, je discute de mes projets avec ma meilleure amie, parce que nous sortons ensemble, le week-end.*

3

The grid shown in the Pupil's Book is reproduced on *Feuille 17*.

Pupils could also present the information in the form of bar charts, using computer database software, if available. If a session in the IT room is planned, you could use it to work with other information as well, for example favourite places (Spread I).

4

The text and sentences 1–8 contain some key vocabulary and phrases which pupils can re-use.

Answers
1 *parents*   2 *Nadia*   3 *Nadia/sa meilleure amie*
4 *assez bien*   5 *deux*   6 *chiens*   7 *sport*   8 *tennis*

For more speaking practice, pupils could work in pairs. A makes a statement and B has to guess whether it is true or false. They continue in this way, swapping roles.

A *Je parle de l'école avec mon amie.*
B *C'est vrai.*
A *Oui.*
B *Je parle de musique avec mes parents.*
A *C'est vrai.*
B *Non, c'est faux!*

5

As preparation for writing, you could go back to the letters in Exercise 4 and help pupils to pick out useful phrases which they could adapt and use.

Ma famille et moi

H Grammaire

Grammar

Present tense (-ir, -re verbs)

Negatives

-ir -re verbs

In Spead D, pupils revised the present tense paradigm of regular -er verbs. Here, we focus on the paradigms of regular -ir and -re verbs. The number of -ir and -re verbs which pupils have met or are likely to need at this level is fairly limited, but the patterns are taught here, to provide complete coverage of the present tense.

1

As well as introducing verbs, this activity is designed to help pupils to develop their awareness of the relationship between the conjugated verb and the infinitive, and the fact that it is the latter that you look up in the dictionary. Point out the noun *les cours* in the first sentence, and ask the class which part of the pattern it corresponds to (i.e. *ils*).

More practice of looking up verbs in the dictionary is given later, on *Feuilles 7* and *8* in Unit 2 (in which verbs are found in the present and perfect tenses).

2

The first section focuses on the singular part of the paradigm. The second part (♣) covers the plural and brings in -er verbs as well.

Negatives

One aim of this book is to ensure that pupils have a firm grounding in basic grammar before moving on to an examination course. Negatives are revised here, as part of that programme. Consolidation of the simple negative form in this unit prepares pupils to move on to other negative forms in Unit 3: *ne … rien/jamais/ personne.*

3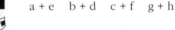

Answers
a + e   b + d   c + f   g + h

4

In this activity, pupils simply have to insert *ne* and *pas* in the correct position. With less able pupils, it would be a good idea to go over the answers before they move on to Exercise 5.

5

In this activity, pupils have to manipulate the verbs as well as making negative statements.

Feuille 11 has more activities practising verbs in the present tense. Exercise 1 focuses specifically on the verb *sortir.*

In Exercise 2, pupils could copy out the verbs with possible subjects before filling in the blanks, e.g.
vous regardez
je/il/elle/on attend

In Exercise 3, pupils practise using a variety of verbs across the whole paradigm.

Ma famille et moi

1 Mon endroit préféré

pp 18–19

Objectives
Talking about places you like, which are important to you

Resources
Presentation sheet 3
Cassette for Exercises 1 and 2

Key language
centre commercial, centre sportif, centre-ville, club des jeunes, gymnase, bof, ennuyeux, matchs, voir, endroit préféré, chambre, parc, campagne, stade, cinéma, piscine, génial, pouvoir, se détendre, être seul, regarder, amis, faire, sport

Grammar
2nd verb infinitives

Ways in
You can introduce and practise places using Presentation sheet 3. Alternatively, your pupils could try matching up the new vocabulary by a process of eliminating known words.

Go through the reasons for Olivier's choice with the class. You can clarify some unfamiliar phrases by means of explanation *(faire les magasins – aller dans les magasins)* and mime *(faire de la musculation).*

You can work the key language further. Pupils close their books. You give a reason *(Là, je peux me détendre* or *Là, il peut se détendre)* and pupils have to identify the place from memory. This can be reversed, with you giving the place and the pupils providing the reason, again in the first or third person.

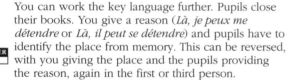

1 – *Quel est ton endroit préféré?*
– *Mon endroit préféré, c'est le centre-ville.*
– *Le centre-ville? Pourquoi?*
– *Parce que là, je peux voir mes amis, et aller chez McDonald's. C'est bien. J'aime aussi ma chambre.*
– *Pourquoi?*
– *Parce que c'est là que je peux être seule. Je peux écouter de la musique ou lire des magazines.*
2 – *Quel est ton endroit préféré?*
– *Mon endroit préféré, c'est le parc.*
– *Pourquoi?*
– *Parce que c'est là que je peux voir mes copains. Je peux jouer au football avec eux. J'aime aussi le centre sportif.*
– *Tu aimes le sport, alors?*
– *Oui, j'aime faire du sport au centre sportif, jouer au badminton ou au squash. J'aime regarder les matchs aussi.*
3 – *Et toi, quel est ton endroit préféré?*
– *Eh bien, moi, mon endroit préféré, c'est ma chambre.*
– *Ta chambre? Pourquoi?*
– *Parce que c'est l'endroit où je peux me détendre. Parfois, j'aime être seule. J'aime aussi l'école.*
– *L'école? Tu blagues?!*
– *Non, c'est vrai! J'aime l'école parce que c'est là que je peux voir mes amis. A midi et à la récréation, on parle ensemble.*
– *Et en classe, aussi!*
– *Ben, oui.*

4 – *Quel est ton endroit préféré?*
– *Mon endroit préféré, c'est le club des jeunes.*
– *Ah bon? Pourquoi?*
– *Parce que là, je peux me détendre, voir mes amis … c'est génial. J'aime aussi le centre-ville.*
– *Pourquoi?*
– *Car je vois mes amis au centre-ville aussi. On va au centre commercial. C'est bien. Il y a un McDonald's.*
5 – *Quel est ton endroit préféré?*
– *Ça dépend. Parfois, c'est le centre-ville.*
– *Pourquoi?*
– *Parce que c'est là que je vois mes amis. On va au cinéma, au café, et au centre commercial. C'est cool. Parfois, mon endroit préféré, c'est la campagne.*
– *Tu aimes la campagne?*
– *Oui, je peux me détendre à la campagne. J'aime faire des promenades, seule ou avec une copine.*
6 – *Quel est ton endroit préféré?*
– *Ça, c'est facile. C'est le gymnase.*
– *Tu vas souvent au gymnase?*
– *Oui. Je fais de la musculation une fois par semaine. C'est cool! En plus, c'est là que je peux voir mes copains. J'aime aussi aller au café.*
– *Au café?*
– *Oui, je peux me détendre au café. Je peux boire un coca avec mes copains. On se raconte des blagues. C'est génial.*

♣ Pupils could add a reason to each exchange, e.g.
B *Pourquoi?*
A *Parce que c'est calme./Parce que j'aime faire des promenades.*

Answers
1 *Jean-Paul, Claude* 2 *Lola, Luc* 3 *Serge*
4 *Véronique*

♣ Pupils could write more questions, for their partner to answer, e.g.
Qui aime les films? Qui aime regarder le sport? Qui aime faire la cuisine?

This exercise acts as a preparation for Exercise 6.

Help pupils individually as necessary, giving them the words and phrases they need to talk about places which are special to them and to give their reasons.

J Ta chambre et ta personnalité pp 20–21

Objectives
Talking about what you have or don't have in your
bedroom

Resources
Presentation sheet 4
Cassette for Exercises 1 and 4

Key language
baskets, jogging, chaîne hi-fi, plante, fleur, trophée, jeux

*vidéo, groupe, calculatrice, bloc à dessins, instrument de
musique, outils, CD, cassettes, radio, animal, poster, ballon,
raquette, ordinateur, préféré, je n'ai pas de*

Grammar
je n'ai pas de

Strategies
Listening: attention to detail (negatives)
Speaking: giving an exposé

Ways in
The items found in the rooms on page 20 are
reproduced on Presentation sheet 4.

1

This provides a good opportunity to revise the
alphabet in French. You say items from the rooms; the
pupils have to say the corresponding letter in French.
They could also do this in pairs.

Answers
1 a   **2** f h   **3** k l m n   **4** o q   *Il est 'techno'.*

COUNTER

1 – *La première chambre: 'fana de sport'.*
 – *Tu as des baskets dans ta chambre, Eric?*
 – *Oui, j'ai des baskets.*
 – *Tu as un ballon et des raquettes?*
 – *Non, je n'ai pas de ballon, ni de raquette. Et
je n'ai pas de jogging, non plus.*
 – *Tu as des trophées?*
 – *Tu blagues?! Non, je n'ai pas de trophées. Je
suis nul en sport! Et je n'ai pas de poster
d'équipes de foot. Je déteste le foot.*
2 – *Et maintenant, la deuxième chambre:
'passionné de musique'. Tu as une chaîne
hi-fi, n'est-ce pas, Eric?*
 – *Oui, j'ai une chaîne hi-fi.*
 – *Mais tu n'as pas d'instrument de musique …*
 – *Non, c'est vrai, Je n'ai pas d'instrument de
musique.*
 – *Mais tu as des CD et des cassettes?*
 – *Oui, bien sûr.*
 – *Est-ce que tu as une radio dans ta chambre?*
 – *Non. Je n'écoute pas la radio.*
 – *Et des posters …?*
 – *Ben non, je n'ai pas de posters de mon
groupe préféré. Ça, c'est pour les filles!*
3 – *Eh bien, la troisième chambre: la chambre
'techno'. Tu as un ordinateur?*
 – *Oui, j'ai un ordinateur.*
 – *Et des jeux-vidéo?*
 – *Ben oui. J'adore jouer aux jeux-vidéo.*
 – *Est-ce que tu as une calculatrice?*
 – *Oui, j'ai une calculatrice pour les maths.*
 – *Et des outils?*
 – *Oui, j'ai des outils, aussi. J'aime réparer les
vieilles radios.*
4 – *Bon, alors, la quatrième chambre:
'passionné de nature'. Tu as un animal
dans ta chambre?*
 – *Euh, oui. Le chat dort souvent sur mon lit.*
 – *Tu as des posters d'animaux?*

 – *Ça non! Je n'aime pas les posters d'animaux!*
 – *Est-ce que tu as des plantes?*
 – *Oui, j'ai des plantes. J'ai trois cactus.*
 – *Et des fleurs?*
 – *Non, je n'ai pas de fleurs.*
 – *Finalement, est-ce que tu as un bloc à
dessins?*
 – *Non. Je n'ai pas de bloc à dessins. Je ne sais
pas dessiner. Je suis nul!*

2

This activity is designed to reinforce the key
vocabulary. By copying it in personalised lists, pupils
are forced to think about the meanings of the words
they write.

The grammar box reminds pupils of the construction
pas de.

3

Pupils could go on to brainstorm ideas for other room
types, and write up list of items to be found in typical
rooms. This could be done as an extension of the
magazine article on page 20. You could give them
ideas to start them off, such as:
Tu adores voyager.
Tu es créatif(ve).
Tu es intello.
Tu es passionné(e) de cinéma.
Tu es fana des sciences.

Pupils might also like to imagine the rooms of famous
people. They could write descriptions of the rooms in
groups, then stick them up round the classroom.
Provide pupils with a complete list of all the people:
can they match them up with the correct rooms?

4a

As preparation, revise with the class all the things they
know how to say, regarding what they do in their
bedroom, e.g. watch TV, listen to music, do their
homework. Focus also on the activities mentioned in
the article. As well as oral practice, you will need to
focus on the first person endings in the written form
(there is a reminder to pupils in the book to do that
when writing their notes).

4b

Answer
Elle est passionnée de musique.

> *J'aime bien ma chambre. J'ai une télé et une radio. J'ai une chaîne hi-fi et beaucoup de CD et de cassettes.*
> *Je regarde la télé dans ma chambre, et j'écoute de la musique.*
> *J'ai aussi un hamster dans une cage, et un aquarium avec des poissons tropicaux.*
> *Aux murs, j'ai des posters de mon chanteur préféré, Michael Jackson, et de mon groupe préféré, Les Négresses Vertes.*

 4c

If possible, pupils could record their presentations on tape.

They could also do a written piece as a follow-up, for example a wall display, with photos or drawings of their rooms.

Feuilles 5 and *6* provide more speaking practice on this topic.

Feuille 12 has further practice of the key language from Spreads I and J.

Ma famille et moi

K Qui t'énerve?   pp 22–23

Objectives
Talking about who gets on your nerves and why

Resources
Cassette for Exercises 1, 2 and *Prononciation*

Key language
lire, magazines, aîné, cadet, x m'énerve, devrait, pourrait, prendre, écouter, jouer, s'entendre, vêtements, CD, stylos, *ordinateur, juste* (and recycled descriptions from Spread E, family members)

Grammar
Present tense 3rd person
lire; prendre

Strategies
Pronunciation: softened c and g

Ways in

1 Read and listen to the photo story. Practise *frère/sœur aîné(e)/cadet(te)* by asking questions round the class. Pupils could then interview each other in pairs and report back.

COUNTER You can encourage pupils to use a broader range of language to explain why some people annoy them, either drawing on language they know or using new expressions. *Il prend* can be used with various items, e.g. *mon vélo, mes cassettes, mes jeux-vidéo …*

2 ♣ Pupils can note the general reason or give more details, if they are able.

> **1** – *Aujourd'hui, nous posons la question: Qui t'énerve? Pour commencer, nous avons en ligne Myrtille. Allô, Myrtille?*
> – *Bonjour.*
> – *Alors, Myrtille, qui t'énerve le plus?*
> – *C'est ma sœur cadette qui m'énerve.*
> – *Ta sœur cadette. Et pourquoi?*
> – *Eh bien, parce qu'elle prend toujours mes vêtements.*
> – *Et est-ce qu'elle te demande la permission?*
> – *Non, jamais. Ça m'énerve!*
> – *Merci, Myrtille.*
> **2** – *Allô. Je t'écoute.*
> – *Bonjour, je m'appelle François.*
> – *Bonjour, François. Alors qui t'énerve le plus?*
> – *Mes parents m'énervent beaucoup. Ils lisent mes lettres.*
> – *Alors ça, ce n'est pas juste! Les lettres sont privées!*
> – *Oui, et en plus, je ne peux pas sortir le week-end avec mes copains. Ce n'est pas juste!*
> – *Eh bien, François, je te conseille de parler avec tes parents. Au revoir.*
> – *Au revoir.*
> **3** – *Bonjour. Tu t'appelles comment?*
> – *Je m'appelle Violaine.*
> – *Et qui t'énerve le plus, Violaine?*
> – *Mon frère aîné m'énerve beaucoup.*
> – *Pourquoi?*
> – *Eh bien parce qu'il entre dans ma chambre sans ma permission. Il écoute ma chaîne hi-fi.*
> – *Il n'a pas de chaîne hi-fi, ton frère?*
> – *Non, il a un ordinateur. Mais moi, je ne peux pas jouer sur son ordinateur. Ce n'est pas juste!*
> – *Non, c'est vrai. Eh bien, merci, Violaine.*

> **4** – *Allô. Je t'écoute.*
> – *Bonjour, je m'appelle Marc.*
> – *Alors, qui t'énerve le plus, Marc?*
> – *Eh bien … au collège mes copains m'énervent beaucoup.*
> – *Ah oui? Comment?*
> – *Quand on fait du sport, ils prennent mes baskets et mon jogging.*
> – *Ils prennent tes vêtements?*
> – *Oui, ils pensent que c'est marrant. Mais moi, j'ai toujours des problèmes avec le prof, parce que je n'ai pas de baskets.*
> – *Ah là là … les copains!*
> **5** – *Bonjour. Tu t'appelles comment?*
> – *Je m'appelle Séverine.*
> – *Il y a quelqu'un qui t'énerve, Séverine?*
> – *Oui, mon frère cadet. Il m'énerve beaucoup.*
> – *Ton frère cadet? Mais qu'est-ce qu'il fait?*
> – *Et ben, il prend toujours mes crayons et mes stylos. Quand j'arrive au collège, je trouve toujours que je n'ai pas de stylos dans ma trousse. C'est vraiment embêtant!*
> – *Oui, ça doit être embêtant! Merci, Séverine, et merci à tous!*

3 For more practice, pupils could play the game outlined in Exercise 3, Spread D.

4 Do plenty of oral practice round the class before pupils split into pairs. Pupils could give reactions to problems mentioned, e.g. *Ce n'est pas juste!/Bof …*

Help them with the vocabulary they need to say other things that people borrow (or other annoying things they do).

More writing practice on this theme is found on *Feuilles 9* and *10*.

Prononciation

A Part A highlights the power of knowledge! Pupils can now apply the pattern to new words: they can work out the pronunciation for themselves without being told. (Most of the words given here occur later in the unit, so pupils will see the benefits very soon!)

The tapescript is not reproduced here, as it is the same as the text in the Pupil's Book.

Answer
1b   **2**c   **3**a   **4**a

L **Atelier**   **pp 24–25**

Objectives
Writing profiles
Finding reasonable solutions to arguments

Resources
Cassette for Exercises 4 and 5

1

Pupils sum up the character and situation of Olivier, drawing together different strands of the unit.

This exercise provides input and a model for productive work in Exercise 3.

2

Here, pupils are invited to reflect on Olivier's character and situation and compare it with their own. There is scope for more able pupils to draw on much of the key language of the unit and use it productively.

3

Pupils can either choose a real person, invent a character, or choose a character from a film or TV programme – get pupils to suggest a few names. You could discuss some of the people together as a class before pupils go on to work in groups.

You could encourage pupils to take this further. It would be an ideal opportunity, for example, to revise physical characteristics, pets and hobbies.

Pupils could work on computer, first drafting their work, then redrafting it for accuracy. If possible, they could also use a photo of the famous person from a magazine.

An alternative would be to make the exercise a guessing game, separating the descriptions from the names of the people. You could then pin up the profiles round the classroom and provide the pupils with a list of names – they have to match them up with the correct profiles.

4

This exercise takes us back to the conflict which opened the unit.

The tapescripts in Exercises 4 and 5 are identical to the texts in the book.

COUNTER

5

♣ Some more able pupils could really have fun with this, inventing various scenarios for different problematic situations. Give them support in this, providing language as necessary. They could act out their scenarios in front of the rest of the class, who have to say whether the teenagers and their parents are behaving reasonably or not.

6

Discuss with pupils how they can go about memorising the scenarios for part **a**. For example, they could cover up some of the words with a pencil or rubber, before attempting to do the whole thing from memory.

CAMARADES 3 (TURQUOISE) OVERVIEW – UNITE 2 – LES FÊTES   National Curriculum Areas of Experience: A, B, C

	Topics/objectives	Key language	Grammar	Skills and strategies	PoS coverage
A	**L'anniversaire** Greetings; talking about presents	*bon anniversaire, c'est pour toi, bon appétit, santé, reçu, de l'argent, produits de beauté, voici, merci, gentil, beaucoup, CD, poster, livre, vêtements* (and family members and friends)	*son, sa, ses*	Pronunciation: *-en, -em, -an, -am*	1 c h 2 f k l 3 f g 4 c e
B	**C'était bien, la soirée?** Describing a party	*fait, mangé, bu, dansé, eu, bavardé, invité, pris, fini, parlé, perdu, préparé, pizza, coca, c'était, génial, nul*	Perfect tense (*avoir*)	Writing: beginning and ending a letter	1 d h i j 2 g j n 3 d e f 4 e
C	**Une journée avec Kévin** Describing a day out and giving your opinions	*patin à roulettes, vu, regardé, écouté, joué, cartes, concert, passé, film, été, mangé, bu, fait, c'était, super, ennuyeux, marrant, intéressant, bête, nul* (and verbs from previous spreads)	Perfect tense (*on*)	Learning vocabulary	1 a d 2 d i 3 b c
D	**Grammaire**		Perfect tense (*avoir*): -er and irregulars (revision); -ir, -re (new)		1 j 2 n 3 f
E	**Infos et jeux** Reading for interest				1 c g i 2 a 4 a c
F	**Une glace à la vanille, s'il vous plaît** Buying ice-cream and drinks from a kiosque	*esquimau, glace, boule, fraise, chocolat, vanille, banane, citron, framboise, cassis, café, coca, limonade, c'est, tout, ça fait, combien* (and prices)	Revise *au, à la*	Listening: anticipate what you're going to hear	1 a b 2 a g
G	**Une visite scolaire** Describing a school day trip	*je suis allé, sorti, rentré, resté, arrivé, venu, parti, chanté, raconté, acheté, musée, visite guidée, souvenirs, glace* (and verbs + opinions from previous spreads)	Perfect tense (*être*)	Writing article: draft, check, redraft	1 c d j 2 i n 3 f h
H	**Grammaire**		Perfect tense (*être*) Possessives		1 b 2 n 3 c f
I	**Des fêtes différentes** Describing festivals (input + manipulation)	*Nouvel An, carnaval, fête, feu d'artifice, défilé, se déguiser, repas spécial, s'offrir des cadeaux, chanter, jeux, repas, décorer, danser, boire, soirée, maison, il y a*		Reading: guessing cognates Dictionary: using information in the dictionary entry to select correct meaning	1 c g i 2 j l 3 d e g 4 c d
J	**Un exposé sur une fête** Describing a special occasion (productive)/Recipe for *crêpes*	*rendre visite à* (and as Spread I)		Speaking: planning an exposé; asking the teacher for help Dictionary: looking up the correct word (part of speech, context); using the French grammar correctly (applying grammar)	1 b g i j 2 b c n 3 d e g
K	**Atelier** Organising a special event				1 a j 2 e g i l n 3 g
L	**Révision** Talking about yourself and your family: appearance and character Describing a typical day				1 a c j 2 a i n

Worksheets

Recommended use of the worksheets (in some cases they can be used later, as revision):

Spread	Worksheet	Spread	Worksheet	Spread	Worksheet	Spread	Worksheet
A	.... 5, 6, 12, 17	D		G		J	.... 9 and 10
B		E	 12	H	 11	K	
C		F		I	.... 3 and 4, 7 and 8, 17	L	

Feuille 1 ♦ and 2 ♣ Vocabulaire

Feuille 3 and Feuille 4 On écoute (Exercice 1b)

Mon beau sapin
Mon beau sapin, roi des forêts,
Que j'aime ta verdure!
Mon beau sapin, roi des forêts,
Que j'aime ta verdure!
Quand par l'hiver, bois et guérets
Sont dépouillés de leurs attraits
Mon beau sapin, roi des forêts,
Tu gardes ta parure!

Toi que Noël planta chez nous
Au saint anniversaire,
Toi que Noël planta chez nous
Au saint anniversaire,
Joli sapin comme ils sont doux
Et tes bonbons et tes joujoux.
Toi que Noël planta chez nous
Par les mains de ma mère.

Feuille 5 On parle ♦ (Exercice 1a)
Pupils could also make their own cards.

1 – *Vendredi enfin!*
 – *Tu rentres chez toi?*
 – *Oui, j'ai fini. Je suis vraiment fatiguée!*
 – *Qu'est-ce que tu fais ce week-end?*
 – *Samedi, je vais en ville, et dimanche, je vais chez mes parents, avec mes enfants. Et toi?*
 – *Moi, je vais passer le week-end à la campagne.*
 – *Génial! Allez, au revoir, et bon week-end!*
 – *Bon week-end!*
2 – *Il est quelle heure?*
 – *Il est onze heures et quart.*
 – *Je suis vraiment fatiguée. En plus, il n'y a rien à la télé. Je vais me coucher. Et toi?*
 – *Moi non. Je vais regarder un film.*
 – *Je vais au lit. Bonne nuit!*
 – *Bonne nuit. Dors bien.*
3 – *Joyeux Noël, Henri. Voici ton cadeau.*
 – *Oh, un CD de Khaled! Super! Merci beaucoup.*
 – *Et toi, qu'est-ce que tu m'as acheté?*
 – *Voilà.*
 – *Un poster de Roc Voisine! Merci, Henri!*
4 – *C'est quand, ton examen, Mireille?*
 – *Mon examen? C'est demain!*
 – *C'est à quelle heure?*

 – *A quinze heures.*
 – *Tu es nerveuse?*
 – *Oui, un peu.*
 – *Oh, ça ira sans problème.*
 – *Je vais réviser ce soir.*
 – *Allez, bonne chance.*
 – *Merci, Sandrine.*
5 – *A table, tout le monde. Le dîner est prêt.*
 – *Mmm! Ça sent bon.*
 – *Bon appétit.*
 – *Maman, je n'aime pas la soupe à l'oignon …*
 – *Mais si, tu l'aimes. Prends un peu.*
6 – *Quelle heure est-il?*
 – *Il est presque minuit – minuit moins dix.*
 – *Allez vite – ouvre la bouteille de champage!*
 – *Voilà, pour toi … et pour toi.*
 – *Merci.*
 – *Bonne année, tout le monde!*
 – *Bonne année!*
7 – *Tiens, Mireille, bonjour!*
 – *Bonjour!*
 – *Qu'est-ce que tu achètes, là?*
 – *Des lunettes de soleil, un maillot de bain, de la crème solaire. C'est pour mes vacances.*
 – *Tu vas où?*
 – *Je vais au bord de la mer.*
 – *Tu pars quand?*
 – *Samedi.*
 – *Super! Allez, au revoir, et bonnes vacances.*
 – *Merci.*
8 – *Bon anniversaire, Henri.*
 – *Bon anniversaire.*
 – *Merci.*
 – *Tu prends un peu de gâteau?*
 – *Oui, s'il te plaît.*
 – *Voici ton cadeau.*
 – *Qu'est-ce que c'est?*
 – *Ouvre-le!*
 – *Un T-shirt – chouette!*

Feuille 6 On parle ♣

1 – *Vendredi enfin!*
 – *Tu rentres chez toi?*
 – *Oui, j'ai fini. Je suis vraiment fatiguée!*
 – *Qu'est-ce que tu fais ce week-end?*
 – *Samedi, je vais en ville, et dimanche, je vais chez mes parents, avec mes enfants. Et toi?*
 – *Moi, je vais passer le week-end à la campagne.*

– *Génial! Allez, au revoir, et bon week-end!*
– *Bon week-end!*

2 – *Il est quelle heure?*
– *Il est onze heures et quart.*
– *Je suis vraiment fatiguée. En plus, il n'y a rien à la télé. Je vais me coucher. Et toi?*
– *Moi non. Je vais regarder un film.*
– *Je vais au lit. Bonne nuit!*
– *Bonne nuit. Dors bien.*

3 – *Alors, Maman, tu as tous les bagages?*
– *Oui, j'ai tout.*
– *Vous arrivez demain à quelle heure?*
– *Nous arrivons demain, vers midi. Je vais vous téléphoner.*
– *Alors, bon voyage!*
– *Au revoir!*
– *Au revoir!*
– *Au revoir, et bonne route!*

4 – *C'est quand, ton examen, Mireille?*
– *Mon examen? C'est demain!*
– *C'est à quelle heure?*
– *A quinze heures.*
– *Tu es nerveuse?*
– *Oui, un peu.*
– *Oh, ça ira sans problème.*
– *Je vais réviser ce soir.*
– *Allez, bonne chance.*
– *Merci, Sandrine.*
– *Bon courage.*
– *Merci.*

5 – *Voilà la clé de notre chambre.*
– *Merci. Alors, vous rentrez chez vous ce matin?*
– *Oui, c'est ça. Mais je voudrais revenir passer mes vacances ici l'année prochaine.*
– *Ça y est, la voiture est prête.*
– *Allez, au revoir, et bon retour chez vous.*
– *Merci. Au revoir.*

6 – *Quelle heure est-il?*
– *Il est presque minuit – minuit moins dix.*
– *Allez vite – ouvre la bouteille de champagne!*
– *Voilà, pour toi … et pour toi.*
– *Merci.*
– *Bonne année, tout le monde!*
– *Bonne année!*

7 – *Tiens, Mireille, bonjour!*
– *Bonjour!*
– *Qu'est-ce que tu achètes, là?*
– *Des lunettes de soleil, un maillot de bain, de la crème solaire. C'est pour mes vacances.*
– *Tu vas où?*
– *Je vais au bord de la mer.*
– *Tu pars quand?*
– *Samedi.*
– *Super! Allez, au revoir, et bonnes vacances.*
– *Merci.*

Feuille 7 ♦ On lit (free-standing)

Feuille 8 ♣ On lit (free-standing)

Feuille 9 ♦ On écrit (free-standing)

Feuille 10 ♣ On écrit (free-standing)

Feuille 11 Grammaire (free-standing)

Feuille 12 En plus (free-standing)

Feuille 13 Que sais-tu?

COUNTER

1 *Moi, j'ai passé un anniversaire super! Pour commencer, j'ai ouvert mes cadeaux. J'ai reçu des cadeaux géniaux! Mes parents m'ont offert un ordinateur, et j'ai reçu des jeux-video de ma grand-mère. A midi, j'ai retrouvé mes copains au centre commercial, où nous sommes allés manger des crêpes. Moi, j'ai mangé une galette jambon fromage, puis une crêpe banane chocolat. C'était très bon. L'après-midi, on a fait du patin à roulettes au centre-ville. Ça, c'était vraiment marrant. Je tombais tout le temps. J'ai pris beaucoup de photos. Et puis le soir, on a fait un grand repas en famille. J'ai invité ma tante et mes deux cousins. C'était bien.*

2 *Hier, c'était mon anniversaire. J'ai eu quatorze ans. Je suis allée en ville avec ma meilleure amie. On a fait les magasins, puis on est allé prendre un coca au café. L'après-midi, on est allé au cinéma. On a vu une comédie, mais c'était vraiment nul, ce n'était pas marrant du tout! Le soir, j'ai fait une soirée. J'ai invité mes amis du collège et du club des jeunes. Il y avait vingt-sept personnes. On a beaucoup dansé. Je me suis très bien amusée. J'ai reçu beaucoup de supers cadeaux!*

3 *Mon anniversaire est tombé un samedi. L'après-midi de mon anniversaire, mes grands-parents sont venus me voir. On a joué aux cartes, mais c'était un peu ennuyeux. Après ça, je suis allé chez Macdo avec mes copains. J'ai reçu un appareil-photo, donc j'ai pris beaucoup de photos de mes copains. C'était marrant. On a mangé des hamburgers et bu des cocas. Le soir, je suis allé au restaurant avec mes parents. On a très bien mangé. Le lendemain soir, dimanche, je suis sorti avec mes copains. On est allé à la discothèque. C'était super bien, on s'est vraiment bien amusé.*

Feuille 14 Révision 1: bedroom (free-standing)

Feuille 15 Révision 2: in the café

COUNTER

1 – *Bonjour, Messieurs-Dames. Vous désirez?*
– *Bonjour. Alors, deux cafés et un thé, s'il vous plaît.*
– *Oui. Et avec ça?*
– *Un croque-monsieur et deux croissants.*
– *C'est tout?*
– *Oui, c'est tout, merci.*
– *Très bien.*

2 – *Bonjour. Vous désirez?*
– *Bonjour. Je voudrais un pain au chocolat, s'il vous plaît.*
– *Oui, et avec ça?*
– *Je prends un coca, s'il vous plaît.*
– *Et pour vous?*
– *Moi, je vais prendre un diabolo, s'il vous plaît, un diabolo menthe.*
– *Très bien.*

3 – *Vous désirez?*
– *Alors, on va prendre un sandwich au fromage, et deux croissants, s'il vous plaît.*
– *Et qu'est-ce que vous prenez à boire?*
– *Qu'est-ce que vous avez comme jus de fruits?*
– *J'ai orange ou pomme.*
– *Alors, moi, je prends un jus d'orange, et … Sylvain, qu'est-ce que tu prends?*
– *Pour moi, un diabolo.*

Feuille 16 A la crêperie
See notes on Spread J.

Feuille 17 Grille
Support for Spread A Exercise 4a; Spread I Exercise 3.

Feuille 18 Réponses
This provides answers for the Unit 2 worksheets.

IT Opportunities

B4/5 Spread B Exercises 4 and 5
Pupils word-process their responses to Exercise 3 rather than write them in their books. Encourage them to check their work for spelling and accuracy. (If a French spell checker is unavailable, it is a good idea to have French dictionaries available near computers so that there is easily attainable reference material.) They save their work and, at a later stage, reload it in order to redraft it into the letter required in Exercise 5.

D Spread D
If word-processors are easily available for pupils, there are advantages to working through this spread with them to hand. For example, pupils could word-process Exercise 1 and use the word-processing functions to *'italicise'* all the participles and **'bold'** the different parts of *avoir*. The act of focusing in on the grammatical element in this way is helpful to some learners and they can correct mistakes easily. They also have a clear record for revision purposes. They could continue in this way for each exercise in the spread, for example, underlining the negatives.

G4 Spread G Exercise 4
i) Write a file, which describes a school visit, for a text manipulator with line jumbler and gapping facilities. Gap the text so that pupils will have to work on the *passé composé*. In preparation for writing their own descriptions, pupils practise putting the text in order and then work on it as a gapped text.
*ii) Pupils use a word-processor to draft an article, check it for accuracy and redraft it. If facilities and photos or illustrations are available, the latter could be scanned in to illustrate the article.
* iii) If multimedia presentation software is available, and a recent school visit has been made, this would lend itself to groups of pupils producing a multimedia presentation of the visit to include sound, text and pictures, for a visiting French audience or for information on a parents' evening. Pupils would need to be capable of using such a package rather than being taught how in French time and co-ordination with the IT co-ordinator is strongly recommended.

H3/4 Spread H Exercises 3 and 4
See note to spread D.

I Spread I
If there is Internet access, other resources could be found which describe national *fêtes*. Search for a text to provide additional reading material for ♣. Alternatively, ask pupils in pairs to search using a search engine, possibly a French one, typing in *Fête Nationale*, and to print out a text and make up some questions for another pair to answer. (If your school has an Intranet system, you might also be able to save a number of useful texts which would facilitate your pupils searching off-line.)

K6 Spread K Exercise 6
* This activity lends itself ideally to pupils using word-processors or desk top publisher software to design and create their posters. Pupils of all abilities will be able to produce a good quality poster. They will need to discuss the purpose and audience of the poster and make decisions about the content and the type of font, borders and illustrations to use. It is a good idea to put a time limit on such an activity, or to extend it into pupils' time where the school computer room is open for extra curricular work.

L7 Spread L Exercise 7
Some pupils might benefit from the following word-processing activity to support Exercise 7.
Word-process a 'typical week-end' and save as a model for pupils to adapt to their own circumstances. (It can be simplified as required for different ability groups.)
As an extra activity when they have adapted it, they could redraft it into a first letter to a French penfriend. They will need to think about what else to add and the work they have done so far in Units 1 and 2 will help them.

Les fêtes

A L'anniversaire

Objectives
Greetings
Talking about presents

Resources
Cassette for Exercises 1 and 2

Key language
bon anniversaire, c'est pour toi, bon appétit, santé, reçu, de l'argent, produits de beauté, voici, merci, gentil, beaucoup,

CD, poster, livre, vêtements (and family members and friends)

Grammar
son, sa, ses
Strategies
Pronunciation: *-en, -em, -an, -am*

This unit revises and extends work on the perfect tense, which was introduced in **Camarades 2.**

Ways in

Read and listen to the photo story.

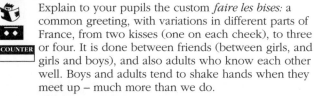

Explain to your pupils the custom *faire les bises:* a common greeting, with variations in different parts of France, from two kisses (one on each cheek), to three or four. It is done between friends (between girls, and girls and boys), and also adults who know each other well. Boys and adults tend to shake hands when they meet up – much more than we do.

Answers
1 F *Elle a vingt ans.*　2 V　3 F *Elle a fait une soirée.*
4 F *Elle aime le petit ami de sa sœur.*

2

Point out that there are seven conversations, and three pictures: some will obviously be used more than once.

Answers
1b　2a　3b　4c　5a　6c　7a

COUNTER

> 1 – *Le dîner est servi. Allez, asseyez-vous, tout le monde.*
> – *Merci.*
> – *Bon appétit.*
> – *Mmm! C'est délicieux!*
> 2 – *Bon anniversaire!*
> – *Merci.*
> – *Tiens. C'est pour toi.*
> – *Merci. C'est très gentil.*
> – *T'as quel âge, maintenant?*
> – *J'ai quatorze ans.*
> 3 – *Tiens.*
> – *Merci.*
> – *Alors, à votre santé!*
> – *Santé!*
> – *Santé!*
> 4 – *Maman, je te présente mon ami, Hamed.*
> – *Bonjour, Hamed.*
> – *Bonjour, Madame.*
> 5 – *Bon anniversaire!*
> – *Merci.*
> – *Voici un petit cadeau pour toi.*
> – *Merci beaucoup! C'est vraiment super!*
> 6 – *Hamed, je te présente mon petit ami, Jérôme.*
> – *Bonjour, Jérôme, ça va?*
> – *Bonjour, Hamed. Tu es dans la même classe que Sophie?*
> – *Oui, c'est ça.*

> 7 – *Ah, bonjour, Henri.*
> – *Bonjour, Hélène. Bon anniversaire!*
> – *Merci.*
> – *Tiens. C'est un petit cadeau pour toi.*
> – *Ah merci beaucoup! C'est très gentil!*

3

This activity picks out different presents and focuses on *son, sa, ses.*

This would be a good time to work on the first part of the grammar section on page 40. In Exercise 1, the focus is on possessives in the singular. Exercise 2 is referred to from Spread I.

4a

COUNTER

As an alternative, pupils could tick the presents on the grid on *Feuille 17.*

> 1 – *Salut, Christelle!*
> – *Salut, Julie, et bon anniversaire!*
> – *Merci.*
> – *Voilà. C'est pour toi.*
> – *Un poster de Gérard Depardieu! Merci beaucoup, Christelle! C'est vraiment super!*
> 2 – *Bon anniversaire, Julie. Tu as quel âge maintenant?*
> – *J'ai vingt ans.*
> – *Ah oui. Tiens, un petit cadeau. J'espère que tu le trouveras utile.*
> – *Oh, un stylo. Merci, Tante Mireille. C'est très gentil.*
> 3 – *Bon anniversaire, Julie! Tiens, un petit cadeau.*
> – *Merci, Henri.*
> – *C'est ma sœur qui l'a choisi. J'espère que tu vas l'aimer.*
> – *Ah! Des produits de toilette! Merci beaucoup. C'est très gentil!*
> 4 – *Bon anniversaire, Julie.*
> – *Merci, Oncle Philippe. C'est pour moi?*
> – *Oui, c'est pour toi.*
> – *Un jeu-vidéo! Merci, Oncle Philippe. C'est super!*
> 5 – *Bon anniversaire, Julie.*
> – *Merci, Thomas.*
> – *Je t'ai acheté un cadeau. Tiens.*
> – *Un CD de Kylie Minogue. Merci, Thomas. Euh, c'est chouette.*
> 6 – *Bon anniversaire, Julie. Je ne savais pas ce que tu aimerais comme cadeau, donc … voilà de l'argent. Tu peux choisir un cadeau que tu aimes.*
> – *Trois cents francs! Merci beaucoup, Mémé.*

7 – *Bon anniversaire, Julie.*
– *Merci, Sandrine.*
– *Je t'ai apporté un petit cadeau.*
– *Qu'est-ce que c'est?*
– *Mais ouvre-le!*
– *Un T-shirt! Merci beaucoup, Sandrine! Il est vraiment bien! Je vais le porter demain soir, quand je sortirai avec toi!*
8 – *Bonjour, Oncle François. Ça va?*
– *Bonjour, Julie, et bon anniversaire!*
– *Merci.*
– *Ton cadeau est dans cette enveloppe.*
– *Qu'est-ce que c'est?*
– *Ouvre-la.*
– *Oh! Deux billets pour le match de football samedi prochain.*
– *Tu aimes le foot, n'est-ce pas.*
– *Oui, oui … j'adore le foot …*

Prononciation

 This gives pupils the opportunity to apply what they have learned to new words.

 Other words pupils have come across in this book and in **Camarades 2** include: *(je te) présente; (20) ans; souvent; roman-photo; enfant; vendredi; quand; dépliant; dans; excellent; attendu; comment; en; France.*

4b **Differentiation**
Pupils could either copy presents from the list in Exercise 3 or invent more of their own. Alternatively, the class could brainstorm a list of possible presents (some nice and some awful).

You could set up the activity using cue cards: pupils make a set of 'present' cards, each with a different present, and reaction cards ('like' or 'dislike'). The cards are then placed face down, and the pupils pick one each then act out the scene.

A productive task for this spread is on *Feuille 12A,* since it involves inventing speech bubbles for a cartoon strip.

This spread would be a good place to revise other greetings, such as *Bonjour, Bonsoir, Salut, Au revoir.* Remind pupils that to say 'Good morning', you have to use *Bonjour.* You might also like to point out that you can say *Bon après-midi,* in the sense of 'Have a good afternoon', and will also hear *Bonne fin d'après-midi* late in the afternoon.

Other greetings are covered on *Feuilles 5* and *6.* You could also revise dates here, and *C'est quand, ton anniversaire?.*

B C'était bien, la soirée?

Objectives
Describing a party

Resources
Presentation sheet 5
Cassette for Exercises 1, 3 and an additional activity

Key language
fait, mangé, bu, dansé, eu, bavardé, invité, pris, fini, parlé,

perdu, préparé, pizza, coca, c'était, génial, nul

Grammar
Perfect tense *(avoir)*

Strategies
Writing: beginning and ending an informal letter

This spread revises the perfect tense with *avoir*. It uses mainly past participles which are familiar, and focuses on the first person singular.

Ways in
You can begin by revising the key verbs using visuals from Presentation sheet 5. You say a sentence for each picture. Pupils only repeat the sentence if it corresponds to the picture.

1

The text of the letter has also been recorded on tape.

Answer
b e d c a

For further exploitation of the letter, you could give pupils a list of words and phrases and ask them to find equivalents in the letter, e.g. *bonjour, à la maison, le shopping, il était assez sympa, parlé, copains, très*.

To help train pupils to listen for detail, read out the letter, making slight alterations to the text. Pupils put their hand up when they hear a 'mistake', and give the correct version.

2

Answers
1D   2A   3E   4B   5C

3

Answers
f-k   c-n   a-l   e-j   d-h   g-i   b-m

– Qu'est-ce que tu as fait pour ton anniversaire, Julie?
– Eh bien, j'ai fait une soirée.
– Ah bon? Et tu as invité qui?
– Ben, j'ai invité des copains du lycée et d'autres copains du club des jeunes.
– Tu as dansé?
– Bien sûr! J'ai dansé avec mon petit ami, Arnaud.
– Et tu as parlé avec qui?
– J'ai bavardé avec tout le monde.
– Qu'est-ce que tu as bu?
– Pour fêter mes vingt ans, j'ai bu du champagne, bien sûr!
– Tu as pris beaucoup de photos?
– Non, j'ai perdu mon appareil-photo. C'est Delphine qui a pris toutes les photos.
– C'était bien, la soirée?
– Ah oui, c'était vraiment chouette!

This would be an appropriate time to refer to the grammar section on pages 32–33, where the perfect tense is re-presented and practised.

You might also want to take this opportunity to remind pupils of the pronunciation of *-é*. Point out that this sound can help them to recognise when someone is talking about the past. An additional listening activity is provided for this: pupils listen to the cassette and say whether the verb ending in *-é* (perfect tense) is number 1 or number 2.

a	**1** *j'ai mangé*	**2** *je mange*
b	**1** *je regarde*	**2** *j'ai regardé*
c	**1** *j'invite*	**2** *j'ai invité*
d	**1** *j'ai regardé*	**2** *je regarde*
e	**1** *je joue*	**2** *j'ai joué*
f	**1** *je prépare*	**2** *j'ai préparé*
g	**1** *j'ai parlé*	**2** *je parle*
h	**1** *je joue*	**2** *j'ai joué*

It is useful to remind pupils that the pronunciation of *-é* is the same as *-er* and *-ez*.

4

To prepare for part **b**, revise words which pupils know for giving opinions: *nul, chouette, super, ennuyeux* etc. Draw pupils' attention to the phrase *c'était*, and contrast it with *c'est*.

5

Prepare this by brainstorming useful words and phrases with the class. You can adapt those presented and practised in the spread, for example to refer to other food and drink.

♦ You may wish to provide less able pupils with a skeleton letter to copy and complete.

If facilities are available, pupils could write their letter using a word-processing package. Encourage them to read through their first draft, checking the verbs in particular. They will then find it easy to revise their letter on computer before printing off a final version.

An attractive wall display could be made up of the letters and any photos pupils have taken.

♣ As an extension activity, pupils could work in pairs to invent an interview with a famous person about a celebrity party they have attended. The interview could either be written up for a magazine, or recorded as a radio interview.

C Une journée avec Kévin
pp 30–31

Objectives
Describing a day out and giving your opinions

Resources
Presentation sheet 6
Cassette for Exercises 1 and 3

Key language
patin à roulettes, vu, regardé, écouté, joué, cartes, concert, passé, film, été, mangé, bu, fait, c'était, super, ennuyeux,

marrant, intéressant, bête, nul (and verbs from previous spreads)

Grammar
Perfect tense *(on)*

Strategies
Learning vocabulary

This spread continues revision of the perfect tense, with specific focus on *on a* + past participle and *vous avez …* . There is also practice of giving and understanding opinions.

Ways in
Practise key verb phrases, using pictures from the top of Presentation sheet 6. You can come back to these later and use them with the happy and unhappy faces to practise opinions.

Answers
1 F   2 F   3 V   4 F   5 F   6 V

This activity focuses on the vocabulary of opinions. A tip for learning the words is given in the *Stratégie* box on page 31.

Before pupils listen, draw their attention to the fact that the interviewer uses *vous* rather than *tu,* and perhaps play the first one on tape. Pupils could look at the answers (sentences 1–5) and say why they think *vous* has been used.

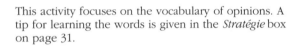
1 – *Qu'est-ce que vous avez fait hier soir?*
  – *On a regardé un documentaire à la télé.*
2 – *Qu'est-ce que vous avez fait hier?*
  – *On a fait du patin à roulettes.*
3 – *Qu'est-ce que vous avez fait hier soir?*
  – *On a écouté un concert à la radio.*
4 – *Qu'est-ce que vous avez fait hier soir?*
  – *On a joué aux cartes.*
5 – *Qu'est-ce que vous avez fait hier?*
  – *On a été au centre commercial.*

1 – *Qu'est-ce que vous avez fait hier soir?*
  – *On a regardé un documentaire à la télé. C'était intéressant!*
2 – *Qu'est-ce que vous avez fait hier?*
  – *On a fait du patin à roulettes. C'était génial!*
3 – *Qu'est-ce que vous avez fait hier soir?*
  – *On a écouté un concert à la radio. C'était affreux!*

4 – *Qu'est-ce que vous avez fait hier soir?*
  – *On a joué aux cartes. C'était marrant!*
5 – *Qu'est-ce que vous avez fait hier?*
  – *On a été au centre commercial. C'était ennuyeux!*

This would also be an appropriate point to remind pupils of the use of *nous,* pointing out that *nous* and *on* can both be used to mean 'we', but that *on* is less formal.

As preparation, work with the class on asking questions with *vous.* For example, mime what you did at the week-end (you can make this up!), or get pairs of pupils to mime. The others have to identify the activities, e.g. *Vous avez été au cinéma?* If no-one is keen on miming, you could do it as a simple guessing game, with the activity noted down on paper first, to avoid accusations of cheating.

As a class, brainstorm activities to mention here, drawing on language from the previous unit, e.g. Spread I *(on a été au …),* or vocabulary learned previously in the course – this is a chance for pupils to show how much they can remember!

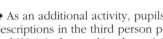
Give less able pupils extra support with language relating to the pictures, if necessary.

♣ As an additional activity, pupils could write descriptions in the third person plural of Delphine and Kévin's date and/or the activities of their classmates, as described in **5b**.

Unité 2 — Les fêtes

D Grammaire pp 32–33

Grammar

Perfect tense: *avoir* + -er/-ir/-re verbs

In this spread, pupils are reminded of the formation of the perfect tense with *avoir* + -er verbs, and some irregular past participles.

In addition, -ir and -re verbs are introduced, as is the negative.

All this is grouped together on one spread, for ease of reference and flexibility of use. You can cover the spread all at once, but you may prefer to have pupils work on it a bit at a time. This will avoid overload, and repeated practice on separate occasions leads to better retention than one long session.

1 The first activity provides pupils with all the necessary components for the sentences, in the form of building blocks.

2 **Differentiation:**
The first five examples focus on the singular paradigm, while 6–10 (♣) practise the plural.

As an additional activity, pupils could translate the sentences into English. Look again at the translations in the box at the top, and discuss with pupils the possible translations and the differences in meaning. For example, the first one is likely to be 'Have you finished your homework?'. The question 'Did you finish your homework?' would relate to some time in the past, e.g. 'last night' or 'before you went out'. Invite pupils to think about how they would explain the difference to a French person learning English.

By discussing these issues, pupils develop a deeper understanding of tenses in French and how they relate to English: there is not a simple one-to-one correspondence, as they might think. This can also lead to pupils reflecting more deeply on their own native language and language structures in general. They might be interested to compare British English with American English: where the British would say 'Have you had lunch yet?', Americans would say 'Did you have lunch yet?' They could listen out for examples on American TV programmes.

3 Pupils could go on to make up other examples using the same verbs.

4 Pupils could also write down in the third person what Olivier hasn't done.

E Infos et jeux   pp 34–35

Objectives
Reading for interest

Resources
Cassette for Exercise 1

Encourage pupils to use a dictionary where they need it. However, to help avoid overdependency on the dictionary and to develop pupils' reading skills, discuss with the class which words they can guess from the context and which they need to look up.

L'âge de la majorité
A quel âge est-on adulte? Ça dépend …
Dès 16 ans, on peut conduire une moto de 125 cm³.
A l'âge de 14 ans, on peut conduire une mobylette de moins de 50 cm³.
Pour conduire une voiture tout seul, il faut avoir 18 ans.
En France, les filles peuvent se marier à partir de 15 ans et 3 mois, avec l'autorisation de leurs parents. Les garçons peuvent se marier à 18 ans.
A l'âge de 16 ans, un jeune peut commencer à travailler à plein temps.
Quand on a 16 ans, on peut travailler pendant les grandes vacances, mais on ne doit pas travailler plus de quatre heures par jour, et pas plus de la moitié des vacances scolaires.
Les Français ont le droit de voter à partir de 18 ans.
On peut prendre une boisson alcoolisée dans un café à partir de 16 ans.

Scolarité
On peut aller à l'école maternelle de deux ans jusqu'à six ans.
On va à l'école primaire de six à onze ans.
On peut quitter l'école secondaire à 16 ans.

Pupils may be interested to know more about learning to drive in France. French people can learn to drive at 16, but must always be accompanied by a qualified driver. This is known as *conduite accompagnée*. However, to drive on their own, they must be 18. They take practical and theory tests (the theory test was compulsory in France long before it was introduced in Britain). Lessons must be given by a qualified instructor: you can't go out practising with family and friends.

2 You will probably need to discuss this in class first. Pupils may be able to pool their knowledge and arrive at a number of statements, or they could research the issue and then report back. Otherwise, you could give alternative ages for a number of situations: pupils say which they think is correct.

Minimum legal ages: Britain
- Ride a motorbike (125cc) – 17
- Ride a motorbike (less than 50cc) – 16
- Drive a car – 17
- Full-time work – 16
- Light part-time work – 13 (but local restrictions on type of work and hours. Certain types of light work permitted before 13.)
- Vote – 18
- Get married
  Scotland – 16
  England and Wales – 18 (16, with parental consent, although if a couple have managed to marry without it, the marriage is still valid)
- Buy alcohol in a bar – 18
- Scotland – Drink alcohol in a restaurant (wine, beer, sherry, with a meal) – 16
  England and Wales – Buy alcohol in a restaurant (beer, cider, porter, perry only) – 16
- Leave school – 16

♦   You could provide support for less able pupils, e.g. a gapped table:

On peut	voter se marier conduire une moto (etc.)	à ……… ans.

The class can then go on to discuss similarities and differences between France and Britain.

Pupils should use a dictionary if necessary, to do this personality quiz.

F Une glace à la vanille, s'il vous plaît   pp 36–37

Objectives
Buying ice-cream and drinks from a kiosque

Grammar
au, à la

Resources
Cassette for Exercises 1, 3 and 5

Strategies
Listening: anticipate what you're going to hear

Key language
esquimau, glace, boule, fraise, chocolat, vanille, banane, citron, framboise, cassis, café, coca, limonade, c'est, tout, ça fait, combien (and prices)

Ways in
To begin, focus on the flavours of ice-cream. Model the pronunciation for pupils to imitate, then go on to ask individuals which flavours they prefer.

1

While working on the dialogues, draw attention to Delphine's bossiness, asking *Delphine est patiente ou impatiente?*.

COUNTER

2
Encourage pupils to memorise the dialogues.

3
COUNTER
Answers
1 f, d 30F   **2** g, a 19F   **3** b, c 55F   **4** a, d 33F
5 h, a 48F   **6** e, g 20F

> **1** – *Une glace à la framboise, s'il vous plaît.*
> – *A la framboise … Une boule ou deux?*
> – *Deux boules.*
> – *C'est tout?*
> – *Non, je vais prendre une glace au cassis, aussi. Deux boules.*
> – *Voilà.*
> – *Merci. Ça fait combien?*
> – *Ça fait 30 francs.*
> **2** – *Bonjour, Madame. Je voudrais une glace, s'il vous plaît.*
> – *Quel parfum?*
> – *Vanille, s'il vous plaît.*
> – *Oui, Monsieur. Une boule ou deux?*
> – *Euh … une boule.*
> – *Et avec ça?*
> – *Un esquimau, s'il vous plaît.*
> – *Voilà, Monsieur. Ça fait 19 francs.*
> **3** – *Deux limonades, s'il vous plaît.*
> – *Voilà. C'est tout?*
> – *Non, je prends aussi une glace au citron.*
> – *Une boule ou deux?*
> – *Deux boules, s'il vous plaît.*
> – *Voilà.*
> – *Merci. C'est tout. Ça fait combien?*
> – *Ça fait 55 francs.*
> **4** – *Bonjour, Madame. Je voudrais deux esquimaux, s'il vous plaît.*
> – *Oui, Madame. Ce sera tout?*
> – *Non, une glace aussi. Qu'est-ce que vous avez comme parfums?*

> – *J'ai citron, cassis, café, framboise, vanille et chocolat.*
> – *Alors, je prends une glace au cassis.*
> – *Une boule ou deux?*
> – *Deux boules.*
> – *Voilà, Madame. Ça fait 33 francs.*
> – *Merci.*
> **5** – *Deux glaces au chocolat, s'il vous plaît.*
> – *Une boule ou deux?*
> – *Deux boules, s'il vous plaît.*
> – *C'est tout?*
> – *Euh, non, deux esquimaux aussi, s'il vous plaît.*
> – *Voilà.*
> – *Merci. Ça fait combien?*
> – *Ça fait 48 francs.*
> **6** – *Deux glaces, s'il vous plaît.*
> – *Quels parfums?*
> – *Une glace au café, et une à la vanille.*
> – *Une boule ou deux?*
> – *Une boule, s'il vous plaît.*
> – *Voilà. Ça fait 20 francs.*
> – *Merci.*

4

There is more work on this theme on *Feuille 12B*. Here are some suggestions for extra practice to use here, or later, as revision:
• Pupils copy out the flavours in their order of preference (remind them that they learned this strategy in Unit 1).
• Do a *mêlée* activity: pupils note down their top 3 flavours then go round asking others what their favourites are, using the phrase *Qu'est-ce que tu aimes comme glace?*. Can they find anyone with the same 3 favourites?
• A member of each group comes out and asks you: *Qu'est-ce que vous avez comme parfums?*. They have to memorise the list you tell them, report back to the group, who write down the choice. Can they get it right?
• Pupils invent a humorous sketch, with an awkward customer or a vendor with a narrow range of ices.

5

COUNTER
You could take this theme further, dicussing who is bossy or childish in TV soaps.

G Une visite scolaire

pp 38–39

Objectives
Describing a day trip

Resources
Cassette for Exercises 1 and 3

Key language
je suis allé, sorti, rentré, resté, arrivé, venu, parti, chanté, raconté, acheté, musée, visite guidée, souvenirs, glace (and verbs; opinions from previous spreads)

Grammar
Perfect tense *(être)*

Strategies
Writing article – draft, check, redraft

Ways in
This spread introduces a selection of verbs which take *être* in the perfect tense. Begin by revising the perfect tense, as pupils have learned it so far.

After completing Exercise 1, invite pupils to look carefully at the texts – do they notice anything different about the verbs? Guide them as necessary into realising that some of the verbs take *être* rather than *avoir,* and get pupils to pick them out.

Answers
1a E, A, B, D, C
1b E: *8h45*; A: *9h15*; D: *14h00*; C: *15h30, 16h15*

COUNTER

> Je suis allée au musée Jeanne d'Arc avec ma classe. Trois professeurs sont venus avec nous.
> On est parti à 8h45.
> On est arrivé au musée à 9h15.
> Le matin, on a visité le musée, où on a vu une exposition sur la vie de Jeanne d'Arc.
> Nous sommes restés au musée pendant deux heures et demie. Après, on a déjeuné.
> Ensuite, vers 14h00, on a fait une visite guidée de l'hôtel de ville. C'était vraiment intéressant.
> A 15h30, nous sommes partis. Je suis rentrée chez moi à 16h15.

More key phrases are presented here.

Answer
1e **2**c **3**d **4**a **5**b

For a summary and activities on verbs taking *être,* see page 41. After working on this, pupils could go through all texts on this spread and pick out useful verbs for describing a day out, listing them in two columns: *avoir/être.*

As preparation, pupils who know the 'yes/no' game could demonstrate it in English. There is also a model of the game on tape. After listening to this, discuss with your pupils strategies for answering (e.g. repeating the sentence; saying *C'est exact*) and for catching the other person out while asking the questions (e.g. repeating their answer: *Tu es allée à Rouen?*).

After pupils have prepared questions, get them to report back to the class, so that they can share ideas. You could ask for volunteers, and select a pair of able

pupils to try the game first in front of the rest of the class, before they split into groups to play.

COUNTER

> – Alors, tu es allée où?
> – Je suis allée à Rouen.
> – A Rouen?
> – C'est exact.
> – Tu es partie le matin?
> – Je suis partie à neuf heures.
> – A neuf heures?
> – Je suis partie à neuf heures.
> – Et c'était bien à Rouen?
> – C'était très bien.
> – Qu'est-ce que vous avez fait?
> – On a visité un musée.
> – Un musée?
> – C'est exact.
> – Qu'est-ce que vous avez fait à midi?
> – On a mangé des hamburgers.
> – Vous n'avez pas mangé des sandwichs?
> – Non, des hamburgers ... Oh zut!! J'ai dit 'non'!

For more practice of describing a day out, try the following game. Pupils describe a day out in groups: as they go round, each person adds one sentence to the description.

Discuss with the class how to structure the article, for example separate paragraphs for morning and afternoon. If possible, build into the draft-redraft process a stage at which you see the article so that pupils can incorporate your corrections into the final version.

By drafting and correcting their work, pupils should end up with a polished article of which they can be proud. Why not display them on the classroom wall or in the corridor?

H Grammaire

Grammar
Possessives
Perfect tense *(être)*

Mon, ma, mes etc.

As elsewhere, activities on page 40 are freestanding, so that pupils can do a section at a time.

1 This focuses on the singular paradigm. Pupils are referred here from Spread A.

Pupils give their personal reactions to items in Delphine's room. You could do similar work based on magazine pictures.

2 Work on the plural paradigm is referred from Spread I.

Draw pupils' attention to No 3: the French custom is to send cards after the 1st January. Invite pupils to tell you in French when Christmas cards are sent in Britain.

Le passé composé avec être

Page 41 outlines the perfect tense formation of verbs which take *être,* and provides practice.

3 Two reflexive verbs are given in the perfect tense here: *je me suis bien amusé(e)* and *on s'est bien amusé.* These phrases are very useful for describing days out and events in the past. They are presented here for pupils to learn as set phrases, although you may wish to exploit the grammar now or later with very able pupils.

Feuille 14 combines differentiated practice of plural possessives and the perfect tense with *être.* Plural possessives are used productively, and more verbs are introduced for pupils to use in the perfect tense.

Unité

2

Les fêtes

1 Des fêtes différentes

pp 42–43

Objectives
Describing festivals (input and manipulation)

Resources
Cassette for Exercise 3
Presentation sheet 7

Key language
Nouvel An, carnaval, fête, feu d'artifice, défilé, se déguiser, repas spécial, s'offrir des cadeaux, chanter, jeux, repas, décorer, danser, boire, soirée, maison, il y a

Strategies
Reading: guessing cognates
Dictionary: using information in the dictionary entry to select the correct meaning

---

This spread provides input for the productive work of the following spread.

Ways in
Read the articles together. Invite pupils to pick out words which they haven't met before; but which they can work out because of their similarity to English. It can be very encouraging for pupils to realise just how many words they can recognise in this way.

Point out also that it is not necessary to understand every word in order to understand the whole text. Go through, paragraph by paragraph, asking pupils to point out any unknown words which prevent them from understanding the gist. Can the class work them out together, using the context as a guide? For words which pupils don't understand and which seem necessary for an understanding of the gist, allow them to look them up in the dictionary. The *Stratégies* box on page 43 gives tips for selecting the correct meaning.

Depending on your pupils, point out any other items of interest. For example, you might like to point out to more able pupils a different use of the reflexive in the article about the Chinese New Year: *se fête* meaning 'is celebrated'. Give them other examples of this use, e.g. *Le pain se vend dans les boulangeries et les supermarchés.*

1 The sentences a–k provide simplified key phrases for talking about festivals.

Remind pupils that *on* can mean 'we' or 'they', so these key phrases can be used for talking about themselves and about others.

2 You could do more work with Delphine's dossier. For example, get your pupils to invent *vrai/faux* questions for their partner, using the key phrases from Exercise 1.

3 Information about important festivals is given on tape.

> **1** – *Mme Goldblum, dans le Judaïsme, quelle est votre fête la plus populaire?*
> – *Alors, notre fête la plus populaire, c'est la Pessah. On fête la Pessah au printemps.*
> – *La fête dure combien de temps?*
> – *Ça dure une semaine.*
> – *Et qu'est-ce que vous faites à la Pessah?*

> – *On fait un repas spécial, qui s'appelle le seder. On mange de l'agneau rôti et du pain spécial.*
> **2** – *M. Kureishi, pouvez-vous me parler de l'Id-al Fitr?*
> – *Oui, alors, nous fêtons l'Id-al Fitr à la fin du ramadan. C'est une fête religieuse qui est très importante pour nous.*
> – *Après le ramadan?*
> – *Oui. Pendant le ramadan, les adultes ne mangent pas pendant la journée. On mange seulement le soir. Donc, nous fêtons l'Id-al Fitr avec un très grand repas.*
> – *Vous faites d'autres choses aussi? Vous envoyez des cartes à votre famille, par exemple?*
> – *Oui, nous envoyons des cartes à notre famille …*
> **3** – *M. Forestier, qu'est-ce que vous faites à Pâques?*
> – *Pour moi et ma famille, la Pâques est une fête religieuse très importante.*
> – *Vous allez à l'église?*
> – *Oui, nous allons à l'église le matin, puis on fait un grand déjeuner en famille.*
> – *Mais ce n'est pas tout le monde qui va à l'église …*
> – *Non, c'est vrai. Certains font un pique-nique, ou rendent visite à leur famille!*
> – *Est-ce que vous donnez des œufs en chocolat à vos enfants?*
> – *Oui, bien sûr! Les enfants reçoivent beaucoup d'œufs en chocolat: de nous, de leurs grands-parents, de leurs tantes et oncles. Ils adorent ça!*

Instead of noting the letters from Exercise 1, pupils could tick the grid on *Feuille 17.*

Feuilles 3 and *4* have activities based on French Christmas songs, while *Feuilles 7* and *8* have reading passages on different *fêtes.*

44

J Un exposé sur une fête

Objectives
Describing a special occasion (productive)
Recipe for *crêpes*

Key language
As Spread I and *rendre visite à*

Strategies
Speaking: planning an exposé
Asking the teacher for help
Dictionary: looking up the correct word (part of speech, context);
using the French word correctly (applying grammar)

Ways in
Begin by revising the work on *fêtes* so far. For example, pupils work in pairs. They quickly brainstorm all they can remember about different *fêtes* – the *carnaval* in Rio, the Chinese New Year etc. – then report back to the class.

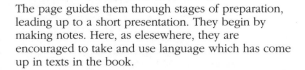
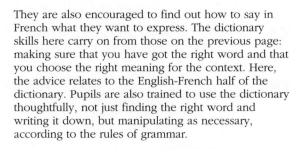

The page guides them through stages of preparation, leading up to a short presentation. They begin by making notes. Here, as elesewhere, they are encouraged to take and use language which has come up in texts in the book.

They are also encouraged to find out how to say in French what they want to express. The dictionary skills here carry on from those on the previous page: making sure that you have got the right word and that you choose the right meaning for the context. Here, the advice relates to the English-French half of the dictionary. Pupils are also trained to use the dictionary thoughtfully, not just finding the right word and writing it down, but manipulating as necessary, according to the rules of grammar.

It is wise to go through the strategies together. Depending on the pupils, and their experience of using the English-French section of the dictionary, it might be a good idea for the class to look up specific words and phrases together, so that you can monitor and comment on the results.

For further work on *visiter/rendre visite à,* give pupils some model sentences – they have to select the appropriate phrase.

Feuilles 9 and *10* give more practice in looking up verbs in the English-French side of the dictionary. More work on looking up words in this part of the dictionary follows in later units.

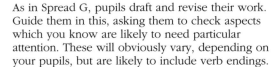

As in Spread G, pupils draft and revise their work. Guide them in this, asking them to check aspects which you know are likely to need particular attention. These will obviously vary, depending on your pupils, but are likely to include verb endings.

Giving a talk in any language can be daunting, so on this first occasion, pupils have the option to read out their talk from a script. If some pupils do choose to work from notes, give them support in selecting key words and phrases. You could do some examples together as a group.

You could do further work on cultural exploitation here, discussing differences and similarities between cultures. This could be done together, as a class, or in groups which report back.

The spread ends with a recipe for *crêpes*. Making *crêpes* for *Mardi gras* was mentioned on page 42. You could also tell pupils that *crêpes* are a speciality of Brittany, where they are traditionally washed down with cider. However, *crêperies* serving sweet and savoury *crêpes* can be found all over France. You can also find mobile vans and stalls (e.g. at camp sites and in the street), where you can buy *crêpes* to take away. Pupils should note that the flour in the recipe is plain, not self-raising.

Feuille 16 is a *crêperie* menu. Use it as a prompt for role-play work after *Feuille 15*, which revises ordering food in a café.

Pupils can begin by looking up unkown words in the dictionary. Can they guess *épinards* from the name of the *galette?* Discuss aspects of the menu, e.g. the difference between *galettes* and *crêpes;* what *Chantilly* is (whipped, sweetened cream); what *flambée* means. The pupils then choose which *crêpes* they like most/least.

As a class, pupils could brainstorm key phrases for dialogues, then do rôle-plays in groups. They could listen to others performing their dialogues, note down their orders and work out the bill.

You could also have a competition to design other fillings for *crêpes*. Pupils could plan their own menu and design and produce it on computer.

K Atelier

pp 46–47

Objectives
Organising a special event

Resources
Cassette for Exercise 2

The *Atelier* brings together elements from the unit in a themed context. It guides the pupils through work on the productive task of planning their own *fête*, in which they use the language of the unit for themselves.

If you wish, you could extend it to include other areas. For example, you could revise food and have pupils plan a menu, write a shopping list and do a role-play on buying food.

1

This provides some ideas for types of activity.

2

COUNTER

The discussion on tape provides a model for pupils' own discussion in Exercise 3.

> – Alors, qu'est-ce qu'on pourrait faire?
> – Eh bien, on pourrait aller au cinéma ... Il y a un bon film.
> – Oui, d'accord. C'est une bonne idée!
> – Ah non, le cinéma, c'est ennuyeux!
> – Alors ... on pourrait organiser une soirée. Un bal masqué, par exemple. On pourrait se déguiser.
> – Ça, c'est une bonne idée!
> – Mais non. Se déguiser, c'est bête!
> – Alors qu'est-ce que tu veux faire, Delphine.
> – Hé, Delphine, on pourrait faire un barbecue au parc!
> – Mais non! Ça va pas, ça. Je suis végétarienne, moi!
> – Bon, alors, on pourrait organiser une soirée chez moi.
> – Chez toi, Delphine?
> – Oui. On pourrait danser, manger des pizzas. Ça va?
> – Oui, d'accord.
> – Bonne idée.

3

The *Expressions utiles* give guidance here. To prepare pupils to integrate them into their own work, play the recording from Exercise 2 again and ask pupils to put their hands up each time they hear one of these phrases.

You could do more work with the construction *on pourrait*. Give pupils a list of problems and ask them to make suggestions, e.g.
problème:
Il n'y a rien à manger à la maison.
suggestions:
On pourrait aller au restaurant.
On pourrait ...

4

This activity prepares pupils to discuss and decide on the details of their *fête* and reminds them of the *aller* + infinitive construction.

5

Remind pupils of the key phrases on p 46 which can be used in this activity as well.

6

Here, you could do some work on preparing different invitations for different people, e.g. for teachers and friends, looking at different styles and levels of formality.

Differentiation
More able pupils who finish early could imagine that the *fête* has already taken place and write up a description in their diary or as a letter. They have to say what they did and what it was like (it could be great or really awful). They can look back at Spreads B, C and G, where they described parties and outings. Give them a model, to start them off, e.g.
samedi 28 juin
Aujourd'hui, c'était la grande fête. Désastre! C'était affreux! La soirée a commencé à huit heures, mais tout le monde est arrivé à neuf heures ...

Unité

2

Les fêtes

L Revision

pp 48–49

Objectives

Talking about yourself and your family: appearance and character
Describing a typical day

Resources

Cassette for Exercise 3

Parler de toi et de ta famille

1 On page 48, pupils revise basic descriptions of themselves and their family. In Exercise 1, key language is re-presented in the context of a letter before pupils are required to use it in later exercises.

Answer

Bruno – f; *Franck* – c

2 Here, the language of description is completed and pupils are required to deal with each word.

Answer

Sophie – a; *Agnès* – b

3

COUNTER

> *Ma sœur Sophie a 18 ans et elle est assez grande. Elle va au lycée, où elle prépare le Bac L: anglais, français et histoire-géo. Comme ma mère, elle a les yeux bleus et les cheveux longs et blonds. Elle est sportive – elle joue au volleyball pour l'école. Elle est assez timide, mais avec ses amis, elle est très sympa, et assez marrante. Je m'entends assez bien avec elle.*
> *Agnès a 16 ans, et elle va au lycée, aussi. Comme Sophie, elle a les yeux bleus et les cheveux blonds. Mais elle a les cheveux courts. Elle porte des lunettes. Agnès est vraiment paresseuse – elle n'aide pas à la maison. Ça m'énerve. En plus, elle est vraiment embêtante. Elle prend toujours mes*

4 A variation on this is to have pupils work in groups. One person chooses someone in the class, but does not say who. To find out who it is, the others ask questions to which the first pupil can only answer *oui* or *non*.

5 If possible, pupils could write their descriptions on computer, since their handwriting might be recognised.

The topic of pets is revised separately, on a worksheet in Unit 3.

Une journée typique

Refer pupils to Unit 1, Spreads B and C, which cover the main points of what is being revised. They can go back and check key language as necessary.

6 This activity reminds pupils of the key language, in context.

7 In Unit 1, pupils described a typical weekday. Here, they write about the week-end.

8 Encourage pupils to be inventive in their sentences – the more outrageous, the funnier the results!

A – Epreuve d'écoute

Exercice 1

Pupils are required in this exercise to pick out details of particular activities and times in short passages. This is typical of performance at **Level 3**.
Total 10 marks.
Award 1 mark for each correct answer.
Pupils scoring at least 7 marks are showing some characteristics of performance at **Level 3**.

Answers
1 c/7.15   **2** e/7.30   **3** g/8.00   **4** j/6.00   **5** i/9.00

Exercice 1

– *La journée de Pierre. Regarde les dessins. Ecoute Pierre. Choisis la bonne lettre et écris l'heure.*
 Exemple:
– *Salut! Je m'appelle Pierre. Je vais décrire une journée typique. D'habitude je me réveille à sept heures.*
– ***Numéro un.***
– *Je me lave dans la salle de bains. Je me lave à sept heures et quart.*
– ***Numéro deux.***
– *Je descends à la cuisine où je prends le petit déjeuner. Je mange des tartines et je bois du thé. Je prends le petit déjeuner à sept heures et demie.*
– ***Numéro trois.***
– *Je quitte la maison et je vais à l'école à huit heures.*
– ***Numéro quatre.***
– *Le soir, après l'école, je fais mes devoirs dans ma chambre. Je fais mes devoirs à six heures.*
– ***Numéro cinq.***
– *Après avoir fini mes devoirs et après le dîner, je me relaxe. J'aime surtout regarder la télé. Normalement je regarde la télé à neuf heures.*
– *Ecoute Pierre encore une fois.*

Exercice 2

Pupils match statements with the content of short conversations using verbs in the perfect tense. The language used in the statements does not reproduce that used in the spoken stimulus. This is typical of performance at **Level 4**, although the inclusion of the past tense means that pupils are working towards **Level 5.**
Total 5 marks.
Award 1 mark for each correct answer.
Pupils scoring at least 4 marks are showing some characteristics of performance at **Level 4**.

Answers
1e   2g   3a   4h   5d

Exercice 2

– *Qu'est ce que les jeunes ont fait? Lis la liste **A** à **H**.*
 Ecoute les jeunes. Choisis la bonne lettre.
 Exemple:
– *Cédric, qu'as-tu fait ce week-end?*
– *Moi, j'ai joué au football dans le parc avec mes amis.*
– ***Numéro un.***
– *Et toi, Delphine. Qu'as-tu fait samedi soir?*
– *Eh bien, samedi soir, je suis allée au cinéma avec mes copains.*
– ***Numéro deux.***
– *Bernard, qu'as-tu fait ce matin?*
– *Je me suis levé. Après ça, j'ai mangé du pain et un croissant, et j'ai bu du café au lait.*
– ***Numéro trois.***
– *Anne. Dis-moi ce que tu as fait ce week-end.*
– *Comme d'habitude je suis allée à la piscine et j'ai nagé pendant deux heures.*
– ***Numéro quatre.***
– *Paul. Samedi, qu'est-ce que tu as fait?*
– *Eh bien, samedi matin, je suis allé dans les magasins. J'ai acheté une nouvelle chemise et puis j'ai acheté un disque. Finalement je suis allé au supermarché où j'ai acheté les provisions pour le déjeuner.*
– ***Numéro cinq.***
– *Catherine. Qu'as-tu fait chez toi hier?*
– *J'ai fait beaucoup de choses pour ma mère. D'abord j'ai fait la vaisselle, ensuite j'ai passé l'aspirateur et finalement j'ai préparé le déjeuner pour la famille.*
– *Ecoute les jeunes encore une fois.*

Exercice 3

Here pupils listen to a longer passage and choose whether given statements are true or false. The text is delivered at near normal speed. This is again typical of performance at **Level 4**.
Total 10 marks.
Award 1 mark for each correct answer.
Pupils scoring at least 7 marks are showing characteristics of performance at **Level 4**.

Answers
1 F   **2** F   **3** V   **4** F   **5** V   **6** V   **7** V   **8** F   **9** V   **10** V

Exercice 3

– *Madeleine parle de sa famille. Regarde les affirmations **1** à **10**.*
 Ecoute Madeleine et coche la case 'vrai' ou la case 'faux' pour chaque affirmation. Ecoute les exemples.
– *Salut! Je m'appelle Madeleine. Je vais vous parler de ma famille. Eh bien, d'abord mon frère. J'ai un frère. Il s'appelle Jean-Paul. Jean-Paul a dix ans.*
– *Continue.*
– *Jean-Paul est très grand. Il aime bien le sport et la musique moderne. Je ne m'entends pas bien avec mon frère. Il n'est pas sympa envers moi.*

Ma mère s'appelle Monique. Elle a quarante-cinq ans et elle est très sympa et très calme. On s'amuse bien ensemble.
Mon père s'appelle Henri. Mes parents sont divorcés, donc mon père n'habite pas avec nous. Il a un appartement à Paris. C'est dommage parce que j'aime mon père. Il est très marrant.
J'ai aussi une grand-mère, Françoise. C'est la mère de ma mère. Elle habite avec nous depuis vingt ans. Elle est très, très vieille – elle a quatre-vingt-douze ans. Elle passe beaucoup de temps à lire. Elle adore les romans policiers.
Je dois aussi vous parler de notre chien. C'est un petit chien brun qui aboie tout le temps, tout le temps. Il est dingue, notre chien – complètement dingue!
– *Ecoute Madeleine encore une fois.*

B – Epreuve orale

Exercice I

Pupils choose one of the two *Fiches*. The B role only is assessed. Pupils are expected to respond to four questions based on daily routine using short phrases, e.g. *Je me réveille à 7h 15*. They use visual cues to help them to respond to brief prepared tasks. This is a typical of performance at **Level 3**.
Total 4 marks.
Pupils gaining at least 3 of the 4 marks show some characteristics of performance at **Level 3**. Teachers who wish to elicit performances at a higher level could give the cue card to Pupil A only and assess the performance in terms of **Level 4**.
Performance at **Level 4** requires pupils to 'take part in simple structured conversations', in response to cues (from A) and to 'adapt and substitute single words and phrases'. A free response from Pupil B to Pupil A would therefore enable some characteristics of performance at **Level 4** to be assessed.

Exercice 2

Pupils choose one of the two *Fiches* and describe a best friend. The differentiation in the exercise is related to outcome. The *Fiche* is intended to cue utterances which enable pupils to display characteristics of performance at several levels.
Total 10 marks.
At **Level 2** pupils should be able to give short, simple responses and name and describe Alain or Lise. Pupils showing characteristics of performance at **Level 2** should be able to communicate meaning but they may need help from the teacher to cue their response and may not always be able to produce a phrase including a verbal construction.

e.g.	Teacher	*Comment est Alain?*
	Pupils	*Cheveux longs et noirs.*
	Teacher	*... et de caractère?*
	Pupils	*Il* (no verb) *sportif.*

At **Level 2** the pronunciation may be approximate and the delivery hesitant. 6 marks of the total 10 are for descriptive language. Pupils gaining 5 or more marks on the first tasks (the age of the friend, family details plus description) are showing some

characteristics of performance at **Level 2**.
At **Level 3**, pupils should be able to produce the above but their utterances will be longer and will often include a verbal form where appropriate (e.g. *Il est sportif. Il a les cheveux longs.*). At **Level 3** pupils should be able to express the likes/dislikes of their friend (e.g. *Il adore regarder la télévision.*).
At **Level 4**, performance will be characterised by generally accurate pronunciation, and the ability to give information on Alain and Lise, their appearance, character, likes, dislikes, reasons for likes/dislikes (e.g. *Mon ami n'aime pas l'école parce que c'est ennuyeux.*). Teachers may prefer to ask pupils to make their own *Fiche,* based on the same headings, this would enable the pupil's ability to adapt and substitute words and phrases to be assessed (also **Level 4**). Pupils scoring at least eight of the set marks are showing some characteristics of performance at **Level 4**.
Teachers may wish to add bonus marks as below. These enable the amount of help/support needed from the teacher to be taken into account. Some pupils may be able to treat the exercise as a presentation and proceed unaided, whereas others may need extra support from the teacher in the form of questions. These marks also give the opportunity to reward the degree of accuracy shown by pupils.
Add bonus marks out of 3 as follows:
1 mark – pupil manages to communicate the basic messages, language is often inaccurate but the meaning of most of the messages is there. Substantial help is needed from the teacher.
2 marks – communicates all the messages despite inaccuracies. Some help from the teacher.
3 marks – communicates the messages well. Language often very accurate. Little help needed.

Exercice 3

This test is aimed to cue utterances which enable pupils to display characteristics of performance up to **Level 5**. Pupils are required to give a short presentation of a party they attended (cued on the invitation). Visual cues are given (6 marks) and an opinion and a reason are requested (2 marks).
Total 8 marks.
Pupils scoring more than half marks and who can communicate but not always in the appropriate tense, who respond in short phrases with generally accurate pronunciation show some characteristics of performance at **Level 4**.
Pupils who manage to gain at least 6 of the set marks and who attempt to communicate in the correct tense are showing some characteristics of performance at **Level 5**.
Teachers may also wish to use the 3 mark bonus scheme (as in Exercise 2) to allow for greater differentiation.

C – Epreuve de lecture

Exercice 1

Pupils show understanding of a short text made up of familiar language based on daily routine. The test is a cloze test, pupils are given the words from which to choose the correct work. (Incorrect spellings are tolerated). This is typical of performance at **Level 3**. Total 5 marks.

Award ½ mark for each item and then round up to give a total out of 5.

Pupils scoring at least 4 or 5 marks are showing some characteristics of performance at **Level 3**.

Answers

1	*lève*	6	*prends*
2	*lave*	7	*fais*
3	*habille*	8	*relaxe*
4	*prends*	9	*écoute*
5	*vais*	10	*couche*

Exercice 2

This test requires the understanding of three short factual texts, of which one is handwritten. Pupils need to understand and note the main points (including likes and dislikes). This is typical of performance at **Level 4**.
Total 8 marks.
Pupils gaining at least 6 marks are showing some characteristics of performance at **Level 4**.

Answers

1 *Paul*
2 *Paul*
3 *Cécile*
4 *Agnès*
5 *Paul*
6 *Agnès*
7 *Cécile*
8 *Paul*

Exercice 3

This test again requires the understanding of short texts but the stimulus material includes the use of past tenses and pupils not only have to note the activity but also an opinion. This is typical of performance at **Level 5**. Pupils fill in the grid, choosing the letter of the activity and ticking the smiling face (positive opinion) or frowning face (negative opinion). Both items (activity and opinion) are needed for a mark.
Total 4 marks.
Pupils scoring at least 3 or 4 marks are showing some characteristics of performance at **Level 5**.

Answers

	Activité	☺	☹
Corinne	a	–	✓
Raoul	f	–	✓
Fabrice	d	–	✓
Dominique	c	✓	–

Exercice 4

This is a test aimed at the more able pupil. Pupils need to show understanding of quite a long text recounting events in the past but which refers to present and, in one case, future events. Pupils need to note the main points concerning the order of events at the party in the first exercise. The second exercise based on the text uses *vrai/faux* + correction to test both factual events and opinions. If teachers felt it appropriate both tests could be used (4 marks per exercise).
Total 8 marks.
Both exercises are tests of performance at **Level 5**, but the second exercise is more demanding in terms of production.
Pupils scoring at least 3 marks on each exercise are showing some characteristics of performance at **Level 5**.

Answers

7h	a	+	f
8h	i	+	k
9h	h	+	e
↓	b		
↓	g	(given)	
12h	d		

Award ½ mark per correct item.
Note: if only one exercise is used, award 1 mark per item.

Answers

1 *Faux: Sébastien est le frère de Marianne.*
2 *Vrai*
3 *Faux:* Accept either *Eliane a trouvé Lucien amusant* or *Eliane a trouvé Philippe bête* (or other appropriate adjective).
4 *Faux: Lucien va téléphoner lundi/demain.*
5 *Vrai*

Award ½ mark for correct *vrai* or *faux* plus ½ mark for correction.
Note: if only one exercise is used, award 1 mark per item.

Epreuve 1

D – Epreuve écrite

Exercice 1
Pupils are required to write a few sentences based on picture stimuli and including a simple expression of like or dislike. The exercise is typical of performance at **Level 3**.
Total 5 marks.
Award 1 mark for each sentence. Spelling need only be approximate, but must be understandable for the award of the mark. Award only $1/2$ mark if there is no expression of opinion included. There is no directive that the opinion should differ each time.
Pupils scoring at least $3^1/2$ marks are showing some characteristics of performance at **Level 3**.

Exercice 2
In this exercise, pupils again write a few sentences based on picture stimuli. The sentences are made more complex, however, in that two elements must be included in each. This exercise is again typical of performance at **Level 3**.
Total 10 marks.
Award up to 2 marks for each sentence. Spelling can be approximate, though teachers might wish to be more severe on spelling errors than in the previous exercise. Award 1 mark for each element of each sentence. Accept any reasonable interpretation of the pictures.
Pupils scoring at least 7 marks are showing some characteristics of performance at **Level 3**.

Exercice 3
The third exercise gives pupils the chance to write a short paragraph using verbs in the perfect tense, based on picture stimuli. At the end of the exercise, pupils are given the opportunity to add further material as they wish, the instruction to do so being represented by question marks. The exercise is typical of performance at **Level 4**, working towards **Level 5**.
Total 10 marks.
Award 1 mark for the rendering of each stimulus. Award only $1/2$ mark if the verb used is not recognisable as a perfect tense. Do not expect a different opinion each time and do not insist on a distinction between the normal and the smiling faces. Tolerate spelling errors – award the mark if the phrase written is readily understandable. Award $1/2$ mark if there is some doubt as to meaning.
Pupils scoring at least 7 marks are showing some characteristics of performance at **Level 4**.

51

CAMARADES 3 (TURQUOISE) OVERVIEW – UNITE 3 – LA VILLE ET LA CAMPAGNE   National Curriculum Areas of Experience: B, C, E

	Topics/objectives	Key language	Grammar	Skills and strategies	PoS coverage
A	**Ma ville, c'est nul!** Saying where you go/don't go and why	*souvent, ne ... jamais, rien, personne, trop cher, loin, ça bouge, patinoire, bowling, aller, magasins, cinéma, piscine, centre sportif, club des jeunes, parc, centre commercial, ville, ennuyeux, génial, souvent, parfois*	*au, à la* (revised) *ne ... personne, rien, jamais*		1 a c f 2 d h k l n 3 c e f
B	**Ça commence à quelle heure?** Asking for and understanding information, e.g. about times and cost	*concert, ça, commence, finit, coûte, se passe, entrée, brochure, à quelle heure, combien, où, ouvre, ferme*			1 i j 2 e j l n 3 e h 4 a
C	**Le concert, c'était génial!** Asking where things are Writing diary of visit	*billet, bar, kiosque des souvenirs, café-bar, toilettes, vestiaires, grande salle, sous-sol, rez-de-chaussée, premier étage, où est, sont, à côté de* (and activities in perfect tense)	Perfect tense (revised from Unit 2)		1 c d i j 2 a e i 3 f h 4 a d
D	**Grammar**		*au, à la* (revised) Negatives		1 i 2 k 3 d f g
E	**Le profil d'une ville** Describing a town	*cathédrale, calme, bruyant, grand, petit, joli, piéton, vieux, quartier, zone, industriel, port de plaisance, rue, marché, église, centre-ville, centre commercial, touristique, historique, jardin public, beau, nouveau, agréable, désagréable, pittoresque, propre, sale, moche*	Adjectives	Dictionary: being referred to another entry Writing: linking sentences with *qui*; ♣ incorporating phrases from text	1 a f i j 2 d g h l n o 3 b d e h
F	**C'est bien, le centre-ville?** Talking about town centre facilities	*marché, banque, hôpital, tabac, pharmacie, hypermarché, épicerie, poste, boulangerie-pâtisserie, boucherie, supermarché, il y a, il n'y a pas de, bien, pratique*	*il n'y a pas de*	Dictionary: using dictionary to check gender	1 a b d f h 2 a g h l 3 e f g 4 d
G	**Fais les magasins ... chez toi!** Reading: information about Minitel				1 g i j 2 d e j l 3 e 4 c
H	**Grammar**		Adjectives		1 j 2 e k n 3 c f
I	**Et la campagne?** Talking about what you can do in the countryside	*au printemps, en été, automne, hiver, vélo tout terrain, randonnée, à cheval, pique-nique, voile, canoë-kayak, bataille de boules de neige, bonhomme, patin à glace, ski alpin, de fond, on peut, barbecue, natation, pêche* (and opinions)	*on peut* + infinitive	Speaking: phrases for giving your opinion	1 a b f 2 g h k l 3 b 4 d
J	**Le temps et les saisons** Talking about the weather and the seasons	*pleut, neige, beau, mauvais, du soleil, du vent, du brouillard, chaud, froid, fait* (and seasons)		Learning vocabulary (diagrams and symbols) ♣ Dictionary: looking up verbs in infinitive	1 b d g h i j 2 a l n 3 b c d e g 4 d
K	**Les impressionnistes et la Normandie** Reading for interest				1 b g i 2 h j m n 3 g
L	**Atelier** Looking at the advantages and disadvantages of a town from different perspectives				1 a b c f j 2 a g h l 3 g 4 d

Worksheets

Recommended use of the worksheets (in some cases they can be used later, as revision):

Spread	Worksheet	Spread	Worksheet	Spread	Worksheet	Spread	Worksheet
A		D		G		J ....7 and 8, 9 and 10	
B ....3 and 4		E		H.................11		K	
C		F 12		I .... 5 and 6		L................. 16	

Feuille 1 and 2 Vocabulaire

Feuille 3 On écoute ◆ (Exercise 1)
Feuille 4 On écoute ♣ (Exercise 1a)

1 – Alors, Léa, qu'est-ce qu'on fait demain?
– Moi, j'ai une bonne idée! On pourrait aller au centre sportif, regarder le match de basket.
– Ça commence à quelle heure?
– Euh, ça commence à 15h00 et finit vers 16h45. J'aimerais bien y aller parce que mon frère y joue. Il est capitaine de l'équipe.
– Bof … on pourrait y aller, mais moi, vraiment, je trouve le basket un peu ennuyeux …
2 – On pourrait aller au nouveau musée en ville. C'est un musée de la musique.
– Ah oui, ce serait super! C'est combien, l'entrée?
– C'est seulement 20F.
– Pas mal.
– Ah non! Impossible! Regarde – le musée est fermé le mardi.
– Zut alors!
3 – Regarde dans le journal. On pourrait peut-être aller au cinéma.
– Bonne idée. Voyons … Oui, il y a 'Le monstre du lac', qui commence à 20h00.
– 'Le monstre du lac'? C'est un film de science-fiction?
– Oui.
– Alors, non. Je déteste les films de science-fiction.
4 – Alors, il y a aussi un film policier.
– Ça commence à quelle heure?
– Ça commence à 19h45.
– Et ça s'appelle comment?
– Ça s'appelle 'Trois coups'.
– Ah non!
– Quoi?
– Je l'ai déjà vu! Je l'ai vu la semaine dernière!
5 – Tu aimerais aller au musée municipal? Il y a une exposition sur les animaux en danger.
– Oui, je veux bien! Ça m'intéresse beaucoup. Je suis membre de Greenpeace, tu sais.
– Bon, alors, ça ouvre à 10h30.
– Et ça ferme à quelle heure?
– Ça ferme à 17h30.
– Et l'entrée, c'est combien?
– C'est gratuit.
– Ça, c'est bien.

6 – Regarde! Il y a un concert de rock, mardi soir. Le groupe, s'appelle 'Les Glaçons'.
– 'Les Glaçons'? J'ai acheté leur CD hier! Il est super bien! Le concert commence à quelle heure?
– Ça commence à 20h30.
– Et ça coûte combien?
– Attends … les billets coûtent 75F. Ça, c'est un peu cher …
– Mais ils sont chouette!
7 – Regarde, il y a une annonce ici. Il va y avoir un défilé mardi après-midi.
– Ah oui, moi, je l'ai vu l'année dernière!
– C'était bien?
– Oui, tout le monde s'est déguisé. Les costumes étaient très très beaux.
– Ah bon?
– Ça commence à quelle heure?
– Le défilé part de l'hôtel de ville à 15h30.

Feuille 3 On écoute ◆

Exercise 2
Ciel bleu
Ciel gris
Soleil ou pluie?
Le printemps rit!

En mars
Le printemps fait des farces!
En avril
L'été se faufile!

Exercise 3
Le mois le plus gentil de l'été,
Le plus ensoleillé
De l'année
C'est juillet.
Sec ou mouillé!

Grand soleil!
Et petit vent
Que le beau temps
règne souvent!
Entrons dans la danse
Des vacances.

Feuille 4 On écoute ♣

> **Exercise 1c**
> – *Salut, Léa. Qu'est-ce que tu as fait hier?*
> – *Eh bien, le matin, Robin et moi, nous sommes allés voir une exposition.*
> – *Quelle exposition?*
> – *C'était une expo sur les animaux en danger, au musée municipal.*
> – *C'était bien?*
> – *Oui, c'était vraiment intéressant. Il y avait beaucoup d'informations sur les animaux. Il y avait aussi une très bonne vidéo.*
> – *Et l'après-midi, qu'est-ce que vous avez fait?*
> – *Eh bien, l'après-midi, on a regardé le défilé, en ville.*
> – *Moi, aussi. Tu n'as pas trouvé ça nul?*
> – *Oui, complètement nul! Il n'y avait pas beaucoup de monde – environ trente personnes. C'était trop petit!*
> – *Oui, tu as raison.*
> – *Et puis le soir, on est allé à un concert de rock.*
> – *C'était qui?*
> – *Un groupe qui s'appelle 'Les Glaçons'.*
> – *Et alors?*
> – *Bof, ce n'était pas mal … La musique était assez bien.*

Feuille 5 On parle ♦

Feuille 6 On parle ♣

Feuille 7 On lit ♦ (free-standing)

Feuille 8 On lit ♣ (free-standing)

Feuille 9 On écrit ♦ (free-standing)

Feuille 10 On écrit ♣ (free-standing)
Pupils could also add quotes from visitors (using the perfect tense and including opinions), e.g. *J'ai visité le musée. C'était vraiment super!* Point out the difference in style between less formal spoken 'quotes' and the more formal text (see the *Stratégies* box).

Feuille 11 Grammaire

Feuille 12 En plus (free-standing)

Feuille 13 Que sais-tu?

> **1** – *Ma ville, c'est complètement nul, tu sais.*
> – *Pourquoi tu dis ça?*
> – *Eh bien, parce qu'il n'y a rien pour les jeunes de mon âge.*
> – *Il n'y a pas de discothèque?*
> – *Tu blagues! Il n'y a même pas de club des jeunes.*
> **2** – *Que penses-tu de ta ville, Xavier?*
> – *Bof, ça va.*
> – *Est-ce qu'il y a beaucoup de choses à faire pour les personnes de ton âge?*
> – *Ça dépend. Pour ceux qui aiment le sport, il y a un centre sportif, et il y a deux cinémas, aussi.*
> – *Ce n'est pas mal, ça, quand même.*
> – *Oui, mais le problème, c'est que tout ça coûte assez cher. Donc je ne peux pas sortir très souvent.*
> – *Ah oui, je comprends.*

> **3** – *Moi, j'aime bien mon village.*
> – *Ce n'est pas ennuyeux?*
> – *Mais non, pas du tout. Il y a beaucoup de jeunes de mon âge – j'ai beaucoup d'amis dans le village. On sort ensemble.*
> – *Qu'est-ce que vous faites, alors?*
> – *Ben, ça dépend de la saison. En été, on fait des barbecues, on fait du canoë-kayak sur la rivière et on fait de la voile sur le lac.*
> – *Génial! Et en hiver?*
> – *En hiver on fait souvent du ski de fond. J'adore ça.*
> **4** – *Moi, je n'aime pas vivre à la campagne.*
> – *Pourquoi?*
> – *Il n'y a rien! Ça m'énerve!*
> – *Comment, il n'y a rien?*
> – *Eh bien, par exemple, il n'y a pas de banque dans mon village. Pour aller à la banque, je dois prendre le bus et aller en ville. C'est assez loin.*
> – *Ah oui, je vois.*
> – *En plus, il n'y a rien à faire le soir. Il n'y a pas de cinéma, il n'y a pas de bon restaurant.*
> – *Oui, c'est embêtant.*
> **5** – *Vous habitez en ville ou à la campagne?*
> – *J'habite en ville, dans une grande ville industrielle.*
> – *Il y a beaucoup de choses à faire, alors.*
> – *C'est vrai. On passe de bons films, il y a plusieurs bons restaurants au centre-ville.*
> – *Alors, vous êtes content d'habiter en ville.*
> – *Hmm, c'est difficile à dire. Parfois, j'aime ça, mais, vous savez, la ville, c'est très sale et bruyant. En ville, je ne peux pas me détendre.*
> – *Oui, je comprends.*
> **6** – *Toi aussi, tu habites en ville, n'est-ce pas?*
> – *Oui, j'habite avec ma mère et ma sœur en plein centre-ville.*
> – *Tu sors souvent?*
> – *Tu parles! Ma copine et moi, on sort presque tous les soirs. On va danser, ou bien on prend un coca dans un café.*
> – *Ça bouge, bein!*
> – *Ah oui. Et le week-end, on va dans les magasins, on va au bowling, ou au Macdo.*
> – *Ça doit être vraiment super!*
> – *Oui, mais il faut avoir beaucoup d'argent. Moi, je dois toujours demander de l'argent à ma mère, et ça m'énerve. En plus, je me couche très tard. Alors, je suis fatigué à l'école. En classe, c'est difficile.*

Feuille 14 Révision 1: describing a *fête* (free-standing)
Discuss the different styles, registers and content with your pupils.
To help pupils write their own description in Exercise 4, they could underline phrases in the perfect tense in the descriptions on the sheet.

Feuille 15 Révision 2: pets (free-standing)

Feuille 16 Grille
Support for Spread L Exercises 1 and 2.

Feuille 17 Réponses
This provides answers for the Unit 3 worksheets.

IT Opportunities

A6 **Spread A Exercise 6**
* Using a word-processor pupils write a first draft of sentences describing their town and their opinion of it. They redraft for accuracy and paragraph it appropriately. They then redraft it into a letter to their *corres français(e)* adding the formalities and some questions and choosing an appropriate font. Remember to have French dictionaries nearby if a French spell checker is unavailable.
◆ Provide a list of different letter greetings and endings for pupils to choose or adapt.

B3/4 **Spread B Exercises 3 and 4**
Extension
If there is access to the Internet, some pupils might like to decide on another French town, e.g. Marseille, and search, using a French search engine or given URLs, for an interesting text to print out to which they write similar type questions to those in Exercises 3 and 4. They could save the text in a word-processor and simplify it. Alternatively, they could search for further information on Rouen and compare it with that in the book.

C1b **Spread C Exercise 1b**
To help pupils become more familiar with the language, write a description of *Le plan du centre Pierre Laval* into a text manipulator with prediction and storyboard options.
◆ Pupils then practise the language, using the prediction option first, with the help of the diagram in the book.
♣ Pupils listen to the cassette without the book, making notes of positions of places and then do the text manipulation exercise (without the book).

E3 **Spread E Exercise 3**
The description could be both prepared and written using a word-processor. For example, pupils can brainstorm in pairs the notes and sentences needed to write their description of their own town. They could then turn these into the description, rearranging as most appropriate. If time and facilities are available, clipart can be used to illustrate the text, or pictures which have been collected could be scanned in.

H4 **Spread H Exercise 4**
◆ Word-process a description of the local town/village without any adjectives and save it. Pupils load up the paragraph and add their own adjectives to each sentence.

J3 **Spread J Exercise 3**
* Pupils use their notes to word-process an article about the climates in French speaking countries.
♣ Pupils could begin the article with something about the climate in the north and south of France, comparing it with the UK. They redraft their article for accuracy, format appropriately and print out to submit to 'the school magazine'.

K3 **Spread K Exercise 3**
* Pupils word-process the report, save it and merge the new file into the description written for Spread E Exercise 3. (Alternatively, they load in the file from Spread E Exercise 3 and add their report in an appropriate place.)

A Ma ville, c'est nul!   pp 50–51

Objectives
Saying where you go / don't go, and why

Resources
Cassette for Exercises 1, 2, 3 and 4

Key language
souvent, ne … jamais, rien, personne, trop cher, loin, ça bouge, patinoire, bowling, aller, magasins, cinéma, piscine,

centre sportif, club des jeunes, parc, centre commercial, ville, ennuyeux, génial, souvent, parfois

Grammar
au, à la (revised)
ne … personne, rien, jamais

The unit begins with recycled names of places, as revision, and as a familiar vehicle for grammar points.

Ways in

Read and listen to the photo story.

Answers
1 c, h   **2** d, e   **3** g, b   **4** f, a   **5** d, b

> **1** – *Tu penses que c'est ennuyeux ici?*
> – *Ben non. Pas du tout! Moi, j'adore le sport. Je vais souvent au centre sportif.*
> – *Ah oui, c'est très moderne.*
> – *Et parfois je vais à la piscine.*
> **2** – *Et toi, Katia. Tu aimes le sport?*
> – *Pas vraiment. Mais il y a beaucoup d'autres choses à faire ici. Le samedi, j'aime aller dans les magasins.*
> – *Et qu'est-ce que tu fais pendant la semaine?*
> – *Une fois par semaine, je vais au club des jeunes.*
> **3** – *Loïc, est-ce que tu penses que c'est ennuyeux ici?*
> – *Mais non! Il y a beaucoup de choses à faire le soir! Moi, par exemple, je vais souvent au cinéma. Il y a un grand cinéma ici.*
> – *Et tu fais du sport?*
> – *Bof. Parfois, je vais à la patinoire … J'aime bien ça.*
> **4** – *Et toi, Sylvie. Tu vas où en ville?*
> – *Eh bien, je vais très souvent au parc, avec mes chiens. C'est un grand parc, et on peut y jouer au tennis, aussi.*
> – *Et le soir?*
> – *Je vais souvent au bowling avec mes copains.*
> **5** – *Qu'est-ce que tu fais le week-end, Hamed?*
> – *Moi, le samedi, je vais au centre commercial avec mes copains. On va dans les magasins, on achète des CD. Parfois, on va chez Macdo …*
> – *Et le soir?*
> – *Je vais souvent à la patinoire. J'adore ça!*

 Do this first as open practice with the whole class, focusing on *parfois* and *souvent*. Encourage pupils to give reasons, too. Re-introduce other places they already know.

The grammar point *au/à la* etc. has arisen before but is revised on Spread D, page 56, as it is a key point, with many applications.

> – *Moi, je ne vais jamais en ville. Il n'y a rien à faire pour les jeunes.*
> – *Mais non, ce n'est pas ennuyeux en ville. Le samedi soir, ça bouge!*
> – *Je ne vais jamais au cinéma, parce que c'est trop cher. Et il n'y a personne de mon âge au club des jeunes …*
> – *Mais beaucoup de jeunes de notre âge vont à la patinoire! Et ce n'est pas trop loin – vingt minutes en bus.*

Suggest that pupils listen in stages:
◆ note the places first, then note ✓ / ✗;
♣ note any reasons on the second hearing.

◆ You could encourage pupils to note any reasons they can make out.
♣ After taking notes, pupils could write up or say the reasons as full sentences. Remind them of likely changes, *e.g.* **mon** *âge* ➪ **son** *âge*.
Remind all pupils to listen carefully for negatives: *il n'y a pas / je ne vais jamais* etc.

Answers
1 *parc ✓; cinéma ✗ (trop cher)*
2 *en ville ✗ (trop loin); chez une copine ✓*
3 *centre commercial ✓ (ça bouge); Macdo ✗ (végétarien)*
4 *centre sportif ✓ (beaucoup de choses à faire pour les jeunes); gymnase ✓ (se préparer pour le match de foot)*
5 *café ✓ (pas cher); club des jeunes ✗ (personne de son âge)*
6 *discothèque ✗ (trop jeune)*

> **1** – *Tu sors le week-end?*
> – *Oui, le samedi, je vais souvent au parc.*
> – *Tu vas souvent au cinéma, le soir?*
> – *Non, je ne vais jamais au cinéma.*
> – *Non? Pourquoi?*
> – *Ben, parce que c'est trop cher.*
> **2** – *Est-ce que tu vas souvent en ville, le week-end?*
> – *Non. Je ne vais jamais en ville.*
> – *Jamais? Pourquoi?*
> – *Eh bien, c'est trop loin. Moi, j'habite dans un petit village à la campagne. Le transport, c'est un grand problème pour les jeunes.*

– *Qu'est-ce que tu fais, alors?*
– *Le week-end? Normalement, je vais chez une copine.*

3 – *Est-ce que tu vas souvent au centre commercial?*
– *Oui, j'y vais souvent avec mes copains.*
– *Vous aimez ça?*
– *Oui, le samedi, ça bouge! On s'amuse bien.*
– *Vous allez prendre un hamburger chez Macdo?*
– *Non, jamais, parce que je ne mange pas de viande. Je suis végétarien.*

4 – *Qu'est-ce que tu fais, le week-end?*
– *Moi, je vais souvent au centre sportif.*
– *C'est bien?*
– *Oui, très bien. Il y a beaucoup de choses à faire pour les jeunes.*
– *Qu'est-ce que tu fais, toi, en particulier?*
– *Alors, moi par exemple, je vais au gymnase le mercredi après-midi pour me préparer pour mon match de football le samedi. Si on joue au foot, l'entraînement est très important.*

5 – *Tu sors le week-end?*
– *Ça dépend. Je vais parfois au café avec mes copines.*
– *Au café?*
– *Oui. On prend un coca. Ce n'est pas cher.*
– *Est-ce que tu vas au club des jeunes?*
– *Tu blagues?! Moi, je ne vais jamais au club des jeunes!*
– *Non? Pourquoi?*
– *Eh bien, parce qu'il n'y a personne de mon âge. Ils ont tous onze ans … douze ans. C'est complètement bête!*

6 – *Tu vas parfois en discothèque, le vendredi ou le samedi soir?*
– *Moi, j'aimerais aller en discothèque, mais je n'y vais jamais.*
– *Pourquoi?*
– *Ben, parce qu'il faut avoir dix-huit ans, et moi, j'ai seulement quatorze ans. J'y suis allé, mais on ne m'a pas laissé entrer!*

This would be an appropriate time to work on negatives on Spread D *Grammaire,* page 57.

◆ Remind pupils to think about grammar: *au/à la* etc.

Differentiation
◆ Pupils could use vocabulary from the spread.
♣ Pupils could use a greater range of vocabulary from earlier in the course or from a dictionary.

Alternatively, you could prepare this together as a class. Give pupils help in talking about particular things in their own town or village.

B **Ça commence à quelle heure?**   **pp 52–53**

Objectives
Asking for and undertanding information, e.g. about times and cost

Resources
Cassette for Exercise 1

Key language
concert, ça, commence, finit, coûte, se passe, entrée, brochure, à quelle heure, combien, où, ouvre, ferme

Ways in
You could begin by revising times in French, especially the 24 hour clock. For example, give times in the 24 hour clock, and ask pupils to give the equivalent in the 12 hour clock, and vice versa.

Pupils could give correct answers to the false statements.

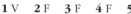

Answers
1 V   **2** F   **3** F   **4** F   **5** F
There is more listening work on this theme on *Feuilles 3* and *4*.

2

♣ As input for this, pupils could research what's on for homework, for example by looking in a local paper, and note the details in French. Otherwise, you could bring in information and read it out in French for them to take notes. Give advice on formulating new questions, such as *C'est ouvert quand?*.

You could read the tourist information on Rouen together as a class before pupils answer the questions individually. Here are some activities:
• Read out sections, then stop suddenly. Pupils have to say the word or phrase which follows.
• Read out sections, making deliberate mistakes, which pupils have to correct.
• Make statements, e.g. *La cathédrale est ouverte tous les jours*. Pupils have to say whether they are true or false.
• Ask for specific information about different places, e.g. the entry price.

3

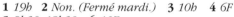
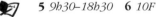
Answers
1 *19h*   **2** *Non. (Fermé mardi.)*   **3** *10h*   **4** *6F*
5 *9h30–18h30*   **6** *10F*

Differentiation
More able pupils could answer in complete sentences.

4

Point out to pupils that they do not have to understand every word in order to answer the questions. Tell them that many of the key words are similar to English words, so they will be able to work them out for themselves, without looking them up. When pupils have completed the activity, discuss with them which words they worked out and which they had to look up. Highlight to pupils that there were a number of words which they didn't need to understand at all.

Ask your pupils to volunteer any information they know about Joan of Arc. She is an important heroine for the French. She lived from 1412 to 1431, during the Hundred Years war between England and France. A simple country girl, she was spurred by visions of saints into leading an army against the English. Declared a heretic, she was burned at the stake. Her story is told in more detail in **Camarades 4**.

C Le concert, c'était génial! pp 54–55

Objectives
Asking where things are
Writing a diary of a visit

Resources
Presentation sheet 8
Cassette for Exercise 1

Key language
billet, bar, kiosque des souvenirs, café-bar, toilettes, vestiaires, grande salle, sous-sol, rez-de-chaussée, premier étage, où est, sont, à côté de (and activities in perfect tense)

Grammar
perfect tense (revised)

Ways in
Presentation sheet 8 has a cross section of a building, as on page 54. The symbols for the places and the labels can be cut out and moved around from one floor of the building to another. As well as asking pupils to say what floor the facilities are on, revise relative positions, using *près de* and *à côté de*.

1a Read and listen to the photo story.

COUNTER

1b **Answers**
1 ✓
2 ✗ *Il est au premier étage, près du kiosque.*
3 ✓
4 ✗ *Ils sont au sous-sol, à côté des toilettes.*
5 ✗ *Il est au rez-de-chaussée, près de la grande salle.*
6 ✗ *Il est au premier étage, à côté du café-bar.*

COUNTER

1 – *Pardon, Madame. Où sont les toilettes, s'il vous plaît?*
   – *Elles sont au sous-sol, à côté des vestiaires.*
2 – *Pardon, Madame. Vous ne savez pas où est le café-bar, s'il vous plaît?*
   – *Le café-bar? Il est au rez-de-chaussée, près de la grande salle.*
3 – *Pardon, Madame. Pourriez-vous me dire où est la grande salle, s'il vous plaît?*
   – *Elle est ici, au rez-de-chaussée, bien sûr!*
4 – *Pardon. Tu ne sais pas où sont les vestiaires, s'il te plaît?*
   – *Les vestiaires … ? Euh, je ne sais pas … Je pense qu'ils sont au premier étage. Oui, ils sont juste à côté du café-bar.*
5 – *Pardon, Madame. Pourriez-vous m'indiquer où est le bar, s'il vous plaît?*
   – *Le bar est au premier étage, Monsieur, près du café-bar. Il y a un escalier ici, à gauche.*
6 – *Pardon. Où est le kiosque des souvenirs, s'il te plaît?*
   – *Oh, je ne l'ai pas vu, mais je pense qu'il est au sous-sol, près des toilettes.*

2 Before pupils start, make sure they have had plenty of practise using *où **est*** and *où **sont*** and using the phrases *près **de*** and *à côté **de*** appropriately. You could use Presentation sheet 8 for this.

3 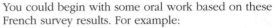 You could begin with some oral work based on these French survey results. For example:
- Ask pupils to pick out percentages, e.g. *Combien de personnes n'ont jamais visité un musée?*
- Ask general questions, e.g. *Lève la main si tu es déjà allé à un cirque. Lève la main si tu n'es jamais allé à un zoo.*
- Ask questions of individual pupils, e.g. *Lauren, tu as déjà assisté à un concert de musique classique?* They can answer with single words or phrases, e.g. *Oui, deux fois* or in whole sentences.
- Pupils could then ask similar questions in pairs.

Differentiation
When pupils come to write their answers, more able pupils could give full sentences, e.g.
Je n'ai jamais assisté à un concert de rock.
Je suis souvent allé dans un parc d'attraction.
Pupils could do a class survey and present the results in a table, as in the Pupil's Book. They could add other questions, for example including places from Spread A.

4 Activities 4 and 5 revise the perfect tense, bringing together *avoir* and *être* verbs from Unit 2.

Answer
c f b i j a h e

5 Pupils can refer back to the brochures on Spread B for ideas about what to do in Rouen, and can also make things up!

D Grammaire

Grammar
au, à la, à l', aux (revised)
negatives *(ne ... rien / personne / jamais)*

---

au, à la, à l', aux

This key point has many uses and arises in a wide range of contexts.

1
◆ Here, its use in the sense of 'to' and 'at' is revised.

2
♣ This exercise also practises *au, à la, à l', aux* in the sense of 'to' and 'at'. Pupils apply the principle to new words which they have looked up in the dictionary.

3
Pupils are also reminded that the principle is applied in set phrases using *à*. Here, we focus on *s'intéresser à*. This helps to make pupils realise that rules and patterns which they learn in one context can also be used elsewhere.

ne ... rien / personne / jamais

4
Answers
1 *jamais*   **2** *personne*   **3** *rien*   **4** *jamais*
5 *personne*

5
♣ This activity gives pupils the opportunity to use the new expressions with less guidance.

E Le profil d'une ville

pp 58–59

Objectives
Describing a town

Resources
Presentation sheet 9
Cassette for Exercise 2

Key language
cathédrale, calme, bruyant, grand, petit, joli, piéton, vieux, quartier, zone, industriel, port de plaisance, rue, marché, église, centre-ville, centre-commercial, touristique,

historique, jardin public, beau, nouveau, agréable, désagréable, pittoresque, propre, sale, moche

Grammar
Adjectives

Strategies
Dictionary: being referred to another entry
Writing: linking sentences with *qui*;
♣ incorporating phrases from text

Ways in
You can introduce and practise places in town using Presentation sheet 9.

1 As you look at the *Stratégie* box together, ask pupils to explain to you the features of the dictionary entry for *beau*. They should remember what *m*, *f* etc. signify.

Part **b** of the exercise gets pupils to extract key vocabulary from text in meaningful lists.
You could now work on Spread H *Grammaire*, which looks at regular adjectives and some irregular ones.

2 This activity focuses on adjectives.

Answers
1 *belle, vieille, touristique*
2 *grand, bel, impressionnant*
3 *joli, agréable, propre*
4 *moderne, moche*
5 *grand, pratique, moche, sale*
6 *super, intéressant*

> **1** *Moi, mon endroit préféré à Rouen, c'est la rue Damiette. Je la trouve vraiment belle. C'est une vieille rue très touristique. Elle a beaucoup de vieilles maisons.*
> **2** *A Rouen, nous avons un grand et très bel hôtel de ville. Tous les touristes trouvent notre hôtel de ville très impressionnant, et moi, je suis d'accord.*
> **3** *Ici à Rouen, nous avons un jardin public en plein centre-ville. C'est le jardin de l'hôtel de ville. C'est un joli jardin, avec beaucoup de fleurs. A midi, j'aime bien manger mes sandwichs là-bas, parce qu'il est agréable et très propre.*
> **4** *Normalement, les églises sont assez vieilles, mais l'église Sainte-Jeanne-d'Arc à Rouen est différente! C'est une église très moderne. Moi, personnellement, je pense qu'elle est moche! Je n'aime pas l'architecture moderne. Je préfère les vieilles églises.*

> **5** *Près de chez moi, il y a un centre commercial. C'est vraiment très, très grand. Il y a beaucoup de magasins, donc c'est très pratique, mais que c'est moche! En plus, le centre est toujours sale: il y a des papiers partout sur le plancher. Moi, je préfère aller en ville.*
> **6** *Il y a beaucoup de musées à Rouen, mais moi, mon musée préféré n'est pas à Rouen. C'est le musée de l'Automobile, qui se trouve à Clères, près de Rouen. A mon avis, c'est un musée super! J'adore les voitures, surtout les anciennes voitures, donc je trouve ce musée vraiment intéressant!*

For extra practice of places and adjectives, try the following activity. Pupils work in groups. One person chooses an adjective. The rest of the group has to say as many places as possible in their town (or a nearby town) which that adjective could be used to describe.
For example:
– *Moderne.*
– *Le supermarché Tesco est moderne; la piscine Edmund Wilson est moderne …*
The class could do this together first then split into groups.

You could also ask pupils to classify adjectives as positive/negative/neutral.

3 Encourage pupils to use the dictionary to look up nouns and adjectives here, and remind them to apply grammar appropriately, using the correct forms according to gender and number.

F C'est bien, le centre-ville?

pp 60–61

Objectives
Talking about town centre facilities

Resources
Presentation sheet 10
Cassette for Exercises 1 and 3

Key language
marché, banque, hôpital, tabac, pharmacie, hypermarché,

épicerie, poste, boulangerie-pâtisserie, boucherie, supermarché, il y a, il n'y a pas de, bien, pratique

Grammar
il n'y a pas de

Strategies
Using dictionary to check gender

Ways in
Presentation sheet 10 has the names of the places and facilities covered on this spread.
You can use them to present the new vocabulary, or use Exercise 1 to present it and Presentation sheet 10 to practise it later.

As you look at the *Stratégie* box, point out to pupils that the dictionary isn't only useful for looking up the meanings of words.

Explain to pupils what is sold in a *tabac:* newspapers, magazines, sweets and stamps, as well as cigarettes and tobacco.

Answers
1 *Mme Lévy*
2 *Le docteur Beauvoir*
3 *Mme Arnaud*
4 *M. Duhamel*
5 *Violaine*

♣ Pupils can note more than one reason, if they are able.

1 *Vous travaillez dans le centre-ville? Venez à la charcuterie Dupont, rue Jeanne d'Arc. Ouverte tous les jours de neuf heures jusqu'à dix-sept heures trente. Pourquoi ne pas acheter une petite quiche ou une pizza pour votre déjeuner ou comme casse-croûte pendant l'après-midi?*
2 *Attention, les amateurs de patin à glace! Pendant le mois de janvier, la patinoire Duchêne sera ouverte jusqu'à vingt-deux heures!*
3 *Le tabac du Pont, rue de la République, a tout ce dont vous avez besoin! Venez acheter votre journal du matin, des magazines sur les voitures, des bonbons … Ouvert dès six heures du matin.*

4 *Moi, j'adore le sport, surtout la natation. Mes copains et moi, nous allons souvent à la nouvelle piscine au centre nautique. Elle est très grande et, en plus, ça ne coûte pas cher! Rouen, c'est vraiment bien pour les sportifs!*
5 *Vous détestez les supermarchés? Vous les trouvez trop grands et trop loin du centre-ville? Vous en avez marre de manger des carottes en boîte? Venez acheter vos légumes frais au marché! Vous trouverez un très grand choix de fruits et de légumes, à des prix raisonnables. Au marché, c'est bon marché!*
6 *Tous les jours, je vais à la boulangerie-pâtisserie Diderot après le travail. Pour acheter du pain pour le dîner, bien sûr. Mais les gâteaux sont **tellement délicieux** – les tartes aux pommes, les religieuses, les tartes aux amandes, les gâteaux au chocolat … Mmmmm! Je ne peux pas y résister!*

Each group could report back to the class as whole. Is there a consensus?

The theme is picked up again on Spread L *Atelier* at the end of the unit.

Feuille 12 provides a crossword, practising key vocabulary from this and previous spreads.

G Fais les magasins ... chez toi! **pp 62–63**

Objectives
Reading: information about *Minitel*

This spread gives background information on teleshopping and other *Minitel* services.

Strictly speaking, *Minitel* refers to the terminal, while the network itself is called *Télétel*. However, the name Minitel is used more commonly.

Some *Minitel* service providers now also have pages on the Internet.

Ask your pupils if they know of any similar services (e.g. the Internet, Prestel; and services such as Ceefax, which are non-interactive).

Suggested answers
1 V
2 F *(Il y a 15 000 / beaucoup de services Minitel.)*
3 V
4 F *(Certains services sont gratuits.)*
5 V
6 F *(On ne peut pas regarder des films sur Minitel. / On peut commander des films sur vidéodisque.)*

Pupils could also write down their own requests. Their partner has to give the appropriate information.

Pupils could also do the following activity:
◆ Pupils say which service(s) they are most interested in.
♣ ◆ + They also give a reason (e.g. *parce que j'aime aller au cinéma*).

If you have access to a computer with a modem, you may wish to access the *Télétel* network. Contact the National Council for Educational Technology (NCET) for the most up-to-date information on how to do so:

National Council for Educational Technology
Milburn Hill Road
Science Park
Coventry
CV4 7JJ
Tel: 01203 416994
Fax: 01203 411418
http://www.ncet.org.uk

H Grammaire

pp 64–65

Grammar
Adjectives *(les adjectifs)*

Les adjectifs

General work on adjectives has been done in previous books: here, we revise standard endings, cover some important exceptions, and look at the position of the adjectives. This lays a firm foundation for pupils going on to do an exam course next year. You could begin by finding out how much pupils remember about adjective endings from their previous work.

1 Go through the first explanatory table together before pupils start on Exercise 1. You could also do this as a spoken activity.
After you have read through the table with the exceptions, pupils can move on to the next exercises. They could try doing them without looking back at page 64, then checking their work afterwards.

2 ◆ Pupils have to select the correct form.

Answers
1 *beau* **2** *vieille* **3** *nouvelle* **4** *jolies*
5 *piétonne* **6** *touristiques* **7** *industrielle*
8 *historique*

3 ♣ In this activity, pupils have to provide the correct form themselves.

Answers
cadet, cadette, paresseux, travailleuse, nouvelles, sportives, vieilles, gentilles

4 The third table deals with the position of adjectives. As in Exercises 2 and 3, pupils doing the ◆ activity have to select from a choice of words, while the ♣ activity requires pupils to think of the correct form and position for themselves.

As an additional ♣ activity, you could give a number of phrases, for which pupils have to write the opposite phrase, e.g.
une vieille cathédrale ⇨ une cathédrale moderne

There is more practice of adjectives on *Feuille 11*.

1 Et la campagne?

Objectives
Talking about what you can do in the countryside

Resources
Presentation sheets 11 and 12 (top)
Cassette for Exercises 1 and 2

Key language
au printemps, en été, automne, hiver, vélo tout terrain, randonnée, à cheval, pique-nique, voile, canoë-kayak, *bataille de boules de neige, bonhomme, patin à glace, ski alpin, de fond, on peut, barbecue, natation, pêche* (and opinions)

Grammar
on peut + infinitive

Strategies
Speaking: phrases for giving your opinion

Ways in
The outdoor activities practised on this spread can be found on Presentation sheet 11 and on the top half of Presentation sheet 12. Alternatively, work from the illustrations on page 66 of the Pupil's Book, and use the OHT sheets for practice or revision later on.

Point out that many French people (and other continental Europeans) do cross-country skiing, on the flat, as well as downhill skiing. The skis for cross-country are different: the boots are attached only at the toe, not at the heel, to allow skiers to propel themselves over the ground.

After reading the text, you could ask pupils to close their books and try to say from memory what activities Caroline mentions for each season.

Pupils listen to the recording several times, listening for different information each time. You may wish to go over the answers to part **b** before pupils do part **c**.

> – *Oui, mais on peut faire de la natation en ville, à la piscine. A mon avis, c'est mieux, parce qu'on peut même faire de la natation en hiver!*
> – *C'est vrai, mais on ne peut pas faire de la voile en ville. On peut faire ça à la campagne. La voile, c'est vraiment chouette!*
> – *On peut faire des barbecues en ville. Nous, on fait un barbecue dans le jardin tous les week-ends, en été.*
> – *A mon avis, c'est mieux à la campagne. En ville, c'est sale! Il y a de la pollution.*
> – *Je ne suis pas d'accord! Rouen est une ville propre! A mon avis, c'est mieux en ville, parce qu'il y a beaucoup de choses pour les jeunes le soir. On peut aller au cinéma, par exemple. Le soir, c'est ennuyeux à la campagne!*
> – *Mais ce n'est pas vrai! On peut aller au cinéma à la campagne. Si c'est loin, on prend le bus! On peut faire des randonnées à cheval à la campagne. On ne peut pas faire ça en ville!*
> – *Oui, c'est vrai …*
> – *Et on peut faire du canoë-kayak à la campagne. On ne peut certainement pas faire ça en ville!*
> – *Mais si! A la piscine!*
> – *Oh là là!*

 This activity introduces phrases for giving opinions, agreeing and disagreeing.
Pupils could go on to make posters of their own.

 This focuses on the phrases introduced in Exercise 3, as preparation for their use in the productive activity which follows.

 As necessary, help pupils to prepare their ideas and arguments before they begin the debate. During the debate, pupils who are not talking at any one time should listen to others and note down the arguments for both sides.

After they have debated in groups, you could stage a whole class debate, with speakers being nominated from each group. Give groups the chance to revise or refine their arguments beforehand, with help from you if required. The whole class votes at the end.

The outdoor activities learned on this spread can be practised further in the activity on *Feuilles 5* and *6.*

J Le temps et les saisons   pp 68–69

Objectives
Talking about the weather and the seasons

Resources
Presentation sheet 12 (bottom)
Cassette for Exercises 3 and 4

Key language
pleut, neige, beau, mauvais, du soleil, du vent, du brouillard, chaud, froid, fait (and seasons)

Strategies
Learning vocabulary (diagrams and symbols)
♣ Dictionary: looking up verbs in infinitive

Ways in
As well as being presented on page 68, weather phrases with pictures can be found on the bottom half of Presentation sheet 12.

1
Read the *Stratégie* box together. Remind pupils that this technique can be used to learn other vocabulary as well. For example, they could draw up a similar diagram to learn activities such as those on Spread I. They could adapt it further, for example putting names of places in town in the circles, and linking them with appropriate adjectives.

Pupils could invent similar spoof adverts, featuring something other than a stone. These could form a wall display.

2
Make sure pupils have understood *hésitation interdite*.

3
Encourage pupils to note as much information as they can.

COUNTER

1 – *Vous habitez quel pays?*
– *J'habite au Canada.*
– *Comment est le climat là-bas. C'est comme en France?*
– *Ben, non, pas exactement. Le climat est plus extrême chez nous. Par exemple, les hivers sont très longs.*
– *Ah bon?*
– *Oui, il fait très froid en hiver.*
– *Il neige beaucoup?*
– *Oui, là où j'habite, il neige beaucoup en hiver.*
– *Et il fait assez froid en été, aussi?*
– *Au contraire! Il fait chaud en été.*
– *Il fait chaud?*
– *Oui, parfois il fait vraiment très très chaud!*
– *Alors vous avez raison. C'est vraiment un climat des extrêmes!*
2 – *Vous habitez quel pays?*
– *Moi, j'habite au Cameroun, en Afrique.*
– *Le Cameroun est situé dans l'ouest de l'Afrique, n'est-ce pas?*
– *Oui, sur la côte Atlantique.*
– *Et quel est le climat du Cameroun?*
– *Alors, ça dépend. Moi, j'habite dans le nord. Il fait très très chaud, bien sûr.*
– *Même en hiver?*
– *Et oui! Il fait chaud en été et en hiver!*

– *Et est-ce qu'il pleut beaucoup?*
– *En général, dans le nord, il ne pleut pas. Pas beaucoup. Mais au printemps, aux mois de mars et avril, c'est la saison des pluies. Alors là, au printemps, il pleut beaucoup beaucoup!*
3 – *Vous habitez en Corse, n'est-ce pas.*
– *Oui, c'est ça.*
– *Vous avez quel climat en Corse? C'est comme le climat italien?*
– *Eh bien, la Corse est très près de l'Italie, donc le climat est similaire. C'est un peu comme le sud de la France. En été, il fait très chaud.*
– *C'est désagréable? Il fait trop chaud?*
– *Ben, non, il ne fait pas trop chaud, parce qu'il fait du vent, aussi.*
– *Et en hiver, il fait froid?*
– *Ben ... non. Pas très froid.*
4 – *Vous habitez en Guadeloupe.*
– *Oui, entre l'Amérique du Nord et l'Amérique du Sud!*
– *Et vous avez quel climat, en Guadeloupe?*
– *Alors, de juin à octobre, il fait très, très chaud, environ 30 degrés.*
– *30 degrés?*
– *Oui, et il pleut beaucoup. C'est la saison des pluies.*
– *Alors, c'est humide.*
– *Oui, humide, c'est ça. Et puis de décembre à avril, il fait assez chaud. 24 degrés.*
– *24 degrés. C'est chaud, quand même!*
– *Mais à la montagne, il fait du brouillard. Il y a beaucoup de brouillard!*
– *Merci.*

4   **COUNTER**
Both poems are also read out on tape.

5
Students could illustrate their poems.

Feuilles 7 and 8 continue the weather theme. *Feuilles* 9 and 10 provide a guided writing activity which draws together the work of the unit.

K Les impressionnistes et la Normandie

Objectives
Reading for interest: Impressionists

This spread gives some information about the links between Impressionist painters and Normandy.

This activity establishes the meaning of key words in the article, as well as introducing the notion of word families.

The five sentences here summarise main points from the text.

Pupils are asked to give their personal response to the paintings. If possible, you could bring in copies of some other Impressionist paintings, for pupils to comment on. Try the art department or the school library.

You could introduce useful vocabulary and phrases, receptively at first, for pupils to use productively later, e.g.
Qui aime les couleurs de ce tableau?
Qui aime le style?
Qui trouve le sujet intéressant?
C'est une scène triste ou heureuse?

Pupils might be interested to know that although Impressionist paintings are very popular today, at the time they were painted they were considered by many to be shocking. Their modern, sketchy style was considered revolutionary, and inferior to 'proper' art.

You could do further work based on the theme of the article. For example, pupils work in groups and prepare questions for an 'interview' with Monet. The groups swap questions and prepare answers (serious or humorous). A representative from each group is then selected to act out mini-interviews.

You could do more work on word families. You could give pupils a partially filled table, with columns for *nom, adjectif* and *verbe*. Pupils have to fill in the blanks, using their dictionaries to help them. They could work individually or in pairs or groups, as appropriate. Here are some ideas, based on words which have appeared on recent spreads:

nom	adjectif	verbe
possibilité		
		discuter
différence		
		pleuvoir
	neigeux	

L Atelier

Objectives

Looking at the advantages and disadvantages of a town from different perspectives

Resources

Cassette for Photo story and Exercise 2

1a

The grid is available on *Feuille 16*. Check that all the categories and aspects have been understood and/or correctly looked up in the dictionary as necessary before pupils go on to complete the activity.

1b

Pupils should revise phrases for giving opinions, agreeing and disagreeing from Spread I, page 67.

2

COUNTER

For both parts of this activity, pupils could answer on the grids on *Feuille 16*.

> 1 – *Vous allez souvent au cinéma?*
> – *Euh non, je ne vais pas très souvent au cinéma.*
> – *Pourquoi?*
> – *Eh bien, parce que c'est cher. Un billet coûte 65F. Alors, pour une famille de cinq personnes, ça fait beaucoup!*
> 2 – *Tu vas souvent au cinéma?*
> – *Oui, je vais souvent au cinéma.*
> – *Vous trouvez ça bien?*
> – *Pour moi, oui. Je suis handicapée, et je ne peux pas prendre le bus. Mais au cinéma, il y a un très grand parking. Il y a une section du parking pour les voitures des personnes handicapées. C'est très bien.*
> 3 – *Vous allez souvent à la piscine en famille?*
> – *Non, jamais. Nous n'avons pas de voiture, et il n'y a pas de bus direct. Il faut changer de bus ... c'est trop compliqué.*
> 4 – *Tu vas souvent à la piscine?*
> – *Oui, j'adore la natation. Et, en plus, ce n'est pas cher. C'est seulement 15F.*
> 5 – *Vous faites les magasins au centre commercial?*
> – *Oui, c'est idéal pour moi. J'ai deux enfants et un bébé, il y a des ascenseurs, donc c'est plus facile avec le bébé. Un ascenseur, c'est essentiel!*
> – *C'est bien alors ...*
> – *Oui, et les toilettes sont bien aussi! Elles sont aménagées pour les familles avec un bébé. Pour changer le bébé, il n'y a pas de problème.*
> – *Mais les magasins, c'est ennuyeux pour les enfants. Il y a un terrain de jeux?*
> – *Oui, il y a un très bon terrain de jeux. Mes enfants adorent ça!*

3

This activity brings together different aspects of work from the unit, and puts pupils in the position of having to see their town from someone else's point of view.

It involves field research – check whether this sort of research has already been done in other subject areas, e.g. geography. If not, help pupils to organise their research. For example, to avoid duplication of visits, pairs of pupils could research particular places, reporting back information as requested by other pairs. Make sure that all pupils know what information is required and how to record it. For example, the class could devise a check-list for all pupils to use, based on the grid in Exercise 1, with any other facilities or adaptations they wish to include.

Once the information has been gathered, pupils could go on to create a database on the town, or present the information in tabular form, print it off and offer it to the local tourist office or town hall, for the use of French-speaking visitors.

CAMARADES 3 (TURQUOISE) OVERVIEW – UNITE 4 LA VIE AU COLLEGE   **National Curriculum Areas of Experience: A, B, C, E**

	Topics/objectives	Key language	Grammar	Skills and strategies	PoS coverage
A	**Si tu continues comme ça …** Talking about possible consequences	*des problèmes de santé, avec la police, au collège, perdre, amis, collège, magasin, devoirs, fumer, alcool, cigarettes, voler, absent, quitter*	Future tense	Dictionary: selecting correct meaning for context	1 a h 2 a i 3 c d f 4 d
B	**Résolutions et promesses** Making promises and resolutions	(as Spread A)	Future tense *plus de*		1 c d h i 2 f i j 3 f g
C	**Comment dire 'non'!** Inviting: refusing politely or suggesting an alternative activity	*désolé, je ne peux pas, je veux bien, libre, on pourrait, dommage, tu veux* (and activities)			1 a 2 a g o l 3 f g 4 e
D	**Grammar**		Future tense		1 a b c d 2 b k 3 f g
E	**Des stars et des héros** Reading for interest: heroes	*quel, chanteur(-euse), groupe, acteur(-rice), sportif(-ve), équipe, préféré*	Adverbs		1 b g h i 2 a h j l m 3 e f
F	**Quel est ton héros?** Saying who you admire and why	*héros, admirer, probablement, énormément, extrêmement, courageux, talent, bien, en plus, marrant, parce que, aussi*		Speaking and Writing: linking clauses together to make compound sentences	1 a b f h k 2 d g h 3 g
G	**Déléguée de classe** Talking about issues in school	*racket, cantine, problème, travail, classe, devoirs, uniforme, moche, trop de, ce n'est pas mal, nul, ça va, facile, difficile*			1 a f i j 2 g h l m 3 c f g 4 d
H	**Grammaire** Pronunciation		Adverbs	Pronunciation: *-au-, -eau-*	1 a b d 2 a f g 3 c f g
I	**Le manifeste d'Isabelle** Proposals for improvements at school	*lutter contre, abolir, choix, plus de, moins de, pour, contre, examens, faire, aller, écouter, donner, parler, demander* (and issues from Spread G)	*plus de, moins de*		1 b d f h j 2 h i l n 3 f
J	**La publicité, c'est bien ou c'est nul?** Discussing adverts	*publicité, choquant, mignon, bête, sophistiqué, marrant, amusant, cool, trouver que, complètement, à mon avis, d'accord*			1 a b f 2 h l 3 e
K	**Atelier** Do your own election campaign			Listening: numbers – silent consonants	1 a c d 2 a h l n 3 f g
L	**Revision** Describing a party; clothes; food; colours				1 a c d k 2 e 3 f i g

Worksheets

Recommended use of the worksheets (in some cases they can be used later, as revision):

Spread	Worksheet	Spread	Worksheet	Spread	Worksheet	Spread	Worksheet
A		D	9 and 10, 11	G		J	3 and 4
B	5 and 6, 7 and 8	E	12A	H		K	
C		F		I	12B	L	

Feuille 1 and 2 Vocabulaire

Feuilles 3 and 4 On écoute ◆ and ♣

1 – *Si vous fumez, vous abîmez votre santé. Vous risquez de mourir du cancer.*
– *En France, le tabac est responsable de 20% des décès par cancer ou par maladie respiratoire.*
– *En fait, chaque année, le tabac est responsable de presque 9% de l'ensemble des décès.*
– *Alors, ne soyez pas stupide! Le tabac, c'est dangereux!*
– *Arrêtez de fumer!*
– *Arrêtez aujourd'hui!*
2 – *La cigarette, ce n'est pas sexy.*
3 – *Qu'est-ce que tu penses des garçons qui fument?*
– *Ils pensent qu'ils sont cools, mais ils sont vraiment bêtes.*
– *Moi, je déteste l'odeur de la fumée. Ça pue! C'est dégoûtant!*
– *Ils n'ont jamais de l'argent pour sortir. Ils dépensent tout leur argent en cigarettes.*
– *En plus, ils ont les doigts et les dents tous jaunes! Beurk!*
– *Ils sentent toujours le tabac, c'est dégoûtant.*
– *Ils toussent tout le temps.*
– *Alors, les garçons! Si vous aimez les filles …*
– *… NE FUMEZ PAS!!*
4 – *J'ai commencé à fumer à l'âge de onze ans … J'ai fait ça pour être cool, mais maintenant, je trouve ça ridicule … C'est cher. Je n'ai jamais l'argent pour sortir avec mes copains … J'ai essayé d'arrêter, mais je ne peux pas … J'ai peur. J'ai peur du cancer … Je voudrais bien arrêter, mais je ne peux pas. C'est trop difficile … Le tabac, c'est une drogue terrible.*
– *Les cigarettes? Refuse la première – c'est plus simple!*
5 – *Tu veux danser?*
– *Ouais …*
– *Je m'appelle Omar, et toi?*
– *Moi, c'est Nadia …*
– *J'aime ton jean.*
– *Merci …*
– *J'aime tes cheveux.*
– *Merci …*

– *Tu aimes mon parfum? C'est du Yves Saint Laurent.*
– *Euh non, ce n'est pas ça … Tu fumes?!*
– *Ouais. Tu veux une cigarette? … Omar? … Omar! Où vas-tu? … Zut!*

Pupils could go on to use the language of the adverts in a short rap or poem, e.g.
Fumer, c'est nul
C'est cher et ça pue
C'est mauvais pour la santé
Ce n'est pas cool

Feuille 3 On écoute ◆
There are five adverts on tape but six posters. As an extra speaking activity, pupils could make a mini advert for the sixth.

Feuille 4 On écoute ♣
Some pupils could also describe the advert, using a dictionary as necessary, e.g.
1 *On parle des risques du tabac. On donne des chiffres sur les décès.*
You could provide useful expressions, e.g.
to cough – *tousser*
deaths – *les décès*
figures – *des chiffres*
to interview – *interviewer*
to light a cigarette – *allumer*
quotes – *des commentaires*
to run off – *s'échapper*
to smell of smoke – *sentir le tabac*

Feuilles 5 and 6 On parle ◆ and ♣
If using these later on, refer pupils back to spread B for ideas and models.

Feuille 7 On lit ◆ (free-standing)

Feuille 8 On lit ♣ (free-standing)
Pupils could also match up similar types of phrase, e.g.
Il y a un an, j'ai été tenté par la cigarette and *C'est l'été dernier que j'ai fumé pour la première fois;*
Sûrement pour frimer… etc. and *Je pensais avoir l'air cool.*

Feuille 9 On écrit ◆ (free-standing)

Feuille 10 On écrit ♣ (free-standing)

Feuille 11 Grammaire (free-standing)

Feuille 12 En plus (free-standing)

Feuille 13 Que sais-tu?

1 – *Tu sais, Elisabeth a encore été absente, la semaine dernière.*
   – *Quand?*
   – *Mardi après-midi et mercredi matin.*
   – *Mais pourquoi? Je ne comprends pas.*
   – *Je ne suis pas sûre, mais on a maths le mardi après-midi.*
   – *Et le mercredi matin, aussi.*
   – *Je sais qu'elle trouve ça difficile, les maths.*
   – *Mais elle est bête! Si elle a des problèmes, elle devrait en parler au prof. Sinon, elle aura des problèmes aux examens.*
   – *Oui, tu as raison.*
2 – *Je m'inquiète pour Sylvia.*
   – *Pourquoi?*
   – *Elle a commencé à voler.*
   – *Vraiment?*
   – *Oui, la semaine dernière, elle a volé un billet de cent francs à sa mère.*
   – *C'est dingue! Pourquoi elle a fait ça?*
   – *C'était pour aller en discothèque. Elle n'avait pas d'argent. Elle aime sortir tous les soirs.*
   – *Si sa mère trouve qu'elle vole de l'argent, oh là là!*
   – *Oui, Sylvia ne pourra plus sortir avec ses copains! Plus jamais!*
3 – *Je n'aime plus Paul et Pierre.*
   – *Pourquoi?*
   – *Eh bien, ils font du racket.*
   – *Du racket?*
   – *Oui, à l'entrée de la cantine. Ils demandent de l'argent aux élèves de sixième.*
   – *Eh bien, ils sont bêtes, ces élèves. Ils ne devraient pas leur donner l'argent.*
   – *Mais Paul et Pierre sont assez violents, tu sais.*
   – *Vraiment?*
   – *Oui. A mon avis, ils perdront leurs amis.*
   – *En plus, s'ils continuent comme ça, ils auront des problèmes avec la police un jour.*
4 – *T'as vu Arnaud pendant le cours de basket ce matin?*
   – *Oui, il jouait très mal. Il ne pouvait pas courir!*
   – *Tu sais pourquoi?*
   – *Non.*
   – *A mon avis, c'est parce qu'il fume.*
   – *Il fume beaucoup?*
   – *Environ vingt cigarettes par jour. En plus, il sort tous les soirs, et il se couche très tard.*
   – *Il sort avec qui?*
   – *Il sort avec des copains plus âgés que lui. Il traîne dans les cafés avec eux, et il boit beaucoup de bière.*
   – *S'il ne fait pas attention, il aura des problèmes de santé un de ces jours.*

Feuille 14 Révision 1: clothes (free-standing)
Colours have already been revised in unit 3.

Feuille 15 Révision 2: buying clothes

1 – *Bonjour. Vous désirez?*
   – *Je cherche un pantalon.*
   – *De quelle couleur?*
   – *Noir.*
   – *Voici des pantalons noirs.*
   – *Merci.*
   – *Alors, ça va?*
   – *Euh non, c'est un peu trop grand.*
   – *Essayez ce pantalon. Il est plus petit ... Ça va?*
   – *Non, désolé. Il est trop court, ce pantalon.*
   – *C'est tout ce que nous avons en noir, mais voici un pantalon en gris foncé.*
   – *Il est bien. Ça fait combien?*
   – *Ça fait 300F. Ça va?*
   – *Oui, ça va. Merci.*
2 – *Bonjour. Vous désirez?*
   – *Je cherche un pull, s'il vous plaît.*
   – *De quelle couleur?*
   – *Bleu.*
   – *Voici un très joli pull. Vous l'aimez?*
   – *Euh non, je n'aime pas la couleur.*
   – *Voici un pull en bleu clair. Vous aimez ça?*
   – *Oui, j'aime bien. Je peux l'essayer?*
   – *Oui ... Alors, ça va?*
   – *C'est un peu trop large. Vous en avez un autre en bleu clair?*
   – *Oui, voici.*
   – *Ça, c'est parfait.*
3 – *Bonjour. Vous désirez?*
   – *Je cherche une chemise.*
   – *De quelle couleur?*
   – *Je ne sais pas ... rouge.*
   – *Regardez cette chemise. Elle est très belle ... Alors, ça va?*
   – *Non, elle est trop juste.*
   – *Il y a cette chemise en rouge et noir, mais elle est à 450F.*
   – *Ah non. Ça, c'est trop cher.*
   – *Vous aimez cette chemise en rose?*
   – *Non. Je pense qu'elle est trop petite, et, en plus, je déteste la couleur!*
   – *Eh bien, je suis désolée, mais il n'y en a plus en rouge.*
   – *Tant pis. Merci.*

Feuille 16 Réponses
This provides answers for the Unit 4 worksheets.

IT Opportunities

B3 Spread B Exercise 3
Write the paragraphs in the correct order into a text manipulator with sentence jumbling and prediction options. Pupils reorder the text ◆ with pictures or ♣ without pictures. It could also help both ◆ and ♣ to work similarly with the text written in the third person, discussing differences. This would prepare pupils to write the story out themselves in Exercise 3b as a ♣ activity.

E3c Spread E Exercise 3c
This set of questions would lend themselves to data collection and finding out class favourites, e.g. a pair of pupils (or the teacher) could create a datafile using the eight key words; *groupe, chanteur, sportive* etc. plus *nom* et *sexe* as field names. Each pupil then writes in his/her own responses to favourite actor, singer etc. Pupils then graph the results to see the class favourite actors, sportspersons etc. and whether there are, for example, big differences between boys' and girls' responses. Results can be reported back either orally or in writing. (This is a useful activity to do if there is a computer with a database in the classroom.)

I6 Spread I Exercise 6
* In pairs at a word-processor pupils brainstorm a list of all the things to put into a manifesto, drawing on the examples they have read and heard in this spread. They check for accuracy and redraft. They then order them using 'cut and paste' acccording to their own priorities and print out. Next they choose which ones to remove and delete from the list and turn it into an attractive, vote-catching manifesto poster. (The first print out could be used a) to compare lists with other pairs and b) for the teacher to compare to the final manifesto and ask for reasons why certain items have been kept or discarded, thus assessing progress made.)

K6 Spread K Exercise 6
* In a computer room pupils work in pairs or groups using a desk top publisher to produce the publicity for their candidate. This should not take up more than a 50 to 60 minute period so long as pupils know how to use the DTP.

A Si tu continues comme ça …   pp 74–75

Objectives
Talking about possible consequences

Resources
Presentation sheet 13
Cassette for Exercises 1 and 3

Key language
des problèmes de santé, avec la police, au collège, perdre,

amis, collège, magasin, devoirs, fumer, alcool, cigarettes, voler, absent, quitter

Grammar
Future tense

Strategies
Dictionary: selecting the correct meaning for the context

Ways in
You can use Presentation sheet 13 before or after working on the photo story.

Answers
1, 2, 4, 6
After pupils have read and listened to the story, you could invite them to give their opinion of Isabelle: *elle est stupide/intelligente/cool* etc.

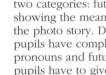

In this activity, pupils match up similar sentences from two categories: future tense and *aller* + infinitive, thus showing the meaning of the future tense verbs from the photo story. Draw closer attention to this after pupils have completed the exercise by saying the pronouns and future tense verbs on their own. The pupils have to give an equivalent phrase using *aller* + infinitive, e.g. *tu auras* ⇨ *tu vas avoir*. Pupils could then go on to Spread D which deals with the future tense.

Answers
1e 2d 3a 4c 5b

Answers
1 *Elle n'a pas fait ses devoirs.* (♣ *prof*)
2 *Il fume des cigarettes.* (♣ *amie*)
3 *Il a eu 2/20 dans un examen.* (♣ *père*)
4 *Elle vole dans les magasins.* (♣ *amie*)
5 *Il est toujours absent.* (♣ *prof*)

1 – *Alice, tu as fait tes devoirs?*
   – *Euh non, Madame.*
   – *Mais pourquoi?*
   – *Euh, j'étais malade, Madame. Je suis désolée.*
   – *Alors, tu feras tes devoirs pour vendredi, d'accord?*
   – *Oui, Madame.*
2 – *Tu as fumé des cigarettes, Jérôme?*
   – *Oui. Et alors?*
   – *Mais, Jérôme! L'odeur! Ça pue!*
   – *Mais non …*
   – *Si, et en plus, si tu fumes, tu auras des problèmes de santé plus tard.*
   – *Oh là là, laisse-moi tranquille!*
   – *Moi, je ne fumerai jamais de cigarettes.*
3 – *Pascal, tu as eu le résultat de ton examen?*
   – *Euh, oui.*
   – *Et alors?*
   – *Euh …*
   – *Tu as eu combien?*
   – *Deux.*

   – *Deux?! Deux sur vingt?!*
   – *Oui, deux sur vingt.*
   – *Oh là là! Ça ne va pas, ça! Bon, alors tu ne sortiras pas ce week-end! Tu n'iras pas au cinéma! Non! Tu vas travailler, mon vieux!*
4 – *J'aime bien ton T-shirt, Catherine. C'était combien?*
   – *C'était gratuit.*
   – *Gratuit? Comment ça?*
   – *Ben, je l'ai volé.*
   – *Quoi?! Tu as volé ton T-shirt dans un magasin?!*
   – *Ben, oui. C'est simple!*
   – *Mais Catherine! Tu ne peux pas faire ça! Je vais le dire à tes parents.*
   – *Tu ne diras rien, d'accord!*
5 – *Youssef, tu étais absent, mardi.*
   – *Oui, Monsieur.*
   – *Pourquoi?*
   – *Euh … mardi, je suis allé chez le dentiste.*
   – *Chez le dentiste. Et mercredi? Tu étais absent mercredi, aussi …*
   – *Alors mercredi, euh, j'étais malade.*
   – *Tu es toujours absent, Youssef. Ça ne va pas! Je veux voir une lettre de tes parents. Demain.*
   – *Oui, Monsieur.*

Pupils could also act out conversations between Véronique and a friend/parent/teacher.

B Résolutions et promesses

Objectives
Making promises and resolutions

Resources
Cassette for Exercise 2

Key language
(as Spread A)

Grammar
Future tense
plus de

1

Ways in
Having worked on Spread D, pupils do further practice with the future tense on this spread. Begin by reading with the class Isabelle's contract. Make sure the pupils have understood the expression *ne ... plus*.

Differentiation
Pupils who finish quickly could invent other resolutions. They give them to a classmate, who has to name the category they fit into.

2a

Answer
1 *Le petit chaperon rouge*
2 *Hansel et Gretel*

COUNTER

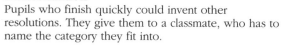

1 – *Alors, Mademoiselle, vous avez eu une aventure terrible, n'est-ce pas?*
– *Oui, c'est vrai. Je ne sortirai plus toute seule.*
– *Vous retournerez dans la forêt?*
– *Ah non! Jamais! Je n'irai plus dans la forêt. C'est trop dangereux.*
– *Et vous ne parlerez à personne ...*
– *Non. Je ne parlerai à personne.*
– *Et votre grand-mère, elle va bien maintenant?*
– *Oui, ma grand-mère va très bien maintenant. Mais je n'irai plus chez elle.*
– *Merci beaucoup.*
2 – *Et vous aussi, Mademoiselle, vous n'aimez pas la forêt. C'est vrai?*
– *Ah, oui, je n'irai plus dans la forêt. Je la déteste!*
– *Ça vous fait peur?*
– *Oui, ça me fait très peur.*
– *Alors, vous n'irez plus chez les vieilles dames?*
– *Absolument pas! Je n'irai plus chez les vieilles dames. Je ne parlerai plus aux vieilles dames!*
– *Et votre frère?*
– *Lui, aussi, il n'ira plus dans la forêt.*
– *Merci beaucoup.*

Discuss with pupils how they were able to identify the people: which clues or key words gave it away? Then let the class hear the tape again and listen out for the clues people have mentioned.

2b

Prepare this thoroughly with your class. If possible, copy the Red Riding Hood tapescript onto OHT to use as a model for their writing. You could work on the text by covering up some words – the pupils have to supply them. Alternatively, copy it onto paper and cut up the lines – pupils have to put them into the correct order. To prepare other characters, you could say or write up sentences – pupils have to say which person might have said each one.
As an additional activity, pupils might have fun inventing resolutions for celebrities.

3

Encourage pupils to use a dictionary if necessary.

Answer
C B E A D

For further exploitation of the article, try the following ideas:
• Give three summaries of the story (in French or English). Pupils have to say which is the most accurate.
• Write up French or English sentences relating to aspects of the story, with words missing for pupils to supply.
• Write up a list of French words or phrases. Pupils have to find the synonyms in the text.

Feuilles 5 and *6, 7* and *8* have activities on the themes of arguments and smoking.

C **Comment dire 'non'!** pp 78–79

Objectives
Inviting; refusing politely or suggesting an alternative activity

Resources
Cassette for Exercises 1 and 3

Key language
désolé, je ne peux pas, je veux bien, libre, on pourrait, dommage, tu veux (and activities)

Ways in

1a The photo story sets the scene.

1b If pupils are able to note down any extra details, encourage them to do so.

Answers
1 *piscine* ✓ 2 *cinéma* ✗ 3 *bowling* ✗ 4 *centre commercial* ✓ 5 *concert / hôtel de ville* ✗

> 1 – *Michael, tu veux aller à la piscine demain après-midi?*
> – *A la piscine? Oui, je veux bien. J'adore la natation. Rendez-vous à quelle heure?*
> – *Rendez-vous à deux heures et demie, d'accord?*
> – *D'accord.*
> 2 – *Tu veux aller au cinéma demain soir, Audrey?*
> – *Oh, je suis désolée. Je ne peux pas. Je dois faire du baby-sitting demain.*
> – *C'est dommage.*
> 3 – *Pascal, tu viens au bowling samedi matin?*
> – *Ah non, je ne peux pas, parce que je sors avec mes parents. Je suis désolé.*
> – *C'est dommage.*
> 4 – *Djamila, tu veux bien aller au centre commercial cet après-midi?*
> – *Oui, je veux bien!*
> – *On prend le bus?*
> – *Oui. Alors, je viens chez toi à deux heures?*
> – *D'accord.*
> 5 – *Il y a un concert ce soir à l'hôtel de ville. Tu veux y aller?*
> – *Ah non, je suis désolé. Je ne peux pas.*
> – *Pourquoi?*
> – *Parce que je vais chez ma grand-mère.*
> – *C'est dommage.*

2 Read the scenarios together. The 'solutions' outline key language.

Answers
a2 b3 c1 d2

3 Answers
1 – 3; 2 – 1; 3 – 3; 4 – 2; 5 – 1

> 1 – *Dis, Julienne, tu veux jouer au tennis samedi?*
> – *Ah, je suis désolée, mais je ne suis pas libre samedi. Mais on pourrait jouer dimanche …*
> – *Dimanche?*
> – *Tu es libre?*
> – *Euh … oui. Je suis libre dimanche matin.*
> – *Bon. Je viens chez toi à dix heures et demie?*
> – *Bon, d'accord.*
> 2 – *Tu veux aller à la pêche cet après-midi?*
> – *Ah non, c'est ennuyeux, ça.*
> – *Qu'est-ce qu'on fait, alors?*
> – *Bon ben … on pourrait faire du vélo.*
> – *Du vélo? D'accord.*
> 3 – *Alain, tu veux aller en discothèque vendredi soir?*
> – *Ah, je suis désolé, mais je ne peux pas. Je sors avec des copains vendredi soir.*
> – *C'est dommage!*
> – *Mais je suis libre samedi soir. On pourrait aller en discothèque samedi …*
> – *D'accord. Bonne idée.*
> 4 – *C'est mon anniversaire, dimanche. Tu peux venir dîner chez nous?*
> – *Euh … je suis désolé, mais je ne peux pas. Je vais chez ma tante dimanche.*
> – *Oh, c'est dommage.*
> – *Tant pis.*
> 5 – *Il fait très beau! Tu veux faire un barbecue?*
> – *Mais non, je n'aime pas les barbecues!*
> – *Mais pourquoi?*
> – *Je suis végétarienne, moi. Je ne mange pas de steak!*
> – *Ah oui, c'est vrai.*
> – *Mais on pourrait faire un pique-nique.*
> – *Bon, d'accord, on fait un pique-nique.*
> – *Je viens chez toi à onze heures?*
> – *Oui, d'accord.*

4 Pupils could go back and act out the situations described in Exercise 3.

5 As preparation, help the class to work out together useful questions to ask each other.

D Grammaire

Grammar
Future tense

1 Go through the explanatory table with the class, before they go on to Exercise 1. Remind them to look out for exceptions, as listed at the bottom of the table.

2 Pupils could read out the resolutions they have written to horrify their parents and teachers. The more amusing and outrageous, the better!

3 You could also encourage pupils to make predictions about current events, for example which teams will win or lose in matches at the week-end; what will happen in the next episode of a popular soap. Pupils write their predictions then come back to them later – who makes the most accurate predictions?
You can provide pupils with useful phrases in the infinitive, e.g.
marquer un but
gagner/perdre un match
être classé numéro un dans le hit-parade.

4 Pupils can improvise their own dice if necessary. Take a six-sided pencil and write the numbers 1 to 6 on the wood at the top, one number above each of the sides. You can then roll the pencil: the number which is uppermost when the pencil comes to a stop is the one you use.

Further work on the future tense can be found on *Feuilles 9* and *10* and *Feuille 11*.

E Des stars et des héros

pp 82–83

Objectives
Reading for interest: 'heroes'

Resources
Cassette for Exercises 2 and 3

Key language
*quel, chanteur(-euse), groupe, acteur(-rice), sportif(-ve),
équipe, préféré*

Grammar
Adverbs

This spread provides input and some key language
for the following one, where pupils go on to discuss
their own heroes.

1

Encourage pupils to use the dictionary as necessary
to answer the questions.

Answers
1c   **2**b   **3**a   **4**c

You could ask further questions on the text, e.g.
Sœur Emmanuelle est de quelle nationalité?
Elle a visité quels pays?
Où se trouve Azbet-el-Nakal?

This would be a good time to look at the section on
adverbs on Spread H.

2

The listening texts include unknown language, but
pupils do not need to understand it all to complete
the tasks. The activity gives them practice in listening
for gist. For the ♣ option of noting other details,
pupils could make notes in French or English.

Answer
c, a

COUNTER

> – *Les Jeux olympiques sont finis, maintenant.
> Mais aujourd'hui commence une autre
> compétition: les jeux paralympiques. Il y a plus
> de 3 500 athlètes ici. Ce sont des personnes qui
> ont surmonté leur handicap – et ce sont de très
> bons athlètes! Nous allons sûrement voir des
> performances exceptionnelles cette année, aux
> jeux paralympiques!*
> – *Ce soir, à 20h30, vous pourrez entendre une
> interview avec Johann Koss, l'athlète norvégien.
> Champion olympique de patinage de vitesse, il
> a quitté la patinoire. Il ne fait plus de
> compétition. En effet, il préfère aller en
> Erythrée, en Afrique, où il fait du sport avec les
> enfants. A son avis, le sport est essentiel en
> Afrique. C'est essentiel pour les enfants qui ont
> connu la misère et la violence.*

3a

3b

COUNTER

There is scope here to practise the structure *aussi …
que.* For example, pupils could make sentences along
the following lines:
*J'aimerais être aussi cool/courageux(-se)/ marrant(e)/
intelligent(e)/sportif(-ve) (etc.) que …* (+ famous
person).

3c

Do plenty of whole-class open practice first, to
practise the key phrases, before pupils do the *mêlée*
activity.

Pupils list the key words: *groupe, chanteur* etc., then
note next to each one the name of anyone with the
same taste.

The top half of *Feuille 12* has a game on this theme.

F Quel est ton héros?

pp 84–85

Objectives
Saying who you admire, and why

Resources
Cassette for Exercises 1 and 3

Key language
héros, admirer, probablement, énormément, extrêmement, courageux, talent, bien, en plus, marrant, parce que, aussi

Strategies
Speaking and writing: linking clauses together to make compound sentences

---

Ways in

Read and listen to the conversation. Ask your pupils whether they also admire the famous people mentioned.

♣ Remind pupils to change **mon** oncle.

Together with the conversation above, this presents key language, including adjectives in their different forms. Make sure that pupils have noted the feminine and plural of adjectives such as *courageux*.

Differentiation

More able pupils could note as much additional information as they can about why the callers admire these people.

Answers
1 *la Mère Térésa – caractère*
2 *Madonna – talent*
3 *Lennox Lewis – talent*
4 *la Princesse Diana – actions*
5 *les agents de Greenpeace – caractère*
6 *sa sœur – caractère*

After checking the answers, you could go on to hold a vote for the *héros de la semaine*, as mentioned on tape.

– *Bonjour à toutes et à tous! Aujourd'hui, nous posons la question: «Quel est votre héros?». Ça peut être une célébrité, un ami, un membre de votre famille. Appelez-nous au 01.45.32.14.98. Alors, pour commencer, nous avons en ligne 1 Anne-France Mirepoix.*
1 – *Bonjour, Anne-France.*
– *Bonjour, Mireille.*
– *Anne-France, quel est ton héros?*
– *Alors, moi, j'admire beaucoup la Mère Térésa.*
– *Ah oui, la Mère Térésa.*
– *Oui, parce qu'elle a beaucoup aidé les gens. Elle a beaucoup travaillé pour les autres.*
– *Merci, Anne-France.*
2 – *Alors, c'est qui en ligne 2?*
– *Je m'appelle Nabila.*
– *Et quel est ton héros, Nabila?*
– *Alors, moi, j'admire Madonna.*
– *Madonna, la chanteuse américaine. Et pourquoi l'admires-tu?*

– *Eh bien, parce qu'elle est superchouette! Elle fait tout! Elle chante bien, elle danse bien, et elle joue même dans les films.*
– *Tu es une fan de sa musique, alors.*
– *Oui, j'ai toutes ses cassettes.*
– *Merci, Nabila.*
3 – *En ligne 3, nous avons Claude, c'est ça?*
– *Oui. Claude Delpais. Bonjour, Mireille.*
– *Bonjour. Alors, Claude, quel est votre héros?*
– *Mon héros, c'est le boxeur, Lennox Lewis.*
– *Lennox Lewis? Et pourquoi?*
– *Eh bien, tout simplement parce qu'il est formidable! C'est un très grand boxeur. Il boxe vraiment bien!*
– *Merci, Claude.*
4 – *En ligne 4, nous avons …*
– *Maryse. Bonjour, Mireille.*
– *Maryse, quel est votre héros?*
– *Moi, j'admire énormément la Princesse Diana, d'Angleterre.*
– *La Princesse Diana? Et pourquoi?*
– *Eh bien, parce qu'elle aide les gens.*
– *Oui?*
– *Ah oui! Elle travaille beaucoup pour les organisations de charité. Elle fait beaucoup pour les autres.*
– *Merci, Maryse.*
5 – *Nous avons qui en ligne 5?*
– *Jean-Pierre. Jean-Pierre Doré.*
– *Bonjour, Jean-Pierre. Alors, qui admires-tu?*
– *Moi, j'admire les agents de Greenpeace.*
– *Ah oui, ce sont des gens qui luttent pour la protection de la nature.*
– *Oui. Je les admire beaucoup. A mon avis, ce sont des gens très très gentils et très sympathiques.*
– *Ils sont admirables, c'est sûr.*
– *En plus, ils sont courageux. Ils travaillent dans des situations dangereuses.*
– *Oui, alors, merci beaucoup, Jean-Pierre.*
6 – *En ligne 6, nous avons Hubert, c'est ça?*
– *Oui, c'est ça. Bonjour, Mireille. Je voudrais dire que j'admire beaucoup ma sœur.*
– *Votre sœur? Elle s'appelle comment?*
– *Elle s'appelle Suzanne.*
– *Et dites-nous pourquoi vous admirez votre sœur.*
– *Eh bien, elle a eu un accident terrible. En voiture. Alors, elle a beaucoup de problèmes, elle va souvent à l'hôpital, mais elle est **très courageuse**. Elle est optimiste, elle raconte des blagues, c'est formidable.*

> *– Elle est vraiment courageuse.*
> *– Oui, elle a beaucoup de courage.*
> *– Merci beaucoup, Hubert ... Alors, lequel de
> ces six héros sera votre 'héros de la
> semaine'? Pour voter, appelez-nous au
> 01.45.32.14.98.*

4

You could exploit the letter in other ways, for example
vrai/faux questions or sentences summarising the text,
with the words jumbled up, e.g.
marrant de Paul L'ami est.

5

Look through the *Stratégies* box before pupils write
their replies.

6

Some pupils may be able to give a short talk on their
choice.

G Déléguée de classe   pp 86–87

Objectives
Talking about issues in school

Resources
Cassette for Exercise 2

Key language
racket, cantine, problème, travail, classe, devoirs, uniforme, moche, trop de, ce n'est pas mal, nul, ça va, facile, difficile

Ways in
Read together the poster and the conversation.

Your class might be interested to know more about class delegates. They are elected near the beginning of the school year, to represent the class in discussions with teachers and the school administration. Pupils should raise problems and issues through their elected representative. Delegates' main responsibility is participation in the *conseil de classe*, which takes place at the end of each term. Here, the staff and head teacher meet the parents to discuss each pupil. The topic of *éducation civique* features in French education from early on – even young primary school classes elect delegates.

1

This activity presents four model questions about school and a range of answers. You may wish to distil these to give simple model answers. To do this, you could provide the following list of sentences. Pupils could either match them up with the answers A–J on page 86, or say whether or not they agree with each one.
Il y a trop de devoirs.
La cantine, c'est nul.
Le racket n'est pas un problème.
Les devoirs ça va.
La cantine, c'est bien.
Le travail de classe, parfois c'est trop difficile.
Pour moi, le racket est un grand problème.
La cantine, ce n'est pas mal.

2

Answers
Christophe: le racket (très grand problème) ☹; la cantine (très bien) ☺; les devoirs (trop) ☹; travail de classe (ça va) ☺
Benoît: le travail de classe (trop difficile) ☹; la cantine (bien) ☺; les devoirs (beaucoup trop difficiles) ☹; le racket (problème pour son frère) ☹
Hélène: la cantine (nul) ☹; les devoirs (ça va) ☺; le racket (une problème pour elle) ☹
François: les devoirs (trop de devoirs; trop difficiles) ☹; la cantine (pas mal) ☺

COUNTER

1 – *Votez Isabelle Vincent! Votez Isabelle Vincent!*
Salut, Christophe. Je vais me présenter aux élections pour les délégués de classe.
– *Ah bon?*
– *Oui. Je prépare ma campagne électorale. Je fais un sondage pour savoir quels sont les problèmes. Je peux te poser des questions?*
– *Oui bien sûr.*
– *Alors, première question, est-ce que le racket est un problème au collège?*
– *Le racket? Oui, à mon avis c'est un très grand problème!*
– *Tu as déjà été victime du racket?*

– *Oui, j'en ai été victime. C'est affreux!*
– *Deuxième question. Que penses-tu de la cantine?*
– *A mon avis, la cantine est très bien!*
– *Tu manges à la cantine tous les jours?*
– *Oui, tous les jours. J'aime bien les repas. J'adore les desserts.*
– *Merci. Alors, la troisième question est sur les devoirs. Ça va avec les devoirs?*
– *Alors là, non. Ça ne va pas! Il y a toujours trop de devoirs!*
– *Bon. Et finalement, le travail en classe, ça va?*
– *Oui, ça va. Ce n'est pas un problème.*
– *Alors, Christophe, tu vas voter pour moi?*
– *Ben, je ne sais pas … Ça dépend …*

2 – *Salut, Benoît. Je vais me présenter aux élections.*
– *Pour les délégués de classe?*
– *Oui. Je fais un sondage pour savoir quels sont les problèmes. Je peux te poser des questions?*
– *Oui, vas-y.*
– *Alors, que penses-tu du travail en classe?*
– *Alors, là, il y a des problèmes. Parfois c'est trop difficile pour moi.*
– *Merci. Et que penses-tu de la cantine?*
– *A mon avis, c'est bien.*
– *Tu manges souvent à la cantine?*
– *Oui, j'y mange tous les jours.*
– *Et que penses-tu des devoirs?*
– *A mon avis, les devoirs sont beaucoup trop difficiles.*
– *Oui?*
– *En plus, on n'a jamais assez de temps pour les faire. Aujourd'hui, mon prof de maths m'a donné des devoirs pour demain. Ce n'est pas juste! Je sors ce soir, et je n'ai pas le temps pour les devoirs. Les profs ne sont pas raisonnables!*
– *Et finalement, le racket. Penses-tu que c'est un problème?*
– *Ce n'est pas un problème pour moi, mais mon petit frère a déjà été victime du racket. Mes parents sont venus au collège, pour parler aux profs.*
– *Et c'est fini maintenant?*
– *Non, malheureusement. Ça continue. Il y a toujours des problèmes.*
– *Merci, Benoît. Alors, tu voteras pour moi?*
– *Peut-être …*

3 – *Hélène, je me présente aux élections pour les délégués de classe. Je fais un sondage. Je peux te poser des questions?*
– *Oui, bien sûr.*
– *Alors, que penses-tu de la cantine au collège?*

– *C'est nul! Vraiment nul!*
– *Tu ne manges pas à la cantine?*
– *Non, jamais! C'est dégoûtant! J'apporte des sandwichs, moi!*
– *Merci. Ensuite, les devoirs. Il y a des problèmes?*
– *Pour moi, non, ça va.*
– *Bon. Finalement, le racket. Penses-tu que le racket est un problème?*
– *Pour moi, malheureusement, c'est un grand problème.*
– *Ah bon? Tu as parlé de ça au professeur?*
– *Euh non … j'ai trop peur.*
– *Alors, vote pour moi. Moi, je dis 'non au racket!'. Tu voteras pour moi?*
– *Oui, je voterai pour toi, Isabelle.*

4 – *François, je fais un sondage. Je prépare ma campagne pour les élections des délégués de classe. Tu veux bien répondre à quelques questions?*
– *Oui, si tu veux.*
– *Alors, que penses-tu des devoirs?*
– *Oh là là, les devoirs! Pour commencer, il y a trop de devoirs. En plus, ils sont trop difficiles!*
– *Merci. Ensuite, que penses-tu de la cantine?*
– *Oh, ce n'est pas mal. J'y vais souvent.*
– *Bon.*
– *En effet, je vais à la cantine maintenant. Je n'ai pas encore mangé. Salut!*
– *Hé, François, tu voteras pour moi?*
– *Moi, non! Je voterai pour Olivier.*
– *Zut!*

 Pupils draw conclusions from the information they have read and heard so far.

 Answer
le racket

 You could go through the letter with the class, asking questions, such as:
Le travail de classe, ça va?
La correspondante a combien d'heures de devoirs par jour? C'est beaucoup, à votre avis?
Elle mange à la cantine? Qu'est-ce qu'elle mange pour le déjeuner?
Est-ce qu'on porte un uniforme dans son collège? Elle aime l'uniforme?

 As preparation, discuss with your pupils which phrases they can pick out and use, and check they have understood them. Practise using the phrases together before pupils start writing.

Pupils are encouraged to write their letter with the exercise book closed, to encourage them to use productively the language they have learned, rather than relying too heavily on the model in the book.

 After pupils have discussed in pairs, they could then join together and discuss the issues in groups. They choose two aspects which they consider to be the most serious in school, then report back to the class.

La vie au collège

H Grammaire

Grammar
Adverbs *(les adverbes)*

Pronunciation
-au-, -eau-

Resources
Cassette for Pronunciation

Les adverbes

Adverbs are taught receptively at this stage. The aim is to alert pupils to the pattern **-ment** / **-ly**. The examples here include adverbs qualifying verbs and adjectives.

You could take it further if you wished, pointing out how adverbs **add** to verbs (and adjectives). The issues of formation and position are more complex.

1

Answers
a-j-p; b-k-r; c-l-m; d-i-q; e-h-o; f-g-n

2

Point out that recognising patterns like this can help them to understand texts in French.

3

Pupils could also invent other sentences to be said in the different styles. They could also add to the different ways of speaking, using a dictionary to help them.

4

Pupils could also discuss aspects of school life.

Prononciation

In the rap in Exercise C, there are a number of variations on the order of the lines. The rap on tape is just one possibility. The backing track is repeated afterwards, so that pupils can do their own rap over it.

COUNTER

Il a fait beau
Je suis allé au château
Il a fait chaud
J'ai acheté un esquimau
Il a fait très chaud
J'ai nagé dans l'eau
J'ai acheté un cadeau
C'est un stylo
Pour l'anniversaire de mon ami, Arnaud

La vie au collège

■ Le manifeste d'Isabelle

Objectives
Proposals for improvements at school

Resources
Cassette for Exercise 4

Key language
lutter contre, abolir, choix, plus de, moins de, pour, contre, examens, faire, aller, écouter, donner, parler, demander
(and issues from Spread G)

Grammar
plus de, moins de

Ways in

1 Read the manifestos together. The future tense is revised here, as Isabelle and Olivier state their intentions as elected delegates.

Answers
Pascal – Olivier
Agathe – Isabelle
Sara – Isabelle
Anne – Olivier
Jean – Isabelle

2 ♣ Pupils may wish to prepare their ideas before discussing in pairs. You could discuss some ideas first, e.g.
Le directeur ne sera pas d'accord.
Ça coûtera trop cher.

3 Encourage pupils to think about which are the main issues to campaign on, based on the number of people who expressed the opinions listed (see the number of tally marks for each one).

4 ♣ Pupils will find it easier to take rough notes while listening and write up correct sentences afterwards.

COUNTER

– *Bonjour, tout le monde. Aujourd'hui, tous les candidats vont présenter leur manifeste. Aline, tu veux commencer? Aline …*
– *Merci, Madame. Bonjour tout le monde. Je vais vous présenter mes promesses.*
Numéro 1: Je demanderai moins de devoirs. En ce moment, nous avons trop de devoirs. Je pense que c'est complètement ridicule!
Ma promesse numéro 2 concerne la cantine. A mon avis, elle est vraiment nulle! Les repas sont affreux. Donc, ma promesse, c'est que je demanderai plus de choix, tous les jours.
Et finalement, numéro 3. Tout le monde déteste les examens. Moi, j'en demanderai moins. Votez Aline Balavoine!
– *Merci, Aline. Maintenant, à toi, Mathieu.*
– *Salut! Bon, voici mes promesses.*
Numéro 1: A mon avis, on fait trop de sport. Donc moi, j'en demanderai beaucoup moins, parce que c'est complètement ennuyeux.
Numéro 2: Tout le monde pense que le racket, c'est un grand problème au collège, surtout pour les élèves les plus jeunes. Moi, je suis contre le racket! Il faut absolument lutter contre la violence au collège, pour avoir une ambiance plus agréable!

Et ma troisième promesse: à mon avis, si on veut vraiment faire des progrès et avoir de bonnes notes aux examens, les devoirs sont très importants. Donc, j'en demanderai plus!
– *Merci beaucoup, Mathieu. Maintenant, on passe à Roulah. Roulah, s'il te plaît …*
– *Merci. Bonjour à tous! Voici mon manifeste. Première promesse: moi, j'adore la musique. J'en demanderai beaucoup plus pour tout le monde: cinq heures par semaine, ou plus! Numéro 2. Je vais tous les jours à la cantine, et je trouve que les sandwichs sont nuls! Fromage ou jambon – il n'y a presque pas de choix! C'est très ennuyeux! Donc, je demanderai plus de sandwichs!*
Et finalement, numéro 3. Le sport, c'est bien pour la santé, c'est amusant et c'est relaxant! Moi, j'en demanderai beaucoup, et pour tout le monde. Merci!
– *Merci, tout le monde.*

5 Remind pupils of the discussion in Exercise 2: what is practical and realistic?

6 ♣ Pupils can make their manifesto as silly or outrageous as they like. They then could present them to the rest of the class or group, who vote for the one they like best.

Feuille 12B has a short activity on the theme of school.

J La publicité, c'est bien ou c'est nul?

pp 92–93

Objectives
Discussing adverts

Resources
Cassette for Exercises 1 and 2

Key language
publicité, choquant, mignon, bête, sophistiqué, marrant, amusant, cool, trouver que, complètement, à mon avis, d'accord

Ways in

1 Read and listen to the conversation. Encourage pupils to work out as much as they can from the context. Which of the new words resemble English ones? They should use the dictionary as a last resort.

Get pupils to pick out the key phrases for giving one's opinion, revised from Unit 3 (e.g. *je trouve que...; je ne suis pas d'accord*). Can they remember any other useful phrases, (e.g. *c'est vrai; ce n'est pas vrai*)?

2

Answers
1F   2D   3E   4E

> 1   – *Que penses-tu de la publicité?*
>   – *C'est mignon, n'est-ce pas? Et c'est assez amusant.*
>   – *Alors, là, je ne suis pas d'accord! C'est assez mignon, oui. Mais le sujet n'est pas amusant. C'est très sérieux. C'est même choquant.*
>   – *Choquant? Ah oui … en effet, c'est vrai. Oui, c'est assez choquant. Un accident comme ça, c'est sérieux …*
> 2   – *Qu'est-ce que tu penses de cette publicité?*
>   – *Je trouve que c'est marrant, et toi?*
>   – *A mon avis, ce n'est pas amusant. C'est sexiste!*
>   – *Sexiste?! Mais comment? C'est la voiture d'une femme!*
>   – *Oui, mais c'est une **petite** voiture et les **grandes** voitures sont pour les hommes.*
>   – *Oh, c'est ridicule, ça. Ce n'est pas sexiste! T'es bête, toi!*
> 3   – *Elle est bien, cette publicité, n'est-ce pas?*
>   – *Oui, elle est sophistiquée, très sophistiquée …*
>   – *Elle est cool, mais assez amusante, aussi, n'est pas? L'image est amusante.*
>   – *Oui, elle est super bien! Il n'y a pas beaucoup de texte.*
> 4   – *Ah regarde, c'est marrant, ça!*
>   – *Tu trouves que c'est marrant?*
>   – *Ben oui. Pas toi?*
>   – *Non! A mon avis, c'est bête! J'aime la photo, elle est très sophistiquée, mais le texte, c'est vraiment bête!*

After discussing the answers, you could reproduce all or part of the tapescript onto OHT for pupils to work on before going on to use the language productively. For example, you could cut up the lines of a dialogue for pupils to put into the correct order, or you could blank out some words for pupils to fill in, either through listening to the tape or by working out from the context.

3 Do some whole-class oral work in preparation for Exercise 3. For example, you and your pupils could bring in adverts and discuss them together.

♣ Go through with pupils possible phrases and extended answers.
Remind pupils of the patterns:
C'est + masculine adjective (invariable)
La publicité / Elle + feminine adjective.

To follow up Exercise 3, you could pin other adverts up round the room. The pupils go round noting down their opinion on each, then they compare with a partner.

The class could also discuss various television programmes. This would help to encourage transfer of the language practised to a different topic area. Pupils might find it fun to write and perform or record their own adverts.

Feuilles 3 and *4* have pupils listening to and discussing anti-smoking adverts.

K Atelier

Objectives
Do your own election campaign

Strategies
Listening: numbers – silent consonants

Resources
Cassette for Exercises 4 and 7

This spread brings together the work of the previous spreads on electing a *délégué de classe*, and provides opportunities for pupils to work collaboratively in groups.
Read the introduction with the class and make sure that pupils have understood the task.

1

In their groups, pupils begin by selecting a candidate. The speech bubbles provide a model for them to follow.

2

Help pupils prepare for the survey: are they going to devise a grid on which to record their answers, or are they going to note down the answers in a list?

3

Pupils could word-process the manifesto, taking care over the design and presentation.

4

After listening to Isabelle's election speech, groups could decide whether they want to change their electoral promises at all, for example by adding others.

Isabelle's speech also provides a model for pupils to follow when writing their own candidate's speech in Exercise 7.

COUNTER

> Bonjour. Je m'appelle Isabelle Vincent. Votez pour moi! Voici mes promesses.
> 1: Si je suis déléguée de classe, j'irai à tous les meetings.
> Ma promesse numéro 2: j'écouterai vos opinions.
> Dans notre collège, le racket est un très grand problème. Ma troisième promesse est ceci: je lutterai contre le racket.
> A mon avis, nous avons trop de devoirs. Voici, donc, ma quatrième promesse: je demanderai moins de devoirs!
> Et finalement, beaucoup d'élèves pensent que les profs ne comprennent rien. Moi, je parlerai aux profs de vos problèmes.
> Votez Isabelle Vincent!!

5

You could discuss the posters together as a class first. Revise vocabulary from Spread J, and ask questions using other known language, e.g. *C'est trop long? C'est trop court?*.

6

Differentiation
The publicity material could be a simple poster or a leaflet, including a profile of the candidate (name; age; brothers and sisters; interests and hobbies).

7a

Before preparing and making their own speeches, pupils should listen again to Isabelle's speech.

Differentiation
More able pupils could give reasons for their promises as well, e.g. *il y a trop de devoirs; la cantine, c'est nul*. Others could just give straight promises, e.g. *Je demanderai moins d'examens.*

7b

Before pupils listen to the results, remind them that, when followed by a consonant, the final consonants of the numbers *six, huit,* and *dix* are not pronounced, e.g. *six francs; huit francs; dix francs*. Point out that the same will apply when the number of votes is read out.

COUNTER

> Alors, voici les résultats des élections pour le délégué de classe:
> Aline – 3 voix, 3 voix;
> Mohamed – 4 voix, 4 voix;
> Mathieu – 2 voix, 2 voix;
> Olivier – 8 voix, 8 voix;
> Roulah – 5 voix, 5 voix;
> Guillaume – 1 voix, 1 voix;
> Isabelle – 11 voix, 11 voix.

At the end of the *Atelier* work, each group could bring together the written documents from the different stages of the electoral campaign, to form a collage for a wall display.

L Révision

Objectives
Describing a party; clothes; food; colours

This spread revises the following topics:
- food items (**Camarades I and 2**)
- shops (Unit 3)
- *du, de la* etc.
- *au, à la* etc.
- adjectival agreements (Unit 3)
- clothes (**Camarades 2**)
- describing a party (perfect tense) (Unit 2).

1

It is useful to remind pupils where items which have come up in **Camarades 3** were originally covered, in case they wish to go back and revise. Shops were covered in Unit 3 Spread F.

2

Answers
clothes: *vert verte jaune vertes jaune*
food: *jaunes vertes jaunes verts vertes*

3

Answers
les frites; le chocolat; les chips; les gâteaux; le jambon; le coca; le fromage; les biscuits; la limonade

4

This game could be reversed: Partner A gives the name of a shop; B has to name two things you can buy there.

5

Pupils can find a list of colours on page 64 of their book.

6

Pupils wishing to refer to previous work could look at Unit 2, Spreads B, G, I and J.

A – Epreuve d'écoute

Exercice 1

An exercise with elements typifying performance at **Level 3** in which pupils pick out specific details of weather and match each with the appropriate visual. Total 5 marks.
Award 1 mark for each correct answer.
Pupils scoring at least 4 marks are showing some characteristics of performance at **Level 3**.

Answers
1a   2d   3f   4g   5c

> **Exercice 1**
> – La météo. Regarde les dessins. Ecoute la météo. Pour chaque ville, choisis la bonne lettre.
> – Et voici maintenant la météo pour aujourd'hui, douze mars. A Paris en ce moment il pleut et il va continuer à pleuvoir.
> – **Numéro un**.
> – A Lyon, pourtant, c'est le beau temps. Il va faire soleil toute la journée.
> – **Numéro deux.**
> – Passons à Marseille où il va faire un temps couvert, mais il va faire chaud également avec des températures élevées pour la saison.
> – **Numéro trois**.
> – Sur les côtes ouest, à Brest, il va y avoir de très forts vents – il fait déjà du vent à Brest.
> – **Numéro quatre**.
> – Il y a un problème à Bordeaux – c'est le brouillard. Il va y avoir du brouillard sur toute l'Aquitaine.
> – **Numéro cinq**.
> – Et finalement, dans les Vosges et à Strasbourg il y a de la neige. Eh oui! Il neige maintenant et il y en aura cinq centimètres au moins avant la fin de la nuit.
> – Ecoute la météo encore une fois.

Exercice 2

Here, a slightly longer passage is presented, from which pupils identify and match up details of places with the appropriate pictures and note briefly, in French, the speaker's opinion of them. This is typical of performance at **Level 4**.
Total 10 marks.
Award 1 mark for each correct answer.
Pupils scoring at least 7 marks are showing some characteristics of performance at **Level 4**. Pupils are not to be marked on the accuracy of their written French when writing the adjectives of description. The mark should be awarded if the French is understandable.

Answers
1 e/moche   **2** g/vieux   **3** b/moderne   **4** f/petit
5 a/belle

> **Exercice 2**
> – Véronique parle de sa ville. Regarde les dessins. Ecoute Véronique. Quels sont les endroits dans la ville? Ecris la bonne lettre. Ecris aussi une description des endroits.
> **Exemple:**
> – Véronique, qu'est-ce qu'il y a dans ta ville?
> – Eh bien il y a un cinéma dans la ville.
> – Et comment c'est, le cinéma?
> – Comment c'est? Eh bien – c'est formidable!
> – **Numéro un**.
> – Et qu'est-ce qu'il y a aussi dans la ville?
> – Eh bien, il y a aussi un parc.
> – Et c'est beau, le parc?
> – Non – moi, je n'aime pas le parc. C'est moche!
> – **Numéro deux**.
> – Et à part ça, qu'est-ce qu'il y a?
> – Eh bien voyons … nous avons l'hôtel de ville.
> – Ah oui, l'hôtel de ville. C'est vieux?
> – Oh oui, il est très vieux, l'hôtel de ville.
> – **Numéro trois**.
> – Et pour faire du sport, qu'est-ce qu'il y a dans ta ville?
> – Nous avons une piscine qui se trouve au centre-ville. C'est une piscine très moderne.
> – **Numéro quatre**.
> – Très bien. Et … euh … il y a autre chose?
> – Qu'est-ce qu'il y a encore? Voyons. Il y a bien sûr le centre commercial.
> – Et comment c'est, le centre commercial. C'est grand?
> – Non, non. Il est tout petit.
> – **Numéro cinq**.
> – Eh bien, c'est très intéressant. C'est tout?
> – Non. Il y a aussi l'église. L'église Ste Anne.
> – Et comment elle est, l'église?
> – Elle est très très belle, je trouve.
> – Ecoute Véronique encore une fois.

Exercice 3

A true/false exercise using a fairly rapidly delivered passage of French including natural hesitation and rephrasing. The passage includes perfect and imperfect tenses and is typical of performance at **Level 5**.
Total 5 marks.
Award 1 mark for each correct answer.
Pupils scoring at least 4 correct answers are showing some characteristics of performance at **Level 5**, though the element of luck in guessing the answers cannot be discounted.

Answers
1 faux   **2** faux   **3** vrai   **4** vrai   **5** vrai

> **Exercice 3**
> – Jean-Luc parle de son chanteur préféré. Lis les affirmations 1 à 5. Ecoute Jean-Luc. Pour chaque affirmation choisis 'vrai' ou 'faux'.

– Je vais vous parler de mon chanteur préféré, qui s'appelle Anthony Dupray. Eh bien, Anthony habite Paris – il y a habité toute sa vie, je pense. Son anniversaire est le 22 septembre et … euh … il est né en 1974. Anthony vient d'une grande famille – il a deux frères et trois sœurs et … euh … ses deux parents travaillent encore. Son père est professeur et sa mère est infirmière – et il faut dire qu'ils s'entendent tous très bien ensemble, Anthony, les parents, les frères et les sœurs.

Eh bien, Anthony s'intéresse à la musique depuis longtemps – enfin, depuis toute sa vie, quoi. Quand il n'avait que huit ans, ses parents l'ont emmené à un concert de Johnny Hallyday qui a beaucoup impressionné le jeune Anthony. Il a adoré ce concert et il a décidé à ce moment-là de devenir chanteur, lui aussi.

Donc il a commencé à chanter, il a fait des enregistrements qu'il a envoyés aux … aux studios, quoi, et son premier disque est sorti en juillet 1993.

Il adore la vie, Anthony. Il a beaucoup de passions. A part la musique, il adore le sport, surtout le ski, la natation et le basket. Je trouve que c'est un chanteur formidable, et j'achète toujours ses disques dès qu'ils sortent.

– Ecoute Jean-Luc encore une fois.

Exercice 4
This is a matching exercise, but more advanced skills of gist understanding are now being tested. The passage is quite long and delivered at normal speed. It uses the immediate future. It is again typical of performance at **Level 5**.
Total 5 marks.
Award 1 mark for each correct answer.
Pupils scoring at least 4 correct answers are showing some characteristics of performance at **Level 5**. Do not penalise incorrectly copied French provided the answer is recognisable.

Answers
1 *à la piscine*
2 *au restaurant*
3 *au stade*
4 *dans les magasins*
5 *à la gare*

Exercice 4
– Où est-ce que les jeunes vont aller ce week-end? Regarde les panneaux. Ecoute les jeunes. Choisis le bon panneau pour chaque jeune.

Exemple:
– Parlons un peu de ce que vous allez faire ce week-end. Adrien, veux-tu commencer?
– D'accord. Moi, je vais aller en ville avec mes amis et on va voir un film américain.

*– **Numéro un.***
– Et Fabienne, que vas-tu faire?
– Moi, je suis très sportive et je vais nager ce week-end.

*– **Numéro deux**.*
– Luc, qu'est-ce que tu vas faire, toi?
– Je vais aller manger un grand repas en ville avec la famille pour célébrer l'anniversaire de ma mère. On va prendre le menu spécial, le menu gastronomique à 200 francs avec de bons vins!
*– **Numéro trois**.*
– Et toi, Hélène?
– Moi, je vais aller voir un match de football. Je vais voir le match Paris St. Germain contre Rennes. C'est un match important – il va y avoir 20.000 spectateurs, je pense.
*– **Numéro quatre**.*
– Jérôme, que vas-tu faire ce week-end?
– Alors samedi, je vais faire des courses. Je dois acheter des livres pour l'école. Ensuite je vais acheter un CD et j'espère m'offrir des baskets en plus.
*– **Numéro cinq**.*
– Et toi, Yvette?
– Alors ce week-end, c'est très important parce qu'il y a mon père qui va venir me voir. Donc moi, je dois aller rencontrer mon père. Il va arriver par le train de dix heures et demie, samedi matin.
– Ecoute les jeunes encore une fois.

B – Epreuve orale

Exercice 1
Pupils work in pairs and invite a friend to a concert or to the cinema using the cue card to help them initiate and respond (**Level 3**). Partner A only is assessed.
Award 1 mark per task.
Total 4 marks.
At **Level 3** short responses only such as *(Tu veux) aller au concert?, vingt heures trente, vingt-trois heures, soixante-cinq francs* are appropriate and would gain the mark. Pupils gaining at least 3 marks are showing some characteristics of performance at **Level 3**. Alternatively, teachers may practise the above situations and then ask pupils to vary the model, substituting different places, times and prices. This would then be a test which could elicit some characteristics of performance at **Level 4**. At **Level 4** pronunciation should be accurate and there should be consistency in pronunciation.

Exercice 2
Pupils choose one of the two *Fiches* and imagine they are Yvette or Olivier. They relate information on the following points:
where they live (1 mark),
situation (1 mark),
activities and season (1 per activity and 1 per season).
They then have to indicate one aspect they feel to be negative about the place where they live, e.g.
C'est très calme, il n'y a pas de club de jeunes, il y a beaucoup de touristes. / C'est bruyant, …
Total 8 marks.
At **Level 4** on this test at least four or five of the above items of information should be conveyed and pupils should be able to give an appropriate negative aspect. An example of **Level 4** language might be:

88

*J'habite Fond-Romeu, à la montagne. En hiver, on peut
jouer dans la neige – mais moi, je ne fais pas de ski.
Au printemps, j'aime / on peut faire des promenades. A
mon avis, à Fond-Romeu il y a beaucoup de touristes –
je n'aime pas ça!*

At **Level 4** pronunciation should be accurate and the
intonation generally consistent. Pupils scoring at least
6 of the available marks are showing some
characteristics of performance at **Level 4**.

Alternatively, at **Level 4**, pupils may prefer to make
their own cue cards based on the profile of Rouen in
the Pupil's Book. They would then have the
opportunity to adapt and substitute words and phrases
which are also characteristics of performance at **Level
4**. Should the teacher have to provide a lot of
prompting on this exercise and should pupils find it
difficult to provide feelings and give responses which
are unconnected short phrases on only two or three of
the set tasks, then pupils may only be showing
characteristics of performance at **Level 3**.

Exercice 3

Pupils are required to give an account of a stay in
France which is cued via the diary entries for a week
and visual cues for further support.

Total 10 marks.

These marks should be awarded each time the pupil
manages to communicate one of the facts given in the
cues. Differentiation on this exercise is by outcome.
Pupils scoring at least 7 marks but who do not always
use the appropriate tense and who use short phrases
with generally accurate pronunciation show
characteristics of performance at **Level 4**. Pupils who
score at least 7 marks and who attempt to
communicate with some consistency in the correct
tense are showing some characteristics of performance
at **Level 5**. Pupils who can score at least 7 marks and
who can manage to develop the set points using
tenses correctly are showing some characteristics of
performance at **Level 6**. Such pupils should be able to
make themselves understood with little or no
difficulty.

Teachers may wish to add bonus marks as below.
These enable the amount of help or support needed
from the teacher to be taken into account. Some
pupils may be able to treat the exercise as a
presentation and proceed unaided, whereas others
may need extra support from the teacher in the form
of questions. These marks also give the teacher the
opportunity to reward the degree of accuracy shown
by pupils.

1 mark – pupil manages to communicate the basic
messages – language is often inaccurate but the
meaning of most of the messages is there. Substantial
help is needed from the teacher.

2 marks – communicates nearly all the messages
despite inaccuracies in short simple responses. Some
help from the teacher.

3 marks – communicates messages well. Language
often very accurate. Little help needed.

C – Epreuve de lecture

Exercice 1

Pupils show understanding of six short texts based on
people's likes and dislikes for food, according to the
proposed five menus. They choose an appropriate
day according to the six texts, and write in the correct
day at the end of each short text. This is a test of
performance at **Level 3**.

Total 6 marks.

Pupils scoring at least 4 marks are showing some
characteristics of performance at **Level 3**.

Answers

Boris – jeudi
Carole – lundi
Thomas – jeudi
Saïd – vendredi
Eléonore – mercredi
Sandrine – mardi

Exercice 2

Pupils show understanding of a factual text, clearly
handwritten, about the town of Bayonne. They show
understanding of both main points and details by
choosing the appropriate word from the list. Accept
incorrect spellings of the word as long as the word is
recognisable as being the correct one, as this is a test
of reading comprehension skills, not writing skills.
This tests characteristics of performance at **Level 4**.

Total 6 marks.

Award ½ mark per correct word. Pupils scoring at
least 4 marks are showing some characteristics of
performance at **Level 4**.

Answers

  1 *touristique*
  2 *cathédrale*
  3 *peintures*
  4 *vieux*
  5 *jardin*
  6 *acheter*
  7 *ennuyeuse*
  8 *aménagé*
  9 *rivière*
10 *hiver*
11 *bouge*
12 *calme*

Exercice 3

Pupils show understanding of an authentic source
which includes different time references. The exercise
requires them to identify and note main points and
specific details. Pupils are required to answer briefly
in French. This tests characteristics of performance at
Level 5.

Total 7 marks.

Pupils scoring at least 5 marks are showing some
characteristics of performance at **Level 5**.

Answers

1 Accept *Québecoise/Canadienne; Québec/Canada*
2 *13*
3 *(Au) Canada / au Québec* + *(en) France* (both countries needed).
4 Accept 2 of the following: *Elle fait le ménage / la cuisine / les magasins.*
5 *Elle a donné de l'argent à une association charitable.* The basic concept is the idea of the gift of money to a charity.
6 *1982*
7 Accept *un concert*. Some pupils will perhaps be able to produce *Elle chantera*. The idea conveyed in *Elle ira à Paris* is not adequate alone.

Exercice 4

Pupils show understanding of a letter to a friend on the subject of bullying and holiday activities. The language used is familiar and uses several time references. Pupils need to show not only understanding of main points and specific detail but also points of view. This necessitates some inference. This tests characteristics of performance at **Level 6**.
Total 6 marks.
Pupils scoring at least 4 marks are showing some characteristics of performance at **Level 6**.

Answers

1 *est la victime du racket*
2 *tout raconter à un adulte*
3 *un bon élève*
4 *faire des courses avec Fabrice*
5 *nager*
6 *gentil*

D – Epreuve écrite

Exercice 1

This exercise tests elements of performance at **Level 3**. Pupils are asked to write five short phrases (based on a model provided) from memory. They can choose any five out of nine activities pictured.
Total 5 marks.
Award 1 mark for each sentence. Spelling should be 'readily understandable'. Award ½ mark if there is some doubt as to meaning.
Pupils scoring at least 3½ marks are showing some characteristics of performance at **Level 3**.

Exercice 2

Here pupils are required to adapt a model provided and write a short text in French. This tests elements of performance at **Level 4**.
Total 10 marks.
Spelling should be accurate. There are ten details to which pupils must refer. Award 1 mark for each correctly written detail. Ignore any accent errors.
Pupils scoring at least 7 marks are showing some characteristics of performance at **Level 4**.

Exercice 3

In the final exercise, pupils are required to write details in the past tense based on visual cues and a model. They include opinions in their writing. This tests elements of performance at **Level 5**, though in some cases the outcome could be judged to represent performance at **Level 6**. Similarly, the outcome could represent inferior performance if the verbs, for example, are poorly handled or if some elements such as the opinions are omitted. This then is an example of an exercise in which the outcome is used to judge the performance.
Total 4 marks.
2 marks for each block of writing. Use ½ marks.
Pupils scoring at least 3 marks are showing some characteristics of performance at **Level 5** or possibly **Level 6**.

CAMARADES 3 (TURQUOISE) OVERVIEW – UNITE 5 A TA SANTE!   National Curriculum Areas of Experience: A, B

	Topics/objectives	Key language	Grammar	Skills and strategies	PoS coverage
A	**De la tête aux pieds** Parts of the body	*tête, bras, jambe, corps, pied, dents, oreille, bouche, nez, main, yeux*	*la tête (etc.) de* …		1 b c 2 a k 3 f
B	**J'ai mal …** Describing symptoms	*j'ai mal, estomac, gorge, dos, genou, œil, doigt, tête, bras, jambe, corps, pied, dents, oreille, bouche, nez, main*	*au, à la, à l'* *en* + present participle		1 b c d 2 g h l 3 f
C	**La santé dans l'assiette** Talking about a healthy diet	*confiture, bœuf, chou, chou-fleur, pain, poisson, riz, biscuits, céréales, frites, gâteaux, haricots, pâtes, salade beurre, coca, fromage, jambon, jus de fruits, poulet, yaourt, limonade, bananes*	*en* (replacing phrases with *de*)	Dictionary: using dictionary to check gender of nouns	1 a g h 2 d f h l 3 c d
D	**Grammar**		*en* (replacing phrases with *de*) *en* + present participle		1 c d 3 f g
E	**Je déteste le sport** Giving opinions on sport	*passion, fana, truc, tellement, s'en passer, vie, individuel, aimer, adorer, détester, préférer, regarder, équipe, ennuyeux, sport, sportif*		Writing and Speaking: using varied language – different ways of saying what you like, don't like	1 c g i 2 h m n 3 c e g 4 a d
F	**Une question de sport** Reading for interest: sport		*quel*		1 b c g i 2 j 4 a c
G	**Le sport pour tous!** Talking about sports	*rugby, badminton, cricket, judo, tir à l'arc, athlétisme, skate-board, planche à voile, jogging, aérobic, patin à glace, karting, escalade, tennis, patin à roulettes, foot, basket, volley, natation, pêche, tennis de table, voile, équitation, ski*		Dictionary: finding phrases embedded in dictionary entry Learning vocabulary Applying known grammar to new situation	1 a c d i j 2 a l n 3 d f g
H	**Grammar** Pronunciation		*quel* *avoir besoin de*	Pronunciation: stress patterns	1 a d 2 b f g 3 c
I	**L'équipement essentiel** Discussing what to take on an outing	*besoin, K-way, couteau suisse, carte, lampe de poche, appareil-photo, lunettes de soleil, trousse de secours, Kleenex, essentiel, utile, pull, grand, lourd*	*avoir besoin de*	Unknown words – (English – French): asking for help; using dictionary	1 a b d 2 c f g h n 3 c d
J	**Premiers secours** First aid	*paire de ciseaux, gaze, sparadrap, coton hydrophile, paracétamol, aspirine, bandage, désinfectant, lampe de poche, argent, stylo, savon, Kleenex*		Reading: skim reading for gist	1 g i 2 j 3 c
K	**Une journée spéciale** Describing a day out	*tout d'abord, après ça, ensuite, cartes postales, plage, lunaparc, château, pin's* (and activities from earlier units)	Perfect tense (3rd person)	Writing: structure, paragraphs; drafting and redrafting Speaking and Writing: phrases for linking	1 c d h i j 2 a n o 3 f h
L	**Atelier** Plans and preparation for a weekend course			Reading: awareness of *faux amis*	1 a i j k 2 g h i l 3 c e

Worksheets

Recommended use of the worksheets (in some cases they can be used later, as revision):

Spread	Worksheet	Spread	Worksheet	Spread	Worksheet	Spread	Worksheet
A		D	11	G	7 and 8	J	5 and 6
B	12	E	9 and 10	H		K	16
C	3 and 4	F		I		L	

Feuille 1 and 2 Vocabulaire

Feuille 3 On écoute ◆

Le marathon
– *Claudie Villiers, vous êtes spécialiste de la nutrition et du sport.*
– *Oui, c'est ça.*
– *Pouvez-vous nous parler d'abord du régime des coureurs de marathon?*
– *Oui. Alors, la veille, il faut manger par exemple de la soupe.*
– *Oui.*
– *Et puis je conseille du poisson, avec une sauce citron et des légumes.*
– *Et comme dessert?*
– *Une banane.*
– *Le jour de l'épreuve, le matin, on doit boire beaucoup: du café, de l'eau minérale, du jus de fruit.*
– *Et à manger?*
– *Je recommande du pain et de la confiture.*
– *Il est impossible de boire beaucoup pendant un marathon, donc après, il faut boire beaucoup. Je conseille à mes athlètes de boire quatre litres d'eau.*
– *Quatre litres?*
– *Oui. Quatre litres sur quatre heures.*

Le football
– *Et pour le football?*
– *Alors, là, il faut bien manger six heures avant le match. De la viande grillée, mais sans sauce.*
– *Sans sauce.*
– *Oui, et avec des pâtes. Puis, comme dessert, on peut manger une banane.*
– *Et puis deux heures avant le match, pour avoir de l'énergie, il faut manger du pain avec de la confiture.*
– *Et qu'est-ce qu'il faut boire?*
– *Du thé ou de l'eau.*
– *Qu'est-ce qu'on doit prendre après le match?*
– *Je recommande de la soupe.*
– *C'est tout?*
– *Non, on peut manger de la viande aussi, mais il ne faut pas manger de viande rouge.*
– *Pas de viande rouge?*
– *Non, il faut d'abord éliminer du corps toutes les toxines.*

La gymnastique
– *Et finalement, la gymnastique.*
– *Alors, au petit déjeuner, on doit manger des céréales avec du lait.*

– *Et avec ça?*
– *Des fruits et du yaourt.*
– *Qu'est-ce qu'on peut boire?*
– *On peut boire du jus de fruits.*
– *On peut déjeuner?*
– *Oui. Je recommande de la viande grillée, avec des légumes.*
– *Et avec ça?*
– *On peut également manger du fromage et un fruit.*
– *Après l'épreuve, il faut boire beaucoup, c'est-à-dire un ou deux litres d'eau.*
– *Et faut-il manger?*
– *Oui, ça c'est important. Je conseille des pommes de terre ou des pâtes.*
– *Claudie Villiers, merci beaucoup.*

For Exercise 3, give pupils ideas about structuring their article, for example a different paragraph for *la veille; avant l'épreuve* and *après l'épreuve*. For extra information, you could give them copies of the transcript of the interviews.

Feuille 4 On écoute ♣

1 – *Ariane, vous faites le marathon, n'est-ce pas? Que mangez-vous la veille de l'épreuve?*
– *La veille, en général, je prends un bon repas riche en protéines, par exemple, je prends de la soupe, suivi de poisson avec légumes et frites.*
– *Et le jour de l'épreuve?*
– *Pour tenir toute la course, je pense qu'il vaut mieux manger beaucoup; autant que possible. Moi, je prends des céréales, des œufs, du fromage, et du pain.*
– *Et vous n'avez pas mal à l'estomac pendant le marathon, après un grand petit déjeuner?*
– *Si, j'ai un peu mal.*
– *Comment récupérez-vous après la course?*
– *Normalement, je bois de l'eau.*
– *Combien?*
– *Je ne sais pas. Ça dépend.*
– *Merci.*
2 – *Quel est votre sport, François?*
– *Je suis footballeur professionnel.*
– *Pouvez-vous nous parler de votre régime alimentaire?*

> – *Bien sûr. Alors, si le match commence,*
>   *disons, à 20h, il faut prendre un repas*
>   *important à 14h, pour avoir le temps de bien*
>   *digérer. Pour ce repas, il faut préférer des*
>   *sucres lents pour avoir de l'énergie, c'est-à-*
>   *dire, du riz, des spaghettis, du fromage etc.*
> – *Et c'est tout ce que vous mangez avant le*
>   *match?*
> – *Ah non, pas du tout! Vers 18h, je prends des*
>   *tartines: deux ou trois tranches de pain,*
>   *avec de la confiture.*
> – *Et après le match?*
> – *La période de récupération est aussi*
>   *importante que la préparation. Il faut faire*
>   *attention à ce qu'on mange. Rien de trop*
>   *lourd. Moi, par exemple, après un match je*
>   *prends un peu de poulet avec des pâtes.*
> – *Avec une bière?*
> – *Certainement pas! J'évite l'alcool le jour du*
>   *match. Je préfère attendre le lendemain,*
>   *quand toutes les toxines sont éliminées de*
>   *mon corps.*
> – *Merci, François.*
> **3** – *Et toi, Alain, tu joues aussi au football.*
> – *Oui, c'est ça, niveau juniors.*
> – *Que manges-tu avant un match?*
> – *Eh bien, ça dépend. Si on joue ici, au club,*
>   *je prends un déjeuner chez moi avant de*
>   *partir, mais autrement, j'emporte des*
>   *sandwichs pour manger dans le car.*
> – *Et après le match?*
> – *Après, j'ai vraiment faim. Ce que j'aime le*
>   *plus, c'est aller dans un café avec l'équipe,*
>   *manger un grand steak.*
> – *Et arroser votre succès avec une bière?*
> – *Une bière ou deux! Oui, bien sûr!*
> – *Merci.*
> **4** – *Charlotte, tu as déjà gagné plusieurs*
>   *trophées en gymnastique, et tu n'as que*
>   *treize ans.*
> – *Oui, je m'entraîne beaucoup, et je fais très*
>   *attention à mon régime alimentaire.*
> – *Le jour de l'épreuve, qu'est-ce tu manges?*
> – *Je prends des cornflakes ou du muesli, avec*
>   *du lait, bien sûr, et du yaourt.*
> – *Tu prends du pain?*
> – *En général non. Je prends plutôt un fruit.*
> – *Qu'est-ce que tu bois?*
> – *Le jour, j'évite le café, c'est trop fort. Je*
>   *préfère le jus de fruits et l'eau.*
> – *Tu déjeunes?*
> – *Oui, mais je prends quelque chose de léger,*
>   *par exemple du poulet ou du poisson.*
> – *Et après l'épreuve?*
> – *C'est là qu'il faut faire attention, pour bien*
>   *récupérer. Moi, je bois toujours deux litres*
>   *d'eau, et je mange une grande assiette de*
>   *spaghettis. Mais ce n'est pas seulement la*
>   *compétition qui est importante. Il faut faire*
>   *attention à son régime pendant*
>   *l'entraînement, aussi.*
> – *Mais tu manges des frites et tout ça avec tes*
>   *copines?*

Feuille 5 On parle ◆

Feuille 6 On parle ♣
Pupils practise more complex rôle-plays, in which they have to deal with problems.

Feuille 7 On lit ◆ (free-standing)
As an extra writing activity, pupils could retell the outline of the invention of the bicycle, in the perfect tense.

Feuille 8 On lit ♣ (free-standing)
To follow up, pupils could select a writing activity: they can imagine that they practise one of these sports, and write a magazine article about their hobby or a race they have just won; or they write an article on someone else (real or fictitious), who is a champion in one of the sports.

Feuille 9 On écrit ◆ (free-standing)
Pupils are trained in writing longer sentences, as appropriate to more formal written work. They also practise using different phrases to give their opinion. They are encouraged to edit and redraft their work.

Feuille 10 On écrit ♣ (free-standing)
In addition to the features also practised on *Feuille 9*, this worksheet provides work on linking sentences and paragraphs and structuring ideas, in the context of giving and justifying opinions.

Feuille 11 Grammaire (free-standing)
Following the introduction in the Pupil's Book of *en*, replacing phrases with *de*, *Feuille 11* provides practice of set phrases with *en: il y en a; il n'y en a pas; j'en ai; je n'en ai pas*. The activities are written, so that the sheet is free-standing and can be used as homework, but pupils could do Exercises 1 and 2 orally. Exercise 1 also revises food items.

Feuille 12 En plus (free-standing)
This worksheet has no specific activities, since the point of reading jokes is simply to enjoy them. If you wish to give a more concrete activity, you could ask pupils to select their favourite jokes and translate them into English to tell their friends.

The jokes also give a good incentive for pupils to look up words they don't know and can't work out for themselves.

Some pupils might also be able to find and bring in different French jokes, for example from French magazines or penfriends. If you have a link class, it could be interesting to swap jokes with them. Are some types of joke found in both countries?

Feuille 13 Que sais-tu?

> **1** – *Mélanie, tu suis un régime équilibré?*
> – *Euh, j'essaie de manger beaucoup de fruits,*
>   *parce que c'est bien pour la santé.*
> – *Tu manges souvent des produits gras?*
> – *Enfin, oui, je suppose. J'adore les frites et les*
>   *chips et j'en mange tous les jours.*
> – *Est-ce que tu fais de l'exercice?*
> – *Pas beaucoup. Je fais des promenades de*
>   *temps en temps, en été, quand il fait beau.*
> **2** – *Bertrand, qu'est-ce que tu manges, en*
>   *général?*
> – *Eh bien, à midi, je vais au Quick prendre*
>   *un hamburger-frites.*
> – *Et qu'est-ce que tu bois?*
> – *Normalement, du coca. Puis, en rentrant de*
>   *l'école, j'achète une tablette de chocolat.*
> – *Tous les jours?*
> – *Ben, oui.*
> – *Est-ce que tu fumes?*
> – *Un peu, oui.*
> – *Combien par jour?*
> – *Ça dépend. Environ neuf ou dix.*

Feuille 14 Révision 1: weather (free-standing)
Pupils could also prepare and record their own weather forecast, perhaps based on information from today's newspaper, using one of the written forecasts on the sheet as a model.

Feuille 15 Révision 2: train travel

Feuille 16 Grille
Support for Spread K Exercise 1.

Feuille 17 Réponses
This provides answers for the Unit 5 worksheets.

IT Opportunities

B3 **Spread B Exercise 3**
◆ In preparation for the listening exercise some pupils could benefit from working with a couple of the dialogues in a text manipulator with line jumbling and gapping facilities. They might also work with the cassette: listening, noting and then rearranging the dialogues in the correct order, also identifying which three were not on the text manipulator.

E5 **Spread E Exercise 5**
* Pupils draft their magazine letters using a word-processor. They are encouraged to write as freely as possible using the language they know. After checking with each other and the teacher, they redraft for accuracy. Finally they redraft for presentation for the magazine.

F **Spread F**
If there is access to the Internet, pupils might like to explore the *Tour de France* site. For example, in pairs, pupils could be asked to find out two new pieces of information not mentioned in the book and then report back to the class.

G4 **Spread G Exercise 4**
* Pupils create and design their poems for display using a word-processor or graphics/drawing program. They use different fonts and colours and import clipart or make drawings to illustrate them.

I3/4 **Spread I Exercises 3 and 4**
To help pupils with the sort of conversation heard in Exercise 3, write Conversation 1 into a text manipulator with gapping and storyboard facilities. Pupils first reconstruct the dialogue filling the gaps and then gradually uncover the text in a storyboard, reading it aloud as they discover each line.

♣ After Exercise 4, pupils could word-process a little playlet dialogue along similar lines for one of the situations they have discussed. They might also put it into the text manipulator for other pupils to do.

K **Spread K Extra**
* Pupils word-process their own 'picture gap' story, like the one in Exercise 1, importing clipart to illustrate the gaps, and print it out for others to do. (Their name must be on their work.) Stories are then shuffled round in groups and other pupils guess the answers, reading aloud the story.

♣ Pupils read a story aloud in the third person. A class book of 'picture gap' stories can be compiled for other classes to do.

A De la tête aux pieds   pp 98–99

Objectives
Parts of the body

Resources
Presentation sheets 14 and 15
Cassette for Exercises 1, 2 and 5

Key language
tête, bras, jambe, corps, pied, dents, estomac, oreille, bouche, nez, main, yeux

Grammar
la tête (etc.) de …

The aim of Spread A is to introduce vocabulary for a restricted number of parts of the body. More parts can be taught in Spread B, where the expression *j'ai mal à* will also be practised.

Ways in
Teach the parts of the body using the labels from Presentation sheet 15 which can be laid on the outline on Presentation sheet 14. If they don't feel it's beneath their dignity, a game of *Simon dit …* could be used for oral practice (*Simon dit: touchez le pied* etc.). Alternatively, start drawing a part of the body on the board. Pupils guess which part of the body it is as soon as they think they know what it is.

Depending on which dictionaries your pupils are using, they may need guidance on how to look up some expressions in the photo story. With your pupils' help, write a list of headwords which they need to look up, e.g. *en retard ⇨ retard, peux ⇨ pouvoir, j'ai mal ⇨ mal, gardien de but ⇨ gardien. J'ai mal* is introduced receptively only. The expression will be exploited in Spread B.

Answers
1 *vrai*   **2** *faux*   **3** *vrai*

Prompt your pupils if they do not recognise one of the names in the box, e.g. *Monica Seles joue au tennis.* A homework task could be for pupils to make up their own quiz on similar lines, using parts of photos cut out of magazines, and writing their own questions.

Answers

> 1 *C'est la tête de Madonna.*
> 2 *C'est le bras de Monica Seles.*
> 3 *C'est la main de Steve Davis.*
> 4 *C'est l'estomac de Frank Bruno.*
> 5 *C'est la jambe de Naomi Campbell.*

Answers
Les yeux / la bouche de sa mère.
Les oreilles / le nez / les dents de son père.

Differentiation
Pupils who finish early could identify the sports represented in the pictures.

Answers
1	*les mains*	6	*la tête*
2	*les jambes*	7	*la bouche / les dents*
3	*la tête*	8	*les oreilles*
4	*les mains*	9	*les yeux*
5	*les bras*		

> 1 – *Je n'aime pas mes yeux.*
> – *Tu n'aimes pas tes yeux? Pourquoi?*
> – *Parce qu'ils sont trop petits.*
> – *Mais tes yeux ne sont pas petits! Tu as de beaux yeux!*
> 2 – *Par contre, j'aime bien mes jambes!*
> – *Ah bon?*
> – *Oui, j'ai les jambes longues et musclées!*
> – *Musclées?!*
> 3 – *Et tes oreilles?*
> – *Alors, là, non! Je déteste mes oreilles!*
> – *Et pourquoi?*
> – *Je les trouve trop grandes!*
> – *Ne sois pas stupide! Tes oreilles ne sont pas grandes du tout!*
> 4 – *Tu as de très belles mains.*
> – *Mais non! Pas du tout! Je n'aime pas mes mains!*
> – *Mais pourquoi?*
> – *Elles sont trop petites. Je joue du piano, et c'est difficile avec des petites mains.*
> – *Ah bon?*
> 5 – *Mais j'ai de belles dents.*
> – *Tu aimes tes dents, alors …*
> – *Eh oui. Elles sont très blanches, tu ne trouves pas?*
> – *Ben oui … Je suppose …*
> 6 – *Par contre, je déteste mon nez!*
> – *Ton nez?! Mais il est bien, ton nez!*
> – *Ah non, il est trop long. Beaucoup trop long!*
> – *Ah là là, t'es ridicule! Ridicule et très vaniteux!*
> – *Qui? Moi?!*

Prepare this by brainstorming some celebrities (including members of staff?) in class.

B J'ai mal … pp 100–101

Objectives
Describing symptoms

Resources
Presentation sheets 14 and 15
Cassette for Exercises 1 and 3

Key language
j'ai mal, estomac, gorge, dos, genou, œil, doigt, tête, bras, jambe, corps, pied, dents, oreille, bouche, nez, main

Grammar
au, à la, à l'
en + present participle

Ways in
Use Presentation sheets 14 and 15 to revise parts of the body and to introduce new ones. For homework, pupils could cut out a picture of a person from a magazine and, using arrows, label the appropriate parts of the body.

Once the pupils feel confident with the vocabulary, use mime to introduce the expressions *j'ai mal au / à la / aux*. Pupils can then come to the front and mime e.g. *j'ai mal aux pieds* and then lay the appropriate *j'ai mal* label from Presentation sheet 15 on the right part of the body on Presentation sheet 14.

You can also cut out the pointer at the bottom of Presentation sheet 15 and use it to point to parts of the body on sheet 14, indicating where it hurts.

Refer to the work on *au / à la* in Unit 3 to reassure pupils that they are not learning 'new' grammar but the application of known grammar in a new context.

1

Normal is easily recognisable; the masculine form *normaux* is less so. Knowledge of the *-al ⇨ -aux* rule therefore eases comprehension. Take a moment to show pupils other examples of these irregular plural forms, e.g. *journaux, chevaux; heureux, silencieux.*

2

Answers
1 *footballeur*
2 *chanteuse*
3 *skieur*
4 *guitariste de rock*
5 *secrétaire*
6 *pilote*
7 *top-modèle*
8 *acrobate de cirque.*

Differentiation
With able pupils, take the opportunity to practise the third person forms, e.g. *Le footballeur, qu'est-ce qu'il a? Il/Elle a mal au / à la …*

3

Answers
1 *genou (footballeur: oui)*
2 *pied (secrétaire: non)*
3 *bras (guitariste: oui)*
4 *mains, yeux (secrétaire: oui)*
5 *tête, gorge (élève: non).*

COUNTER

1 – *Bonjour, M. Pollet.*
 – *Bonjour, Docteur.*
 – *Alors, qu'est-ce qui ne va pas?*
 – *J'ai très mal au genou.*
 – *Voyons … . ah, oui. Comment avez-vous fait ça?*
 – *J'ai fait ça en jouant au football. En fait, je suis footballeur professionnel. J'ai un match demain. Est-ce que je peux jouer?*
 – *Ah non. Je suis désolée, mais vous ne devriez pas jouer demain.*

2 – *Bonjour, Docteur.*
 – *Bonjour, Madame. Quel est votre problème?*
 – *J'ai mal au pied.*
 – *Faites voir … Ça fait mal ici?*
 – *Aïe! Oui, ça fait mal!*
 – *Et comment avez-vous fait cela?*
 – *Je suis tombée en faisant du patin à roulettes.*
 – *Bon, alors je vais vous faire un bandage.*
 – *Merci.*
 – *Quelle est votre occupation?*
 – *Je suis secrétaire. Je vais au travail en bus, donc ce n'est pas un problème.*

3 – *Bonjour, Monsieur. Qu'est-ce qui ne va pas?*
 – *Eh bien, j'ai très mal aux bras.*
 – *Faites voir …*
 – *Ça fait mal quand je joue de la guitare.*
 – *Alors, ne jouez pas de la guitare!*
 – *Mais je suis guitariste professionnel! Je joue dans un groupe!*

4 – *Bonjour, Docteur.*
 – *Bonjour. Quel est le problème?*
 – *J'ai très mal aux mains et j'ai mal aux yeux. Surtout quand je travaille sur mon ordinateur.*
 – *Qu'est-ce que vous faites dans la vie?*
 – *Je suis secrétaire.*
 – *Et vous travaillez beaucoup sur ordinateur?*
 – *Mais oui, tous les jours!*

5 – *Bonjour, Docteur.*
 – *Bonjour, Cyril. Alors, qu'est-ce qu'il y a?*
 – *J'ai mal à la tête et à la gorge.*
 – *Ouvre la bouche, s'il te plaît.*
 – *Aaahhh.*
 – *Je vais te donner des antibiotiques. Tu ne devrais pas aller au collège.*
 – *Ça, ce n'est pas un problème – on est en vacances!*

This would be an appropriate time to work on Spread D *Grammaire*, page 104: *en …ant.*

4

Having given their opinions, pupils could imagine that they themselves have been invited out but don't want to go. They write their own excuses, modelled on those in the book.

5

Use pairs of sentences to explain the meaning of the new grammar point, e.g.

J'ai joué au tennis. Je suis tombée.

= Je suis tombée en jouant au tennis.

When pupils practise their dialogues, their partners could comment on whether their excuses are good or not – as in Exercise 4.

C La santé dans l'assiette

Objectives
Talking about a healthy diet

Resources
Presentation sheets 16, 17 and 18
Cassette for Exercise 2

Key language
confiture, bœuf, chou, chou-fleur, pain, poisson, riz, biscuits, céréales, frites, gâteaux, haricots, pâtes, salade, *beurre, coca, fromage, jambon, jus de fruits, poulet, yaourt, limonade, bananes*

Grammar
en (replacing phrases with *de*)

Strategies
Using dictionary to check gender of nouns

Ways in
Use Presentation sheets 16, 17 and 18 to introduce and practise the key vocabulary. You could play Kim's game, starting with a few items only and then increasing the number. Or play this team game: members of the team call out items on a shopping list, while one of their team stands at the OHP and places on it the items which have been called out. How many can he/she do in one minute? Can the next team do better?

1 Pupils use the dictionary here not only to check on the meanings of any unknown words, but to establish the gender of nouns shown in the plural. Remind pupils of the importance of learning and noting the gender of any new words. In their books, pupils should always note the gender in the same way, e.g. *pomme* (f) apple, or *une pomme* an apple.

2

> – *Qu'est-ce que c'est, Marc, cette brochure?*
> – *Oh, c'est un truc pour bien manger …*
> – *Je peux voir? Ah, oui … Alors, le groupe C, produits laitiers, j'adore ça! J'adore le fromage. Et toi?*
> – *Oui, moi aussi, j'adore ça! Surtout le camembert. J'en mange tous les jours.*
> – *Et le yaourt, tu aimes ça?*
> – *Ben, oui, je suppose. Ce n'est pas mal … J'en mange parfois.*
> – *Et le groupe A, fruits et légumes, j'aime tout ça aussi. Et toi? Tu aimes les pommes, par exemple?*
> – *Les pommes? Non, je n'en mange jamais!*
> – *Mais tu aimes les bananes?*
> – *Ben … oui. J'en mange de temps en temps.*
> – *Et les légumes? Voyons … tu aimes le chou?*
> – *Ah non! Ça, je n'en mange jamais!*
> – *Moi, j'aime bien! Tu aimes le chou-fleur, alors?*
> – *Non! Ça, c'est dégoûtant, aussi! Beurk!*
> – *Tu aimes la viande? Tu n'es pas végétarien?*
> – *Moi? Non! J'adore le bœuf! Un steack avec des frites, c'est mon plat préféré! J'en mange souvent.*
> – *Tu aimes le poulet aussi?*
> – *Ben oui, j'aime bien. Le poulet-frites – mmm! Ça aussi, j'en mange souvent.*
> – *'Pain et céréales', c'est facile. Tu aimes le pain …*
> – *Bien sûr. J'aime bien le pain. J'en mange beaucoup.*
> – *Et les pâtes?*
> – *Ah oui, j'adore! Les spaghettis, les macaronis. C'est bon, ça!*

> – *Alors, pour les produits sucrés, je sais que tu aimes les gâteaux. C'est vrai?*
> – *Oui, j'adore les gâteaux et les biscuits. J'en mange tous les jours.*
> – *Et tu aimes le coca?*
> – *Ça, non. Je n'aime pas beaucoup. Je préfère le lait.*
> – *Et les bonbons, aussi, je suppose …*
> – *Ah oui. J'en mange tous les jours. J'adore ça. En effet, je pense que je mange très bien!*
> – *Très bien?! Tu blagues!*

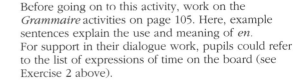

The *Stratégie* box draws the pupils' attention to a skill much needed in target language exams (such as GCSE): not listening out for a word which they have seen in print (e.g. *souvent*) but listening instead for an equivalent expression (e.g. *tous les jours*). To make the point, play the tape a second time: pupils put up their hand each time they hear an expression of time (*de temps en temps, jamais* etc.). Pause the tape and write the expression on the board. It will help pupils to visualise the expressions, and pupils will be able to refer to the list on the board when they do their dialogue work in Exercise 3.

3 Before going on to this activity, work on the *Grammaire* activities on page 105. Here, example sentences explain the use and meaning of *en*. For support in their dialogue work, pupils could refer to the list of expressions of time on the board (see Exercise 2 above).

4 Make sure pupils understand the distinction between the past and the future.

If a few days elapse before the next lesson, a homework task could be for pupils to keep a diary of what they eat each day. They can then refer to their diary when they do Exercise 4.

5 Pupils get the chance to use the new language to make real and valid recommendations.

Feuilles 3 and *4* have activities based on recommended diets for different sports.

D Grammaire   pp 104–105

Grammar

en + present participle
en (replacing phrases with *de*)

---

en ...ant (while/through ...ing)

Answers
En arrivant à Quimper, nous avons visité la
cathédrale.
J'ai eu peur en montant la tour de la cathédrale.
J'ai acheté des cartes postales en quittant la
cathédrale.
Je me suis fait mal au genou en jouant au foot après
le déjeuner.
J'ai dépensé tout mon argent en achetant des
souvenirs.
Dans le car, en rentrant, on a raconté des blagues.

2 **Differentiation**

All pupils write similar sentences, but abler pupils are
challenged to produce the present participles
themselves. They may of course refer to page 150 in
the Grammar Section.

To start pupils off, you might show them some
pictures of people doing things, cut out of a
magazine. This might prompt sentences such as e.g.
J'ai mangé du poisson en dansant le limbo and give
pupils an idea of the sort of sentences you are
looking for.

en (it/them/some/any)

For homework, pupils could answer the eight
questions for themselves.

For further practice, ask pupils **when** they eat
particular foods, e.g.
– *Tu manges souvent du poulet?*
– *Non, je n'en mange pas souvent.*
– *Tu en manges à midi, parfois?*
– *Non, j'en mange le soir.*

4 Before starting on Exercise 4, look back, with your
pupils, at the explanation at the top of the page and
focus this time on the position of *en* in the sentence –
i.e. just before the verb.

Tackle the first item in the exercise (*elle en mange*)
on the board for the class as a whole. This will help
pupils to avoid mistakes in word order.

On *Feuille 11*, pupils can practise using en in set
phrases: *il y en a / il n'y en a pas and j'en ai / je n'en*
ai pas.

E **Je déteste le sport!** pp 106–107

Objectives
Giving opinions on sport

Strategies
Writing and Speaking: using varied language – different ways of saying what you like, don't like

Resources
Cassette for Exercises 1 and 4

Key language
passion, fana, truc, tellement, s'en passer, vie, individuel, aimer, adorer, détester, préférer, regarder, équipe, ennuyeux, sport, sportif

---

1

Ways in
Ask questions on the storyline, e.g.
– *Il y a un match de football aujourd'hui?*
– *Et Marc: il veut jouer? Pourquoi (pas)?*
– *Qu'est-ce que tu penses: Marc est-il vraiment malade?*
– *A ton avis, Marc, qu'est-ce qu'il va faire? Il va jouer au tennis?*

Differentiation
Exploit new phrases from the letters (e.g. *Céline: c'est un moyen de …*) to allow pupils to express their own opinions.

2

Answers
1 *Pierre-Charles*   2 *Guillaume*   3 *Céline*
4 *Valentine*   ♣ 5 *Guillaume*   ♣ 6 *Valentine*

3

To reinforce the new phrases, write the two headings from Exercise 1 on the board:

aime le sport   n'aime pas le sport

Pupils come to the board and write the new phrases in the appropriate column.

For more oral practice, use the questions from the survey in Exercise 6: pupils answer using one of the new expressions.

4

Pupils could take notes and then write up their answers in full sentences.

Answers
1 ✗ *pas son truc, ennuyeux*
2 ✓ *sa passion, sa vie, souvent*
3 ✓ *bien, sportive*
4 ✗ *peut s'en passer*
5 ✓ *fana de sport à la télé*
6 ✗ *pas son truc*

COUNTER

1 – *Marion, est-ce que tu aimes le sport?*
– *Moi, le sport, ce n'est pas mon truc.*
– *Non? Pourquoi?*
– *Ben, je trouve ça ennuyeux!*
– *Ennuyeux? Comment ça?*
– *Eh bien, la semaine dernière, par exemple, j'ai regardé un match de foot à la télé.*
– *Et tu n'as pas aimé ça?*
– *Non, pas du tout. C'était un match très ennuyeux. Le score était: 0-0!*

---

2 – *Et toi, Robin, tu aimes le sport?*
– *Moi, le sport, c'est ma passion! C'est ma vie!*
– *Tu fais souvent du sport?*
– *Oui, j'en fais très souvent. Par exemple, je joue au volleyball chaque semaine. Je suis dans une équipe.*
– *Vous jouez bien?*
– *Oui, très bien, en fait. Nous gagnons tous nos matchs! Nous avons déjà gagné cinq trophées.*

3 – *Gaëlle, tu fais du sport, toi?*
– *Ben oui. Le sport, c'est bien. Je suis assez sportive.*
– *Pourquoi fais-tu du sport?*
– *Parce que c'est un moyen de me détendre. C'est une activité anti-stress!*
– *Tu es stressée, alors?*
– *Oui, parfois je suis très stressée.*
– *Pour quelles raisons?*
– *Oh … j'ai des problèmes au collège. Je trouve le travail trop difficile. Les maths en particulier.*
– *Ah bon?*
– *En plus, je suis victime d'un racket.*
– *Oh là là, c'est affreux. Tu devrais en parler à un professeur.*
– *Oui, mais j'ai peur …*

4 – *Toi, tu aimes le sport, Laurent?*
– *Bof! Le sport, je peux m'en passer!*
– *Cela ne t'intéresse pas?*
– *Ben, non. Le sport, c'est bien, mais je préfère la musique. La musique, c'est ma vie! Je joue dans un groupe, tu sais.*
– *Ah bon? Tu joues de quel instrument?*
– *De la guitare. Et je chante aussi, parfois.*
– *Vous faites des concerts, de temps en temps?*
– *Oui, au club des jeunes. Tu devrais venir nous écouter!*
– *Oui, j'aimerais bien!*

5 – *Tu es une fana de sport, Caro?*
– *Oui, je suis une grande fana de sport … à la télé! Je trouve ça passionnant!*
– *Qu'est-ce que tu aimes regarder à la télé?*
– *Alors, j'adore regarder le tennis … la gymnastique … le judo … et la Formule 1.*
– *La Formule 1?*
– *Oui. Damon Hill est mon héros!*
– *Tu es déjà allée le voir?*
– *Oui, je l'ai vu pendant mes vacances en Angleterre. On est allé à Silverstone, et je l'ai vu gagner. C'était vraiment chouette. J'ai même eu son autographe!*

6 – *Et toi, Marc, tu fais du sport?*
– *Ben, oui, mais le sport, ce n'est pas mon truc.*
– *Mais tu joues au foot, n'est-ce pas?*
– *Oui, mais je déteste ça! Je suis vraiment nul! Si on perd, c'est toujours de ma faute. Je déteste les sports d'équipe!*
– *Est-ce que tu aimes regarder le sport?*
– *Oui, ça, j'aime beaucoup. Samedi prochain, je vais aller au stade avec mon oncle. On va regarder une compétition d'athlétisme. Ça va être génial.*

5

From now on, make a point of eliciting one of the new expressions when pupils express their opinions.

6

Pupils could record answers for *filles* and *garçons* in different columns. They could then report on whether they find significant differences or not.

On *Feuilles 9* and *10,* pupils work on developing higher-level writing skills, including writing longer and more complex sentences, different ways of giving their opinions, and redrafting.

F **Une question de sport** pp 108–109

Objectives
Reading for interest: sport

Grammar
quel

Ways in
To encourage pupils not to read the text before
answering the questions, display the questions
initially on the board or OHP.

When pupils come to read the text, refrain from
helping them too much. This is a good opportunity
for them to make use of the dictionary skills which
they have learnt.

Answers
1 *bleu, jaune, noir, vert, rouge*
2 *Athènes, 1896*
3 *Roland-Garros*
4 *Miguel Indurain*
5 *jaune*
6 *la natation, le cyclisme*
7 *la natation, la gymnastique*
8 *le football, la natation, la danse, le judo*

Discussion of the *Tour de France* is a good
opportunity to show a map of France, drawing
pupils' attention to where the principal mountain
ranges are. The *tour* often passes through one of the
neighbouring countries (including, sometimes,
Britain), so it's a good time to revise the names of
these countries too.

If time allows, pupils could compare the sporting
scene in France with that in Britain. Show your pupils
a way of drawing simple comparisons:
• pupils describe an aspect in France (e.g.
  popularity of hang-gliding or cycling, preference
  of boys for judo, preference of women for
  gymnastics);
• they give their opinion about the comparison (two
  useful phrases: *chez nous, c'est différent / c'est la
  même chose*) – they then describe the equivalent
  aspect in Britain.

For productive work on *quel,* see Spread H
Grammaire, page 112.

Follow-up tasks (e.g. for homework):
• pupils cut out pictures of their favourite sports and
  pastimes from colour magazines and make a
  poster with captions in French (e.g. publicity for
  gymnastics, or a defence of skate-boarding);
• following work on *quel* in Spread H, pupils make
  up their own quiz about sport.

G Le sport pour tous!

Objectives
Talking about sports

Resources
Presentation sheets 19 and 20
Cassette for Exercise 2

Key language
rugby, badminton, cricket, judo, tir à l'arc, athlétisme, skate-board, planche à voile, jogging, aérobic, patin à

glace, karting, escalade, tennis, patin à roulettes, foot, basket, volley, natation, pêche, tennis de table, voile, équitation, ski

Strategies
Dictionary: finding phrases embedded in dictionary entry
Applying known grammar to new situation

Ways in
Before opening the books, ask pupils how many different sports they think they can say in French. Then challenge them to give you the names of as many sports as they can remember. List them on the board or OHP (with gender, of course). See whether they actually know as many as they thought (or, more likely, more).

1
Focus on sports which pupils did not mention in your introductory activity. Even if pupils deduce the meaning of the new words from the visuals, get them to check their hunches in the dictionary. This will give them practice in looking up words embedded in the dictionary entry (e.g. *tir à l'arc*).

For further practice with the new nouns use Presentation sheets 19 and 20.

2
Answers
1 *le rugby*
2 *le jogging*
3 *la planche à voile*
4 *l'aérobic*
5 *l'équitation*
6 *le basket*
7 *le cyclisme*
8 *le patin à glace*

Pupils first hear the clues on their own, and have the opportunity to guess the right answers. They then hear the clues again together with the right answers.

COUNTER

– *On fait ce quiz sur les sports?*
– *D'accord. Toi, tu lis les questions.*
– *OK. Numéro 1. 'C'est un sport d'équipe, pratiqué en général par les garçons et les hommes. Beaucoup de gens considèrent que c'est un sport assez violent. Chaque année, il y a un grand championnat pour les équipes nationales de France, d'Ecosse, d'Angleterre, d'Irlande et du Pays de Galles.'*
  Numéro 2. 'C'est un sport individuel. On peut faire ça dans les rues, dans le parc – n'importe où! C'est un sport plus populaire chez les adultes que chez les jeunes. Beaucoup de gens pratiquent ce sport pour la santé, pour rester en forme.'
  Numéro 3. 'C'est un sport nautique. On peut faire ça sur la mer ou sur un lac. C'est un sport individuel. L'équipement coûte assez cher.'

Numéro 4. 'C'est un sport individuel que l'on pratique à l'intérieur. Il y a beaucoup de clubs pour faire ça. En général, ce sont les adultes qui pratiquent cette activité. Ils font ça pour garder leur forme. Beaucoup de gens s'amusent bien en faisant cette activité. Ils trouvent ça amusant.'
Numéro 5. 'C'est un sport qu'on pratique beaucoup à la campagne. Si on veut, on peut faire des compétitions. Il y a des compétitions pour les enfants, ainsi que pour les adultes. Pour pratiquer ce sport, il faut aimer les animaux!'
Numéro 6. 'C'est un sport d'équipe. On peut y jouer dans un gymnase ou dans la cour du collège, si on a l'équipement nécessaire. C'est plus facile si on est assez grand. C'est un sport très populaire aux Etats-Unis.'
Numéro 7. 'C'est un sport que l'on pratique en général à l'extérieur, mais il y a des compétitions à l'intérieur. Les compétitions ont lieu sur plusieurs distances. Ça peut être un sport individuel ou d'équipe. Tout le monde peut faire ça, adultes et jeunes, dans les rues ou à la campagne. C'est un sport très populaire en France.'
Numéro 8. 'En général, on pratique ce sport à l'intérieur. C'est un sport que l'on peut faire en compétition seul ou avec un partenaire. On gagne des points pour la technique et le style. On le considère comme un sport d'hiver.'

COUNTER

Les réponses:
– *Numéro 1. 'C'est un sport d'équipe, pratiqué en général par les garçons et les hommes. Beaucoup de gens considèrent que c'est un sport assez violent. Chaque année, il y a un grand championnat pour les équipes nationales de France, d'Ecosse, d'Angleterre, d'Irlande et du Pays de Galles.'*
– *Eh bien, ça, c'est le rugby, n'est-ce pas?*
– *Attends … . oui, le numéro 1, c'est le rugby.*
– *Numéro 2. 'C'est un sport individuel. On peut faire ça dans les rues, dans le parc – n'importe où! C'est un sport plus populaire chez les adultes que chez les jeunes. Beaucoup de gens pratiquent ce sport pour la santé, pour rester en forme.' Ça doit être le jogging … Oui, c'est ça, le jogging.*

- *Numéro 3. 'C'est un sport nautique. On peut faire ça sur la mer ou sur un lac. C'est un sport individuel. L'équipement coûte assez cher.'*
- *C'est la voile?*
- *Non, la voile, ça coûte très cher. Moi, je pense que c'est la planche à voile.*
- *Regarde les réponses.*
- *Oui, c'est la planche à voile.*
- *Numéro 4. 'C'est un sport individuel que l'on pratique à l'intérieur. Il y a beaucoup de clubs pour faire ça. En général, ce sont les adultes qui pratiquent cette activité. Ils font ça pour garder leur forme. Beaucoup de gens s'amusent bien en faisant cette activité. Ils trouvent ça amusant.' Alors là, je n'ai aucune idée.*
- *Ça pourrait être l'aérobic …*
- *Ah oui, c'est ça, l'aérobic.*
- *Numéro 5. 'C'est un sport qu'on pratique beaucoup à la campagne. Si on veut, on peut faire des compétitions. Il y a des compétitions pour les enfants, ainsi que pour les adultes. Pour pratiquer ce sport, il faut aimer les animaux!'*
- *Ça, c'est facile, c'est l'équitation!*
- *Oui, tu as raison.*
- *Numéro 6. 'C'est un sport d'équipe. On peut y jouer dans un gymnase ou dans la cour du collège, si on a l'équipement nécessaire. C'est plus facile si on est assez grand. C'est un sport très populaire aux Etats-Unis.' C'est quoi, ça, le volley?*
- *A mon avis, c'est plutôt le basket. Ça, c'est très populaire aux Etats-Unis.*
- *Attends … oui, c'est le basket.*
- *Numéro 7. 'C'est un sport que l'on pratique en général à l'extérieur, mais il y a des compétitions à l'intérieur. Les compétitions ont lieu sur plusieurs distances. Ça peut être un sport individuel ou d'équipe. Tout le monde peut faire ça, adultes et jeunes, dans les rues ou à la campagne. C'est un sport très populaire en France.'*
- *C'est l'athlétisme?*
- *Moi, je pense que c'est le cyclisme. Attends … oui, j'ai raison, c'est le cyclisme.*
- *Numéro 8. 'En général, on pratique ce sport à l'intérieur. C'est un sport que l'on peut faire en compétition seul ou avec un partenaire. On gagne des points pour la technique et le style. On le considère comme un sport d'hiver.'*
- *Un sport d'hiver? Ça doit être le ski.*
- *Sois pas stupide. C'est un sport que l'on pratique à l'intérieur. Ça doit être le patin à glace.*
- *Oui. C'est ça. Le patin à glace.*

To make sure all pupils understand the categories, suggest one or two sports for each category before the game begins.

This is an opportunity for pupils to learn a short poem by heart – either their own, or one from the book.

Feuilles 7 and *8* have reading material on the theme of cycling. Reading authentic articles such as these, and successfully completing the tasks can be very motivating for pupils. Point out that they do not have to understand every word in order to do the activities and that, with the help of the dictionary, they are able to read articles which go beyond the key language taught in the book.

H Grammaire

Resources
Cassette for Pronunciation

Grammar
quel (which, what)
avoir besoin de

Pronunciation
Stress patterns

---

quel (which; what)

1

Answers
1b   2b   3a   4b   5c   6c

The gender of each noun is given so that pupils have the opportunity to apply the principles shown in the grid.

2

If necessary, show your pupils that they can derive the gender of the nouns from the use of *ton* or *ta*. Point out that both *quel* and *préféré* need to agree with the gender and number of the noun.
Following work on *quel,* pupils could make up their own quiz questions about sport, modelled on that in Spread F.

avoir besoin de

Note: Pupils will first meet *avoir besoin de* in Spread I. It is therefore recommended that pupils tackle Spread I first and then come back to this section for further practice of the grammatical point.

3

For pupils who need more support, list possible items on the board, keeping countables separate from uncountables, e.g.
– *coca, pain, fromage etc.*
– *une bouteille de limonade, un melon, un ouvre-boîte etc.*
Show pupils that they use *avoir besoin **de*** with the first group, and *avoir besoin **d'un** / **d'une*** with the second.

4

The equipment and ingredients are listed on page 45 of the Pupil's Book.

Prononciation: l'accent

This section focuses on a key difference in the stress patterns between English and French: the tendency in French is for the stress to fall on the second syllable, not the first. Getting the stress right is a fast route to 'sounding French'.

The pronunciation work exploits cognates, most of which have featured in the unit.

While focusing on stress patterns, pupils should not forget other principles of pronunciation which they have met, e.g. the nasal *-on (melon, poivron, saumon)*, the nasal *-in (raisin)*, or the soft 'c' (*cerise*).

A ta santé!

I L'équipement essentiel   pp 114–115

Objectives
Discussing what to take on an outing

Resources
Presentation sheet 21
Cassette for Exercises 1 and 3

Key language
besoin, K-way, couteau suisse, carte, lampe de poche, appareil-photo, lunettes de soleil, trousse de secours,

Kleenex, essentiel, utile, pique-nique, grand, lourd

Grammar
avoir besoin de

Strategies
Unknown words (English – French): asking for help; using a dictionary

Ways in
Begin with revision of *aller, pouvoir* + infinitive. For example, display two teenagers on the board or OHP, one with strict parents and one with lax parents. Gather suggestions from the class as to what sort of things each can do, e.g.
Gérard (parents stricts)
Il ne peut pas aller à la discothèque.
Il ne peut pas téléphoner à ses amis.
etc.
Perrine (parents pas stricts)
Elle peut aller à la discothèque.
Elle peut téléphoner à ses amis.
etc.

When you have a few suggested sentences on the board, highlight the infinitive endings. From then on, invite pupils to write sentences suggested by others in the class, and check the infinitive ending in each case.

 Read the photo story. Contrast *une promenade à vélo, à cheval, à pied.*

 Use Presentation sheet 21 to practise the new nouns.

COUNTER

 At this point, encourage pupils to focus on the vocabulary from page 114 rather than to spend a lot of time looking up new words.

Differentiation
Pupils who finish early could compare their own lists with their partners'. Have they thought of the same items?

 Pupils make notes. From their notes, they guess what activities the French people are planning.

Answers
3a (Notes)
1 ✓ *K-ways, carte, sandwichs, lunettes de soleil*
   (♣ *raquettes de tennis* – trop lourdes; *ballon de foot* – trop grand)
2 ✓ *argent, appareil-photo* (♣ *sandwichs* – il y a un café)
3 ✓ *lampe de poche, trousse de secours, couteau suisse* (♣ *gameboy* – pas à la campagne)
3b (Activities)
1 *promenade à la campagne*
2 *visiter un musée*
3 *camping*

COUNTER

1 – *Pour cet après-midi, qu'est-ce qu'on va emporter?*
  – *Alors, nous avons besoin de K-ways. Il pourrait faire mauvais. On ne sait jamais.*
  – *Oui, bonne idée.*
  – *J'emporte mes raquettes de tennis?*
  – *Ah non, les raquettes sont trop lourdes. En tout cas, nous n'avons pas besoin de ça. On ne va pas jouer au tennis.*
  – *Nous avons besoin d'une carte, n'est-ce pas?*
  – *Oui, c'est vrai. C'est essentiel, ça.*
  – *On emporte quelque chose à manger? Des sandwichs?*
  – *On pourrait trouver un petit village avec un café …*
  – *Non, emportons des sandwichs. C'est plus pratique.*
  – *On va emporter un ballon de foot? On pourrait jouer au football!*
  – *Ah non, un ballon de foot, c'est trop grand. Ce n'est pas pratique!*
  – *Moi, je vais emporter mes lunettes de soleil. Je pense qu'il va faire beau.*
  – *Moi aussi.*
  – *Bonne idée!*
2 – *Qu'est-ce que nous allons emporter?*
  – *Ben, nous avons besoin d'argent. L'entrée, c'est quarante francs.*
  – *On emporte des sandwichs aussi, pour faire un pique-nique après?*
  – *Mais non. Nous n'avons pas besoin de ça. Il y a un café là-bas.*
  – *Oui, bonne idée. On mange au café.*
  – *Moi, je vais emporter mon appareil-photo.*
  – *Oui, moi aussi.*
  – *La photographie, c'est permis?*
  – *Oui, on peut prendre des photos.*
3 – *Bon, pour ce week-end, nous avons besoin de quoi?*
  – *Alors, nous avons besoin d'une lampe de poche.*
  – *Bonne idée. Tu as une lampe de poche, toi?*
  – *Oui, oui, je peux l'emporter.*
  – *C'est très utile, pour aller aux toilettes la nuit!*
  – *Moi, j'ai une trousse de secours.*
  – *Oui, ça, c'est essentiel, en cas d'accidents.*
  – *Moi, je vais emporter mon gameboy.*
  – *Mais non!*
  – *Tu ne vas pas emporter ton gameboy à la campagne!*

> – *Bon, d'accord.*
> – *Moi, j'ai un couteau suisse. Je l'emporte?*
> – *Oui. Ça va être utile.*

3b
COUNTER

> – *Bon, alors, c'est décidé:*
> *jeudi, nous allons faire une promenade à la campagne;*
> *vendredi, nous allons visiter le musée;*
> *et ce week-end, nous allons faire du camping à la campagne.*

4

Groups could decide on just three essential items for each situation. Groups could then report back to the class (e.g. with suggestions written on an OHP transparency) and see whether all groups decided on the same priorities.

J Premiers secours

Objectives
First aid

Resources
Cassette for Exercise 1

Key language
*paire de ciseaux, gaze, sparadrap, coton hydrophile,
paracétamol, aspirine, bande, désinfectant, lampe de poche,
argent, stylo, savon, Kleenex*

Grammar
avoir besoin de

Strategies
Reading: skim reading for gist

Ways in

1 Pupils work on the activity before they listen to the tape.

Answers

1c   2d   3a   4b

2 The vocabulary introduced in this exercise prepares pupils for the longer reading text in Exercise 3.

Practise the pronunciation of the new words as a class activity before starting the pair work. Pupils will then be able to compare their lists orally for further practice of the new words.

For extended pronunciation practice, four pupils could come to the front of the class. Each should mouth one of the items, using their mouths to make the word as clear as possible, but making no sound at all. Pupils write down which word they think each 'mouther' is saying. Each 'mouther' gets one point for each correct guess.

Nothing interests pupils more than the real thing. If you have a first aid box (or can borrow one from the school office) bring it into the lesson. You can then play games such as:

- Kim's Game: Show eight items on a tray. Remove them from sight: pupils, working in pairs, then have to list the items they can remember seeing. Make the task more difficult by adding other items – a ruler, a pencil, a book etc.
- *C'est qui?*: Divide the class into teams of about eight pupils. One team comes to the front: each member takes one item from the first aid box and keeps the item hidden. Another team guesses who has which item (each member has one guess). A point is scored for each correct guess.

Differentiation

Extend abler pupils by asking why certain items are included in a first aid box, e.g.
Il y a une paire de ciseaux. Pourquoi? – pour couper le sparadrap
de l'argent – pour téléphoner au médecin
un stylo – pour écrire un message
une lampe de poche – s'il y a un accident, la nuit

3

Answers
♦ **1e**   **2b**   **3a**   **4d**   **5c**

Draw your pupils' attention to the importance of recognising key words by asking them which word (or words) gives away the answer in each case.

For further practice, tell your pupils to cover sentences **a–c**. Display a gapped version of the same sentences, with key words displayed in a box. The pupils then fit the right words in the appropriate gaps, e.g.

1 *Passe l'endroit brûlé sous ...... froide pendant au moins dix minutes. Si la brûlure est ...... , va voir un ....*
2 *Fais un ...... stérile retenu par du ....*

As a homework task, pupils could make a first aid poster, giving advice on how to cope with a particular wound or accident.

Pupils can go on to use the key vocabulary more actively in rôle-play sitatuions on *Feuilles 5* and *6*.

K Une journée spéciale

pp 118–119

Objectives
Describing a day out

Resources
Cassette for Exercises 1 and 3

Key language
*tout d'abord, après ça, ensuite, cartes postales, plage,
Lunaparc, château*

Grammar
Perfect tense (3rd person)

Strategies
Writing: structure, paragraphs; drafting and re-drafting
Speaking and Writing: phrases for linking

Telling and writing a narrative in the past tense are skills which secure higher grades at GCSE. In addition to mastery of the perfect tense, narrative skills include:
• thinking of enough things to say,
• linking the different elements with idiomatic phrases,
• making use of set phrases in the imperfect tense (e.g. *il y avait, c'était, il faisait* + weather).

On this spread, pupils are shown a model narrative passage which displays the features outlined above. Pupils are then given guidance on how to structure a narrative of their own.

Ways in

1

Check that all pupils understand the real meaning of *une journée* (i.e. **not** 'a journey'!)

The gapped text has been reproduced on *Feuille 16*.

To fill some gaps, pupils will need to do some grammar manipulation. Draw your pupils' attention to this by working through the first five items with them, showing them that for numbers **4** and **5** they need to supply *mes* and *mon*. Pupils can then work on numbers **6–16** in pairs.

Differentiation
Weaker pupils will need more support. Limit their choice by giving them a list of alternatives, e.g.
1 *mon/mes?*
2 *le/la?*
3 –
4 *mon/mes?*
5 *mon/ma?*
etc.

Answers
1 *mes copains*
2 *le vélo*
3 *appareil-photo*
4 *mes lunettes de soleil*
5 *mon K-way*
6 *à huit heures*
7 *beau*
8 *vingt kilomètres*
9 *son vélo*
10 *un village*
11 *au café*
12 *visité*
13 *cartes postales*
14 *deux*
15 *à quatre heures*
16 *je suis allé*

2

Answers
a *Marc est allé à la plage avec Alexandre, pas avec les filles.*
d *Ils ne sont pas rentrés en voiture – ils sont rentrés en train.*
f *Ils n'ont pas fait de pique-nique – ils ont mangé dans un café.*

3

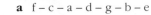

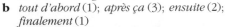

Answers
a *f – c – a – d – g – b – e*
b *tout d'abord* (1); *après ça* (3); *ensuite* (2); *finalement* (1)

> *Normalement, la mariée porte une longue robe blanche, et elle a un bouquet de fleurs. Tout d'abord, il y a le mariage civil. On va à l'hôtel de ville, où le couple est marié par le maire. Après ça, on va à l'église pour la cérémonie religieuse. Le mariage religieux n'est pas obligatoire. Le couple décide s'il veut une cérémonie religieuse ou non. Après la cérémonie, tout le monde jette du riz et des confettis sur les mariés.*
> *Ensuite, tout le monde va dans un hôtel ou dans un restaurant. Là, on boit du champagne, et on porte des toasts aux nouveaux mariés. Après ça, on fait un grand repas.*
> *Ensuite, tout le monde danse! Il y a une soirée dansante ou une disco.*
> *Après ça, tout le monde se couche. Mais, dans certaines régions, il y a encore une tradition! A quatre ou cinq heures du matin, on réveille le couple. On lui donne une sorte de soupe bizarre: du vin, du jus d'orange etc., avec des confettis dedans.*
> *Finalement, le couple part en vacances. Les vacances après un mariage s'appellent la lune de miel.*

4

Make sure your pupils realise that they may make up events – the wilder the funnier!

You could play this as a Chain Game: pupil A says the first sentence, pupil B says the first sentence and adds a second, pupil C says the first two sentences and adds a third, and so on. The game goes on until a pupil cannot remember one of the preceding sentences. A new sequence then begins.

5

This activity gives pupils the opportunity to focus on the third person singular. You could omit it if your pupils are still having difficulty with the perfect tense in the first person.

6 Make sure that pupils use the link words in the *Stratégie* box on page 118.

Differentiation

Extend abler pupils by focusing on *il faisait beau* in Marc's letter on page 118. Elicit other phrases with *il faisait* and teach *il pleuvait* and *il neigeait*. Pupils should then make use of these set phrases in their written work.

L Atelier

Objectives
Plans and preparation for a weekend course

Resources
Cassette for Exercises 2 and 4

Strategies
Awareness of *faux amis*

As usual, the *Atelier* spread provides a themed context in which pupils can practise the language and structures which they have acquired in the unit.

1

Read through the *Stratégie* together.

Answers
1 *pour les jeunes*
2 *deux jours*
3 *quatre*
4 *non, au centre du village*
5 *oui*
6 *non, à chaque étage*

2

Answers
le football, le volleyball et le basketball, voile, la planche à voile, la natation, le tennis, le judo, la gymnastique, l'athlétisme, l'équitation et le vélo tout terrain.

COUNTER

– *Centre Chevalier, allô.*
– *Bonjour, Monsieur. Je voudrais des renseignements sur le stage sportif pour les jeunes.*
– *Le stage sportif, ne quittez pas ... Bon, j'ai tous les détails ici. Qu'est-ce que vous voulez savoir?*
– *Euh, je voudrais savoir quels sports on peut pratiquer.*
– *Eh bien, oh, il y a un grand choix de sports. Vous avez trois sports d'équipe: le football, le volleyball et le basketball.*
– *Le foot, le volley et le basket.*
– *C'est ça. Il y a plusieurs sports nautiques. Vous avez la voile, ainsi que la planche à voile.*
– *La voile et la planche à voile.*
– *Et la natation, aussi, bien sûr.*
– *Oui.*
– *Il y a un grand choix de sports individuels. Par exemple, il y a le tennis, le judo et la gymnastique.*
– *Tennis, judo et gymnastique ...*
– *Ou si vous préférez pratiquer un sport en plein air, il y a l'athlétisme, l'équitation et le vélo tout terrain.*
– *L'athlétisme, l'équitation et le VTT.*
– *Et voilà.*
– *Merci beaucoup, Monsieur. Il y a un très grand choix!*
– *C'est tout? Vous voulez d'autres renseignements?*
– *Non, c'est tout, merci. Au revoir, Monsieur.*
– *Au revoir.*

3

Make sure that pupils understand that they must agree on four sports only, one for each slot on their weekend course.

4

Possible answers:
à manger/boire: sandwich, jus de fruit, biscuits, fruits, tablettes de chocolat
équipement sportif/vêtements: baskets, raquette de tennis, pull, short, T-shirts, maillot de bain, sweat-shirt.
autre: magazines, appareil-photo, lunettes de soleil, baladeur, cassettes, gameboy

COUNTER

– *Alors, Carole, qu'est-ce que tu vas emporter pour le voyage? Tu veux un sandwich pour le train?*
– *Oui, d'accord, je prends un sandwich, et du jus de fruit.*
– *Tu prendras des magazines pour le train?*
– *Ah, oui, bonne idée!*
– *Tu vas emporter tes baskets.*
– *Oui, bien sûr, Maman. Je vais emporter ma raquette de tennis, aussi.*
– *N'oublie pas ton appareil-photo!*
– *Ah non, ça, c'est essentiel!*
– *Tu as un sweat-shirt, pour le football? Il peut faire froid ...*
– *Oui, Maman, j'ai un sweat-shirt!*
– *Je vais te donner des biscuits, aussi.*
– *D'accord. Merci.*
– *Tu peux emporter des fruits, aussi ...*
– *Ah non, Maman, ça suffit, vraiment! Il y a une salle à manger, tu sais!*
– *Oui, mais ...*
– *OK, j'emporte des fruits.*
– *Et des tablettes de chocolat, aussi ...*
– *Oui, d'accord.*
– *Si tu vas faire de l'équitation, tu auras besoin d'un pull chaud.*
– *Oui, tu as raison. Je vais emporter mon pull bleu.*
– *Et s'il fait du soleil, tu auras besoin de tes lunettes de soleil.*
– *Oui, c'est vrai.*
– *Et tu as ton short et tes T-shirts?*
– *Oui, oui, ils sont déjà dans mon sac!*
– *Bon. Et ton maillot de bain, pour la natation?*
– *Ah là là! J'avais oublié mon maillot de bain!*
– *Tu vois?!*
– *Tu vas prendre ton baladeur et tes cassettes?*
– *Oui, ça, c'est une très bonne idée. Je peux écouter de la musique dans le train.*

5 Pupils could write their lists individually and then compare their ideas with their partner's.

6 Remind pupils to use some of the link words (*tout d'abord, après ça etc.*) which they learnt in Spread K.

CAMARADES 3 (TURQUOISE) OVERVIEW – UNITE 6 VIVENT LES LOISIRS!   **National Curriculum Areas of Experience: B, D, E**

	Topics/objectives	Key language	Grammar	Skills and strategies	PoS coverage
A	**Tu as un petit job?** Talking about part time jobs (details and pros and cons)	*indépendence, expérience, temps libre, important, petit job, reçois, argent de poche, baby-sitting, x livres, école, famille, aider, maison, travailler, tous les jours, week-end, chez, quand, où, combien, beaucoup*	Question words	Speaking: agreeing and disagreeing	1 a b f j 2 e h l m 4 c d
B	**Mimi, baby-sitter** Reading for pleasure: BD				1 d g i j 2 j k 4 a
C	**Quels sont tes passe-temps?** Talking about hobbies and spare time activities	*pêche, bricoler, jeux-vidéo, chanter, chorale, peinture, collectionner, autocollants, timbres, danse, théâtre, ça m'intéresse, pas grand-chose, faire, chanter, sport, musique, regarder, télé, écouter, chez, copains, ville, apprendre à, s'intéresser à, se passionner pour, membre*	*ce, cette, ces*	Dictionary (English – French): cross-referencing; applying grammar	1 b i i 2 a l m n 3 c d g
D	**Grammar**		Question words (*qui, quand, où, combien, pourquoi, comment, qu'est-ce que) jouer à/de*		1 b c g 2 e f g 3 g
E	**Tu fais ça souvent?** Talking about hobbies and spare time activities	*ce matin, cet après-midi, ce soir, cette semaine, tous les jours, x fois par semaine* (and hobbies from Spread E, opinions from previous spreads)	*ce, cette, ces* Perfect tense *aller* + infinitive	Referring to past and future events	1 a c d f 2 e i m 3 c f g
F	**Un coup de téléphone** Making phone calls	*allô, est-ce que je peux parler à, elle n'est pas là, rentrer, vers, désolé, beurre, c'est, qui* (and suggesting activites)			1 a d i k 2 a l m n o 3 b c i
G	**Es-tu rap ou techno?** Reading for interest: music				1 g i j 2 h j n 4 a c
H	**Grammar** Pronunciation		*ce , cette, ces aller* + infinitive	Pronunciation: *-ation; -ition* etc.	1 a b h 2 f h 3 c f
I	**Les grandes vacances** Discussing plans for the summer holidays	*stage de …, colonie de vacances, louer, rester, maison, vacances, sortir, famille, partir, voir, copains, faire, sport, camping* (and activities from earlier units)	Perfect tense *aller* + infinitive	Writing: writing a letter Reading and Writing: recognising tenses and using them appropriately	1 a c j k 2 i j l 3 f g 4 c
J	**Atelier** Making friends on holiday	(asking for and giving information about family and hobbies; commenting on weather; suggesting activities)			1 a c d 2 a d e g h i 3 c g
K	**Revision** (Board game)	(food, sport, various activities)			1 c e 2 b d h i 3 c e

113

Worksheets

Recommended use of the worksheets (in some cases they can be used later, as revision):

Spread	Worksheet	Spread	Worksheet	Spread	Worksheet	Spread	Worksheet
A	16	D		G		J	
B		E	9 and 10, 12, 16	H	11	K	
C		F	17	I	3 and 4, 5 and 6, 17		

Feuille 1 and 2 Vocabulaire

Feuilles 3 and 4 On écoute ♦ and ♣

These are jig-saw listening activities. Pupils work in pairs and listen to one recording each. They then share and discuss the information they have noted. Discuss with your pupils what questions they might ask. Pupils could listen to the different recordings simultaneously at different listening posts, if available. Otherwise, the activity could be carried out as part of a 'carousel' of activities, in which groups move round from one activity the next. The pairs could come together at the end to complete the task on *Feuilles 3* and *4*. If you prefer not to do it as a jig-saw activity, pupils could simply listen to both parts.

Feuille 3 On écoute ♦

Partenaire A

Anne
- *Vous avez quel âge, Anne?*
- *J'ai 17 ans.*
- *Bon, alors parlez-moi un peu de vous. Quels sont vos passe-temps?*
- *Eh bien, je fais de la natation.*
- *Souvent?*
- *Assez souvent, une fois par semaine. Il y a une piscine près de chez moi. Je suis membre d'une chorale, aussi.*
- *Vous aimez la musique, alors.*
- *Oui, beaucoup. J'aime aussi les enfants.*
- *Vous avez des petits frères ou sœurs?*
- *Oui, j'ai une sœur de trois ans.*
- *Qu'est-ce que vous avez fait l'été dernier?*
- *J'ai passé mes vacances en Angleterre.*
- *Et vous avez aimé ça?*
- *Non, c'était nul! Je n'ai pas aimé l'Angleterre. Il a fait très mauvais tout le temps!*
- *C'est dommage.*

Valérie
- *Valérie, vous avez quel âge?*
- *J'ai 19 ans.*
- *Quels sont vos passe-temps?*
- *Mes passe-temps. Eh bien, je fais un peu de sport.*
- *En particulier?*
- *Ah, je joue au badminton, et je fais de l'aérobic.*
- *Oui?*
- *Je fais aussi du théâtre. J'adore ça. C'est passionnant.*

- *Et qu'est-ce que vous avez fait l'été dernier?*
- *J'ai voyagé avec une copine. On a été au Pays de Galles, près de Cardiff.*
- *C'était bien?*
- *Ah oui, c'était fantastique! J'adore voyager à l'étranger. J'aime bien la Grande-Bretagne.*
- *Vous avez travaillé aussi?*
- *Oui, j'ai travaillé un peu dans un magasin.*

Suzanne
- *Quel âge avez-vous, Suzanne?*
- *J'ai 18 ans.*
- *Et vous avez des passe-temps?*
- *Oui, je suis passionnée de sport.*
- *Quels sports?*
- *Je joue principalement au tennis, et je fais aussi du jogging.*
- *Vous faites souvent du sport?*
- *Oui, tous les jours.*
- *Qu'est-ce que vous avez fait l'été dernier, Suzanne?*
- *Alors, j'ai joué beaucoup au tennis. J'ai fait beaucoup de compétitions.*
- *Vous avez bien joué?*
- *Oui, j'ai gagné toutes mes compétitions.*

Partenaire B

Anne
- *Quel est votre numéro de téléphone, Anne?*
- *C'est le 02 35 12 40 28.*
- *Parlez-moi un peu de vous. Vous avez déjà travaillé?*
- *Oui, j'ai travaillé dans l'épicerie de mes parents.*
- *Vous avez aimé ça?*
- *Oui, c'était bien. Je fais aussi du baby-sitting pour ma sœur, de temps en temps.*
- *Et quelles sont vos ambitions, Anne?*
- *Oh, je ne sais pas. J'aimerais avoir beaucoup d'argent un jour, et habiter une très grande maison.*

Valérie
- *Valérie, je peux noter votre numéro de téléphone?*
- *Oui, c'est le 02 35 17 61 42.*
- *Parlez-moi de votre expérience. Vous avez déjà travaillé?*
- *Oui, je fais du baby-sitting pour une amie.*
- *Vous faites ça régulièrement?*
- *Oui, trois fois par semaine, de quatre à six heures.*
- *Il y a combien d'enfants?*

- Trois enfants, âgés de cinq à huit ans.
  J'adore les enfants. J'ai aussi travaillé un
  peu dans un magasin, mais c'était un peu
  ennuyeux.
- Et quels sont vos ambitions?
- Euh … j'aimerais peut-être travailler dans
  un hôpital.
Suzanne
- Suzanne, pouvez-vous me donner votre
  numéro de téléphone?
- C'est le 02 35 16 59 72.
- Parlez-moi un peu de vous. Vous avez déjà
  travaillé?
- Oui, l'année dernière, j'ai travaillé dans un
  hôtel pendant les grandes vacances.
- Dans un hôtel?
- Oui, dans le restaurant et le bar. C'était
  vraiment bien, j'ai beaucoup aimé ça.
- Et avez-vous des ambitions?
- Ah, oui, être joueuse professionnelle de
  tennis. Un jour, je serai championne
  mondiale de tennis!

- Oui, j'ai travaillé un peu, ici en France,
  dans un magasin.
Suzanne
- Vous avez des passe-temps, Suzanne?
- Oui, je suis passionnée de sport. Je joue
  principalement au tennis.
- Vous faites souvent du sport?
- Ah oui, pour être en forme, j'en fais tous les
  jours. Si je ne joue pas au tennis, je fais du
  jogging et de la musculation.
- Vous avez d'autres passe-temps?
- Je ne fais que du sport. Je n'ai pas le temps
  de faire autre chose.
- Et qu'est-ce que vous avez fait l'été dernier,
  Suzanne?
- La plupart du temps, j'ai joué au tennis. J'ai
  fait beaucoup de compétitions, et beaucoup
  d'entraînement, par exemple du jogging.
- Vous avez bien joué?
- Oui, j'ai gagné toutes mes compétitions. Mais
  ça coûte cher, vous savez, acheter de
  l'équipement et faire les compétitions. Donc
  cet été, je dois gagner beaucoup d'argent.

COUNTER

Feuille 4 On écoute ♣

Partenaire A
Anne
- Anne, parlez-moi un peu de vous. Quels sont
  vos passe-temps?
- Je chante dans une chorale une fois par
  semaine.
- Vous aimez la musique, alors.
- Oui. J'aime aussi les enfants.
- Vous avez des petits frères ou sœurs?
- Oui, une sœur de trois ans. J'aime aussi les
  sports qu'on fait en plein air, à la campagne.
- Qu'est-ce que vous avez fait l'été dernier?
- J'ai passé mes vacances en Angleterre avec
  une amie.
- Et vous avez aimé ça?
- Non, pas du tout! Il a fait un temps affreux
  tous les jours, et la nourriture était nulle!
- C'est dommage.
- Oui. Cette année je préfère rester en France!
  Je dois trouver du travail, parce que je n'ai
  pas d'argent.
- Et vous cherchez quelle sorte de travail?
- Bof. Ça m'est égal. Mais ça doit être bien
  payé.
Valérie
- Dites-moi, Valérie, quels sont vos passe-
  temps?
- Mes passe-temps? Je fais des costumes pour le
  théâtre. Ce sont mes deux passions: j'adore
  bricoler et je me passionne pour le théâtre.
- C'est intéressant.
- Je fais un peu de sport, aussi.
- En particulier?
- Je joue au badminton, et je fais de l'aérobic.
- Et qu'est-ce que vous avez fait l'été dernier?
- J'ai voyagé avec une copine. On a été au
  Pays de Galles, près de Cardiff.
- C'était bien?
- Ah oui, c'était fantastique! En général,
  j'adore voyager à l'étranger, et je trouve la
  Grande-Bretagne un pays très intéressant.
- Vous aimez travailler à l'étranger?
- Beaucoup. C'est un très bon moyen de voir
  un pays et de rencontrer de nouvelles
  personnes.
- Vous avez travaillé aussi?

Partenaire B
Anne
- Anne, est-ce que vous avez déjà travaillé?
- Oui, j'ai été serveuse dans un restaurant,
  mais j'ai arrêté après deux semaines.
- Pourquoi?
- Parce que j'ai trouvé ça assez ennuyeux.
- Et avez-vous fait autre chose comme travail?
- J'ai travaillé dans un magasin, aussi, mais
  j'ai trouvé ça trop fatigant. En ce moment, je
  fais aussi du baby-sitting pour ma sœur,
  mais seulement une fois par mois.
- Et quelles sont vos ambitions, Anne?
- Oh, je ne sais pas. J'aimerais être très riche
  un jour, habiter une très grande maison,
  acheter un restaurant, peut-être.
Valérie
- Valérie, parlez-moi de votre expérience. Vous
  avez déjà travaillé?
- Oui, en ce moment, je garde les trois enfants
  d'une amie.
- Vous faites ça régulièrement?
- Oui, trois fois par semaine, de quatre à six
  heures.
- Et ils ont quel âge, les enfants?
- Ils sont âgés de cinq à huit ans. Ils sont
  vraiment mignons, je m'amuse très bien
  avec eux. On fait beaucoup de choses
  ensemble, on se raconte des blagues.
- Et quelles sont vos ambitions?
- Euh … j'aimerais peut-être travailler dans
  un hôpital. Ou bien faire quelque chose avec
  les enfants.
Suzanne
- Parlez-moi un peu de vous. Vous avez déjà
  travaillé?
- Non, je n'ai jamais eu de petit job, parce que
  je n'ai jamais eu le temps de travailler.
- Vous avez fait autre chose, alors.
- Oui, pour moi, le sport est plus important
  que le travail.
- Et avez-vous des ambitions?
- Ah, oui, être joueuse professionnelle de
  tennis. Un jour, je serai championne
  mondiale de tennis!

115

Feuille 5 On parle ◆

This worksheet draws on language from previous units as well as the current one. It has work on semi-structured conversations which include reference to the past and future, giving opinions and some improvisation. Give pupils any help they need at the preparation stage.

Feuille 6 On parle ♣

Feuille 6 is similar to *Feuille 5*, but has less structured conversations, which include unprepared and unpredictable elements.

Feuilles 7 and 8 On lit ◆ and ♣

Following the unit theme of leisure activities, pupils follow instructions and use a dictionary to learn how to do a card trick. If you intend to work on this in class, ask pupils in advance to bring in packs of cards. Alternatively, pupils could improvise cards using pieces of paper: only 11 are needed for *Feuille 7* and 15 for *Feuille 8*. The sheet could also be used for homework: pupils have to learn the tricks at home and perform them in class.

Feuilles 9 and 10 On écrit ◆ and ♣ (free-standing)

As in previous units, specific guidance is given to develop pupils' writing skills. Focus here is on structure (writing in paragraphs), redrafting, giving opinions, and using the dictionary for checking and for variety of expression.

Feuille 11 Grammaire (free-standing)

Feuille 12 En plus

This activity could be approached in different ways: pupils could work as groups of six individuals, or some pupils could work in pairs, sharing a picture. (Alternatively, you could divide the whole class into six groups, giving a picture to each one.)

- Each person spends time looking at their card and preparing what they can say to describe it, ready to answer others' questions. They also prepare some questions to ask others. You can give help here and encourage pupils to use dictionaries as necessary.
- The groups then come together. Going round in a circle, each person asks one or two questions at a time about someone else's picture. All pupils note the information.
- They try to establish the correct order of the cards and piece together the story, still only looking at their own card.

Feuille 13 Que sais-tu?

Feuille 14 Révision 1: family relationships (free-standing)

Feuille 15 Révision 2: buying food

Feuille 16 Grille

Support for Spread A Exercise 2; Spread E Exercise 2.

Feuille 17 Grille

Support for Spread F Exercise 2; Spread I Exercise 2.

Feuille 18 Réponses

This provides answers for the Unit 6 worksheets.

IT Opportunities

B   **Spread B Extra**
Some pupils might be interested in the popularity of the BD in France. They could be directed towards searching for more information about them on the Internet by keying in, for example, *Bandes Dessinées* or *Astérix* or *Tintin*.

C4   **Spread C Exercise 4**
* Using a word-processor or DTP, pupils design, write and illustrate a form to send away for a French correspondent.

F2   **Spread F Exercise 2**
It is useful practice for pupils to rearrange jumbled telephone conversations. For example, write one or two of the longer tapescript conversations (e.g. 3, 5 or 7) in a text manipulator. Pupils listen, make notes and then rearrange the text. Pupils could then pull it up as a prediction exercise and predict each word in the conversation.
Another useful exercise is to word-process one side of the telephone conversation and save the file for pupils to work on. Pupils listen to the conversation once, load in the file and then fill in the missing dialogue.

G3   **Spread G Exercise 3**
* Pupils use a word-processor to write their articles. For homework they are encouraged to collect together information about their favourite group and make a list in French of words, phrases and expressions they might use. Then, they word-process a first draft of their article. They check for accuracy and interest (with teacher, other pupils, reference material) and then redraft it with corrections, amendments and for presentation. If it is possible to scan in pictures of the group, they do so in an appropriate place, make any alterations necessary (i.e. make smaller, add a frame) and finally print out for display.

I4   **Spread I Exercise 4**
* If there is access to the Internet, an activity which works well is to ask pupils in groups to search for destinations in a region of France and plan a holiday. They write up an account of what they are going to do (or did) on their Internet tour, picking out places and ◆ one or ♣ more interesting fact/s about them or present it orally to the class.

A Tu as un petit job?

pp 122–123

Objectives
Talking about part time jobs (details, and pros and cons)

Resources
Cassette for Exercises 1 and 2

Key language
indépendance, expérience, temps libre, important, petit job, reçois, argent de poche, baby-sitting, x livres, école, famille,

aider, maison, travailler, tous les jours, week-end, chez, quand, où, combien, beaucoup

Grammar
Question words

Strategies
Speaking: agreeing and disagreeing

Ways in
Read and listen to the conversations together. Invite pupils to tell you to point out any words they don't understand, then help them to work out what they mean. Encourage them to use the context and their common sense wherever possible, only resorting to the dictionary as a last resort. Check that they have understood the meaning in this context of words for which they know alternative meanings, e.g. *gagner* (to win; to earn); *temps* (weather; time).

Answers
1 *Delphine; Marc*
2 *Fatima*
3 *Alexandre*
4 *Delphine*
5 *Fatima*

The grid is reproduced on *Feuille 16*.

Answers
1 *oui; non; –; –; –; n'a pas le temps / trop de devoirs*
2 *oui; oui; supermarché; vendredi soir, dimanche; 250F; elle achète des vêtements*
3 *non; oui; pharmacie; samedi; 200F; acheter des CD, aller à des concerts*
4 *oui; non; –; –; –; joue dans des matchs*
5 *oui; oui; baby-sitting; parfois; 50F; pour aider sa tante*
6 *non; oui; café; week-end; pas beaucoup; plus d'indépendance*

1 – *Pascal, est-ce que tu reçois de l'argent de poche?*
   – *Oui, mes parents me donnent de l'argent chaque semaine.*
   – *Tu as un petit job?*
   – *Non, mais j'aide à la maison.*
   – *Pourquoi tu ne travailles pas?*
   – *Parce que je n'ai pas le temps. J'ai trop de devoirs et ça, pour moi, c'est le plus important.*

2 – *Est-ce que tu as un petit job, Marion?*
   – *Oui, je travaille dans un supermarché.*
   – *Tu travailles quand?*
   – *Normalement le vendredi soir et le samedi.*
   – *Tu gagnes combien?*
   – *Je gagne 600 francs. C'est bien, parce que ça me permet de m'acheter des vêtements.*
   – *Est-ce que tu reçois de l'argent de poche?*
   – *Je reçois un peu d'argent de mes grands-parents, chaque semaine.*

3 – *Tu reçois de l'argent de poche, Gilles?*
   – *Non, mais j'ai un petit job. Je travaille dans une pharmacie.*
   – *Tu travailles le samedi?*
   – *Oui, c'est ça.*
   – *C'est bien payé?*
   – *Pas mal. Je gagne 350 francs.*
   – *Tu aimes le travail?*
   – *Non, je le trouve vraiment ennuyeux! Mais j'ai besoin de l'argent pour acheter des CD, ou s'il y a un bon concert …*

4 – *Céline, est-ce que tu as un petit job?*
   – *J'ai de la chance, parce que je reçois de l'argent de poche si j'aide mes parents à la maison, donc je ne travaille pas.*
   – *Qu'est-ce que tu fais pour aider?*
   – *Je fais la vaisselle, je fais les courses. Des trucs comme ça. De toute façon, je ne pourrais pas travailler le week-end, parce que je fais du sport. Il y a toujours des matchs le week-end.*

5 – *Jean-Marie, est-ce que tu reçois de l'argent de poche?*
   – *Oui, un peu, mais pas beaucoup.*
   – *Alors, tu travailles aussi?*
   – *Oui, parfois.*
   – *Qu'est-ce que tu fais?*
   – *Je fais du baby-sitting pour ma tante.*
   – *Tu gagnes combien?*
   – *Pas beaucoup: 70 francs. Mais je fais ça pour aider ma tante. Elle ne sort pas souvent.*

6 – *Et toi, Evelyne, est-ce que tu as un petit job?*
   – *Oui, je travaille au café de mon oncle.*
   – *Tu travailles quand?*
   – *Je travaille le week-end, seulement. Ma mère m'a dit que je ne dois pas travailler pendant la semaine. Elle dit que je dois faire mes devoirs.*
   – *Tu gagnes combien?*
   – *Pas beaucoup! Mais c'est bien, parce que je ne reçois pas d'argent de poche.*
   – *Non?*
   – *Donc, avec l'argent que je gagne au café, j'ai un peu plus d'indépendance.*

There is specific practice of question words on Spread D, page 128.

3

Give the class advice about writing their list of questions in part **a** and taking notes in **b**. Are they going to number their questions so that they can write down a separate list of numbered answers? Or are they going to leave space next to each question? In making their notes during the interview, it will be too time-consuming to write complete sentences. Discuss the sort of notes they can make, for example:

- key words (e.g. *baby-sitting, tante*)
- abbreviations and symbols (e.g. *£3/heure, ven. + sam.*)

For part **c**, suggest that pupils use a word-processor if possible. Encourage them to produce a first draft, to check it through, focusing specifically on spelling and verb endings, then make corrections.

If told to 'check their work', many pupils just read through in a passive way. Active checking for particular points is more effective and can be tailored to focus on any particular point of grammar or style being practised, or on recognised weaknesses on the part of the individual pupil. If a piece has be written on computer, pupils may find it easier to check a printout for mistakes. Many people find that they notice mistakes in a printed version which they missed on the screen.

4

♣ This activity provides opportunities for high level speaking. While they are preparing their notes, give pupils support in expressing their ideas and opinions in French.

In the picture story, Katy mentions the fact that fewer young people in France have a part time job than in this country. If your class has a link class in France (or in any other country), it might be interesting to write, fax or e-mail them to make comparisons regarding part time jobs. How many in that class have jobs; what kind of jobs do they have; how long/often do they work; what is the pay like; do they get pocket money? Your class could then use the information to write up a report or article, with graphs or diagrams to illustrate the results.

B Mimi, baby-sitter

pp 124–125

Objectives
Reading for pleasure: cartoon strip

Encourage pupils to read the cartoon strip on their own first. Since the pictures carry most of the story, pupils might be pleasantly surprised at how easy it is to follow.

You could then look in more detail at some of the language. For example, can they interpret Kévin's baby talk *(B'zour, Mimi; R'var maman; Kévin pas dodo)*?

The class might have fun working in groups and reading out the different parts. Practise this first, modelling phrases for the class to repeat.

1

Suggested answers

a *Le baby-sitting, c'est dur!*　**b**3　**c**3

You could ask pupils to imagine other details about the story, e.g.
Où vont les voisins ce soir?
Qu'est-ce qu'ils vont faire?
Pourquoi Mimi fait-elle du baby-sitting?
Qu'est-ce qu'elle voudrait acheter?

Pupils could also tell you about their own experiences. For example, ask them:
Qui a déjà fait du baby-sitting?
Pour qui?
Il/Elle a quel âge?
Il/Elle est comment? (mignon(ne)/gentil(le)/bête)
C'était comment? (facile/bien/affreux)

2

Answers
◆ **h c f a d g b e**

Pupils could work in groups to invent a similar cartoon strip. They could record a sound track with some of them playing the parts and others providing appropriate sound effects.

C Quels sont tes passe-temps?

pp 126–127

Objectives
Talking about hobbies and spare time activities

Resources
Presentation sheets 22 and 23
Cassette for Exercise 3

Key language
pêche, bricoler, jeux-vidéo, chanter, chorale, peinture, collectionner, autocollants, timbres, danse, théâtre, ça m'intéresse, pas grand-chose, faire, chanter, sport, musique, regarder, télé, écouter, chez, copains, ville, apprendre à,
s'intéresser à, se passionner pour, membre

Grammar
ce, cette, ces

Strategies
Dictionary (English – French):
cross-referencing;
applying grammar

Ways in
You could begin with some revision. Present some of the pictures on Presentation sheets 22 and 23, and ask pupils to give you appropriate sentences. These might include *J'aime regarder la télé. J'adore la musique.* Then present and practise the alternative phrases shown on the sheets: *J'aime me détendre devant la télé* etc.

From there, build up to the complete set of pictures, concentrating on a few at a time.

1

Having done this initial preparation, pupils will find the article easier to approach. As well as presenting key language in context, the article gives models of more complex and varied language. This is exploited in the ♣ activity. More simple constructions, which can serve as general models for all pupils, are found in the quotes in Exercise 2.

In Exercise 1, all pupils have to say which category or categories their own hobbies fall into. You could ask them round the class to give examples, to show why they have noted these particular categories.

Do some further work based on the article. For example:
- You say a sentence about a hobby mentioned in the article, e.g. *Je m'intéresse à la nature;* pupils race to say which category it is.
- Pupils have to find phrases in the text which are equivalent to: *je chante; je ne fais pas beaucoup; je reste au lit* etc.

2

Point out to pupils that the speech bubbles for the six friends contain key phrases. You could read through them together first, then ask pupils to close their books. Read out individual sentences from the speech bubbles. Pupils have to identify the person from memory. They could then play the same game in pairs.

They then go on to do the activity outlined in the book, which involves a shift from the first to the third person.

3

Differentiation
Pupils could answer in single words, in phrases, or they could make notes including additional information, which they write up more fully afterwards.

Pupils could go on to compare and discuss their answers, as in Exercise 2.

COUNTER

1 – *Quels sont tes passe-temps, Florence?*
– *Eh bien, j'aime aller à la campagne. En été, je fais des randonnées chaque week-end avec des copains. Je suis membre d'un club.*
– *Et en hiver, qu'est-ce que tu aimes faire?*
– *En hiver, quand il neige, j'aime faire du ski de fond.*

2 – *Jérôme, quels sont tes hobbies?*
– *Mes hobbies? Eh bien, j'aime aller à la pêche, quand il fait beau.*
– *Tu vas à la pêche avec des amis?*
– *Parfois avec des amis, parfois tout seul. Ça dépend. Je joue aussi du piano dans un orchestre de jeunes. C'est génial. On s'amuse vraiment bien!*

3 – *Tu aimes le sport, Omar?*
– *Non, ça, ce n'est pas mon truc. Moi, personnellement, je préfère bricoler. Je fais du modélisme. Je fabrique des jeux pour mes petits frères. En ce moment, je fabrique des cadeaux pour Noël.*
– *Tu as d'autres passe-temps?*
– *Oui, j'aime jouer sur mon ordinateur …*
– *Oui.*
– *Et regarder les films à la télé.*

4 – *Anne-Valérie, quels sont tes passe-temps?*
– *J'ai beaucoup de passe-temps. Par exemple, je fais du théâtre. Je suis membre d'un club de théâtre en ville. On répète tous les samedis.*
– *Et tes autres passe-temps?*
– *Je fais de la danse.*
– *Quelle sorte de danse?*
– *Je suis des cours de danse moderne et classique. Et en plus, je collectionne des T-shirts.*
– *Des T-shirts?*
– *Oui, quand je vais en vacances, j'achète un T-shirt avec le nom de la ville ou de la région. J'en ai déjà neuf.*

5 – *Paul, quels sont tes hobbies?*
– *Moi, j'adore le dessin. Je fais de la peinture.*
– *Qu'est-ce que tu peins?*
– *J'adore les animaux, donc je fais des peintures de mes chiens.*
– *Tu as d'autres passe-temps?*
– *Oui, je chante.*
– *Dans une chorale?*

> – *Non, non, dans un groupe. C'est moi le chanteur, puis mon frère joue de la guitare, et un copain joue de la batterie. C'est super chouette!*
>
> 6 – *Emmanuelle, qu'est-ce que tu as comme passe-temps?*
> – *Alors, moi, je m'intéresse aux arts martiaux, comme le judo et le karaté.*
> – *Tu fais ça au collège?*
> – *Non, dans un club au centre sportif.*
> – *Tu fais autre chose, aussi?*
> – *Oui, je me passionne pour l'informatique. J'écris des programmes pour mon ordinateur. Je trouve ça amusant. J'invente des jeux.*
>
> 7 – *Et toi, Ben, quels sont tes hobbies?*
> – *J'apprends à faire de la photographie. Prendre et développer des photos en noir et blanc. C'est passionnant, mais ça coûte cher!!*
> – *Tu as d'autres passe-temps?*
> – *Non, je n'ai pas le temps. Je travaille dans un fast-food quatre soirs par semaine!*

To focus on the patterns *jouer à* and *jouer de*, you could work at this point on Spread D, page 129.

As preparation for this, revise sports from Unit 5. Presentation sheets 19 and 20 can help you with this.

For this activity, encourage pupils to avoid simply listing their hobbies and interests and writing the simplest of sentences. Prepare by asking questions orally round the class. Insist on complete sentences, with 'added' ingredients. For example, instead of *Je joue au football,* encourage responses such as *Je joue au football avec mes amis,* or *Je joue au football le samedi,* or even *Je joue au football le samedi. Je suis membre d'un club.*

The *Stratégie* box gives hints on using the English – French half of the dictionary effectively. Read through it together, and do some whole-class practice, in which they look up words required by individual pupils. That way, you can talk them through the process and ensure that they are comfortable with cross-checking in the French – English section. You can also get them into the habit of remembering to take account of grammar as they use the words they have looked up.

Pupils could pin up their profiles round the classroom, then go round reading them all, taking notes. They try to work out who should get on well together, based on similar interests.

They could play a version of *Blind Date.* A volunteer comes out to the front and is blindfolded. Three others, of the opposite sex, come out and answer questions on their hobbies put by the first person. They can disguise their voices as they speak, and invent whacky hobbies if they wish. The rest of the pupils have to predict which person will be chosen. Having heard the answers, the first person chooses one of the three, then removes the blindfold to reveal his/her blind date.

D Grammaire

Grammar

Question words: *qui, quand, où, combien, pourquoi, comment, qu'est-ce que*

jouer à / de

Les questions

1

Answers

◆ 1C 2D 3F 4J 5G 6I 7B 8E 9A 10H

2

Answers

♣ 1 *combien* 2 *comment* 3 *qui* 4 *quelle*
5 *Où* 6 *Quand* 7 *combien* 8 *Qui* 9 *Qu'est-ce que*

This page focuses on question words, receptively at
◆ level. You may also wish to revise different ways
of forming a question:

- simple statement, using rising intonation
  Tu aimes le football?
- using *est-ce que*
  Est-ce que tu aimes le football?
- putting the verb first
  Aimes-tu le football?

At ◆ level, you may prefer to concentrate on the first
two ways. The third way is more formal and is less
useful for pupils, except when forming questions
with question words, e.g.
Pourquoi aimes-tu le football?
Quand vas-tu au club?

You could give pupils a list of simple questions of the
first type, to which they have to add *est-ce que*, e.g.
Tu joues au tennis de table?
Tu fais du skate-board?
Tu aimes le sport?
Tu préfères faire du sport ou regarder le sport?
Tu as fait du vélo, le week-end dernier?
Tu vas faire du sport ce week-end?

Some pupils confuse *est-ce que* with *qu'est-ce que*.
While some manage to learn that *qu'est-ce que* means
'what', others find it easier to memorise two common
sentences, which they can then refer back to. Choose
questions which your pupils are already familiar with,
e.g. *Est-ce que tu as un animal?* and *Qu'est-ce que tu
fais, le week-end?*

Having practised using *est-ce que*, pupils could go on
to do an activity in which they have to choose
between the two. For example, they have to fill in the
blanks:

.... *tu fais, normalement, le samedi?*
.... *tu aimes le sport?*
.... *tu as fait, lundi dernier?*
.... *tu fais le soir?*
.... *tu as des frères ou des sœurs?*
.... *tu manges pour le petit déjeuner?*

---

jouer à, jouer de

3

Answers

◆
1 *de la* 2 *de la* 3 *au* 4 *au*
5 *au* 6 *d'* 7 *du* 8 *du*

♣
Suzanne joue au badminton.
Nicolas joue de la batterie.
Evelyne joue au golf.
Alain joue au rugby.
Sabine joue de la guitare.
Hervé joue aux boules.
Camille joue du clavier.
Didier joue du violon.
Samia joue au basketball.
Mathieu joue du piano.

4

Give pupils a minimum number of people to include
in their quiz (say, eight).

E Tu fais ça souvent?

pp 130–131

Objectives
Talking about hobbies and spare time activities

Resources
Cassette for Exercises 1, 2 and 4

Key language
ce matin, cet après-midi, ce soir, cette semaine, tous les jours, x fois par semaine (and hobbies from Spread E, opinions from previous spreads)

Grammar
ce, cette, ces
Perfect tense
aller + infintive

Strategies
Referring to past and future events

Ways in

Go through the photo story together. Pupils could use their dictionaries to look up the expression *J'en ai marre*.

Spread H, page 136 has an explanation and practice of *ce, cette, cet* and *ces*.

Differentiation

A grid for recording the answers is available on *Feuille 16*. More able pupils could note down extra information as well, for example **what** Fatima does when she goes out.

There are two more difficult sections at the end for the ♣ level. They contain familiar language in unfamiliar contexts, and some unfamiliar language, non-essential for completing the task.

Answers
Fatima …
1 *travaille au Quick – 3 fois par semaine*
2 *fait ses devoirs – tous les jours*
3 *sort – rarement/jamais*
4 *aide à la maison – tous les jours*
5 *fait du baby-sitting – 1 fois par semaine*
6 *fait du théâtre – jamais*
7 *aide sa sœur – 4 fois par semaine*
8 *lit – tous les jours*

1 – *Maman, je serai en retard ce soir. Je travaille au Quick.*
  – *Quand est-ce que tu travailles, exactement, Fatima? J'ai oublié.*
  – *Je travaille trois fois par semaine, le mercredi après-midi, le vendredi après l'école et le samedi soir.*
2 – *Et est-ce que tu as beaucoup de devoirs pour l'école, cette année?*
  – *Ben, oui, évidemment. J'ai quelque chose à faire tous les jours, tu sais. C'est nul! J'ai une heure, deux heures, tous les jours!*
3 – *Oui, mais il faut quand même sortir avec tes copines, Fatima …*
  – *Oui, en ce moment, je sors rarement. Je ne vais jamais en ville avec mes copines.*
4 – *En plus, je dois aider à la maison tous les jours. Ce n'est pas juste!*
  – *Mais ce n'est pas beaucoup, quand-même. Je te demande seulement de faire ton lit et d'aider à faire la vaisselle.*

  – *Et faire les courses, et promener le chien …*
5 – *En plus, je garde Rania le dimanche soir.*
  – *Garder ta petite sœur une fois par semaine n'est pas difficile, Fatima! Tu pourrais faire tes devoirs en même temps …*
  – *Mais j'aimerais sortir le dimanche!*
6 – *Tu fais du théâtre cette année? Tu es membre du club au collège?*
  – *Non, je ne fais jamais de théâtre. Le club, c'est le mercredi après-midi, quand je suis au Quick. C'est vraiment embêtant!*
7 – *En plus, je dois aider Rania à faire ses devoirs de français. Ça, ce n'est pas juste! Pourquoi moi? Tu pourrais l'aider, toi!*
  – *Mais tu es plus forte en français que moi. Et en plus, je suis occupée.*
  – *Mais, Maman! C'est tellement ennuyeux!*
  – *C'est vraiment trop, te demander d'aider ta sœur?*
  – *Mais elle a français lundi, mardi, jeudi et vendredi!*
  – *Et alors?*
  – *Alors ça fait beaucoup de devoirs!*
  – *Oh là là! Tu est tellement égoïste, Fatima!*
8 – *Je n'ai pas assez de temps pour mes passe-temps!*
  – *Mais tu as toujours le nez dans un livre, ou dans un magazine.*
  – *J'aime lire après l'école, mais je lis pendant une demi-heure, au maximum, avant de faire mes devoirs.*
  – *Tu lis le week-end, quand même.*
  – *Oui, un peu, je suppose, le samedi après-midi, et le dimanche matin, mais …*
  – *Ecoute, Fatima, est-ce qu'il est absolument nécessaire que tu travailles?*
  – *J'aime avoir de l'argent.*
  – *Oui, mais l'argent n'est pas tout, quand même!*

This activity sets out the key questions which pupils will work on answering on the rest of the page. Ask students why they think the questions are in the *vous* form (i.e. a job interview is a formal occasion, so more formal language is used).

The aim of this page is to bring together references to past, present and future, each of which has been thoroughly practised earlier in the course. Take time now to revise the perfect tense, if necessary. The immediate future, using *aller* + infinitive is revised on Spread H, page 137.

4

The conversations on tape model the type of language pupils themselves will be using.

Differentiation

Invite pupils to note down any other information they can.

After completing the activity, listen together as a class, pause the tape and get pupils to say whether a person is talking at that moment about their habits (present tense), the past, or the future. Draw pupils' attention to the forms of the verbs, and time marker phrases.

1 – *Alors, Guillaume, parlez-moi un peu de vous. Quels sont vos passe-temps?*
   – *Je fais de la natation une fois par semaine. J'adore ça. Je nage assez bien. Je fais des compétitions.*
   – *Vous faites autre chose aussi?*
   – *Oui, je m'intéresse à l'informatique.*

2 – *Vous faites souvent de l'informatique, Guillaume?*
   – *Oui, je joue sur mon ordinateur tous les jours. Parfois, je fais des jeux, et parfois j'écris des programmes.*

3 – *Stéphanie, qu'est-ce que vous allez faire la semaine prochaine? Vous avez déjà décidé?*
   – *Oui, en fait, samedi prochain, je vais chanter dans un concert. Je suis dans une chorale.*
   – *Qu'est-ce que vous allez chanter?*
   – *Nous allons chanter des chansons françaises et anglaises.*

4 – *Vous allez souvent à la chorale? Vous répétez souvent?*
   – *Je vais à la chorale une fois par semaine, le lundi soir. Mais je chante chez moi plus souvent, deux ou trois fois par semaine. Je répète les chansons.*

5 – *Pierre, qu'est-ce que vous avez fait la semaine dernière?*
   – *Eh bien, samedi dernier, je suis allé à la patinoire avec des amis. C'était vraiment amusant, parce que c'était très difficile! Je suis tombé plusieurs fois! Et puis, mercredi, je suis allé au stade, où j'ai fait de l'athlétisme. C'était vraiment bien, mais très fatigant.*

6 – *La semaine prochaine, je vais faire une randonnée à la campagne. Je vais partir avec mon père. On va partir samedi matin, vers huit heures, et on va passer toute la journée à la campagne. Ça va être chouette! On va emporter du papier et des couleurs, et on va faire de la peinture.*

7 – *Moi, je fais du théâtre. Je trouve ça vraiment passionnant! Je suis membre du club de théâtre au collège. C'est la prof de français qui organise le club. J'y vais avec deux copines, et on s'amuse vachement bien! Je bricole, aussi. Je fabrique des cadeaux pour mes amies. J'adore bricoler!*

8 – *Je fais de la danse deux fois par semaine. J'ai une leçon de ballet le lundi de cinq heures à six heures, puis le mercredi après-midi, je fais de la danse moderne dans un club à la Maison des Jeunes.*

9 – *Ben, je ne sais pas. Je n'ai pas encore décidé. Je pense que je vais aller au centre sportif. Je vais jouer au tennis de table ou au badminton.*
   – *Vous allez jouer avec qui?*
   – *Avec ma sœur aînée, probablement.*

10 – *Lundi dernier, je suis allé chez ma petite amie, et on a regardé la télé.*
   – *Qu'est-ce que vous avez regardé?*
   – *Ben, on a regardé un film de science-fiction. Et mardi, j'ai un peu joué de la guitare. J'ai reçu une guitare électrique pour mon anniversaire. C'est super bien!*

 5

You might want to discuss further the issue of register. In formal situations such as a job interview, phrases like *c'est super, nul, chouette, génial* would not be appropriate.

To exploit the example further before pupils write their own answers, they could practise changing as much information as possible in each sentence, taking it in turns with a partner.

Encourage pupils to look back at their vocabulary notes and their work from Spread C (talking about their own hobbies) and Unit 5 (sports). Encourage pupils working at ♣ level to make use of the more complex and varied expressions they have noted, e.g. Spread C Exercise 1. Give them further assistance in talking about themselves, as necessary.

Build in a checking stage between Exercises 5 and 6, so that pupils check their own (or each other's) work, and redraft it. You could also check it, if possible, so that the language being used in Exercise 6 has been corrected and refined.

 6

Give pupils guidance in using the work they have done in Exercise 5. They should avoid reading out their answers. If possible, get pupils to learn key phrases as homework, in preparation for the 'interview'. If necessary, they could have a note of some key words and phrases to refer to during the interview – suggest a maximum of six.

Pupils will also need practice in asking the questions 1–4 given at the top of the page, and in following them up (e.g. *Avec qui? Quand?*).

If time allows, it would be good to do some work on interview technique – body language (smile), dress, how to sound pleasant and interesting (avoid speaking in monosyllables) and so on.

Pupils could record their interviews on tape or video them. They listen to them critically afterwards: did they make a good impression? Did they give interesting answers to the questions?

An observer or the interviewer could take notes and write a report, describing the interviewee (i.e. in the third person).

Some pupils might have fun writing a humorous sketch, in which the interviewee has strange hobbies or talks non-stop or answers in monosyllables.

As an extra activity, pupils could do a presentation to the class or their group about their hobbies. They bring in photos or props to illustrate their talk.

Feuilles 9 and *10* continue the work on this theme: pupils write a letter about their hobbies, making reference to the past, present and future.

F Un coup de téléphone

pp 132–133

Objectives
Making phone calls

Key language
allô, est-ce que je peux parler à, elle n'est pas là, rentrer, vers, désolé, heure, c'est, qui (and suggesting activites)

Ways in

1

Read and listen to the conversations together. The matching activity focuses on key 'telephone' phrases.

Pupils could read the conversations in pairs.

2

Feuille 17 has a grid for noting the answers to this exercise.

Answers

1 ✗ *5h*
2 ✓ *patinoire, vendredi, 7h30*
3 ✓ *badminton, vendredi, 3h30*
4 ✗ *6h00/6h30*
5 ✓ *samedi, vélo, 2h00*
6 ✗ *9h00/9h30*
7 ✓ *dimanche, musique, 8h00*

1 – *Allô.*
– *Bonjour. Est-ce que je peux parler à Marjolène, s'il vous plaît?*
– *Je suis désolé, mais elle n'est pas là. C'est qui à l'appareil?*
– *C'est son amie, Valentine. Marjolène va rentrer à quelle heure?*
– *Je ne sais pas. Vers cinq heures, peut-être.*
– *Bon, alors merci.*
– *Au revoir.*
2 – *Allô.*
– *C'est Anne-Laure?*
– *Oui, c'est moi.*
– *Salut, c'est Perrine!*
– *Salut, Perrine, ça va?*
– *Ecoute, tu veux venir à la patinoire ce soir?*
– *Ce soir? Oui, je veux bien. Il y a un bus?*
– *Oui, le 39 va à la patinoire.*
– *Alors, je viens chez toi vers sept heures et demie?*
– *D'accord, sept heures et demie. Au revoir.*
– *Au revoir.*
3 – *Allô.*
– *Est-ce que je peux parler à Roger?*
– *C'est moi.*
– *Ah bonjour, Roger. C'est Jeanne. Ça va?*
– *Ça va, et toi?*
– *Ça va. Dis, tu es libre cet après-midi? Tu aimerais jouer au tennis?*
– *Euh … je suis libre cet après-midi, mais … je n'aime pas trop le tennis.*
– *Alors, on pourrait jouer au badminton.*
– *Oui, d'accord, j'aime bien le badminton.*
– *Donc on se voit au centre sportif à quelle heure?*
– *A trois heures et demie? Ça va?*

– *Oui, ça va. Alors, à plus tard!*
– *Au revoir.*
4 – *Allô.*
– *Bonjour, Madame. Est-ce que je peux parler à Michaël, s'il vous plaît?*
– *Je suis désolée, mais il n'est pas là. Il est chez sa grand-mère.*
– *Ah, zut!*
– *C'est qui à l'appareil?*
– *C'est Gilles. Vous ne savez pas à quelle heure il va rentrer?*
– *Si, vers six heures, six heures et demie.*
– *OK, merci. Au revoir.*
– *Au revoir, Gilles.*
5 – *Allô.*
– *Est-ce que je peux parler à Violaine?*
– *C'est moi. C'est … Henri?*
– *Oui. Ecoute, Violaine, est-ce que tu es libre demain après-midi?*
– *Attends … Oui, demain après-midi je suis libre.*
– *Tu veux aller au bowling?*
– *Ah non, je déteste ça! Je suis nul!*
– *Qu'est-ce que tu aimerais faire, alors?*
– *On pourrait faire du vélo. Il va faire beau. Tu as un vélo, toi?*
– *Oui, j'ai un vélo tout terrain.*
– *Bon, alors on part à quelle heure? A une heure?*
– *Non, à deux heures. D'accord?*
– *D'accord. Au revoir.*
– *A demain.*
6 – *Allô.*
– *Bonjour. Est-ce que je peux parler à Mme Rabany?*
– *Je suis désolée, mais ma mère n'est pas là. Elle est au travail. C'est qui à l'appareil?*
– *C'est Michel Perronne. Elle va rentrer à quelle heure?*
– *Oh, vers neuf heures, neuf heures et demie.*
– *Merci beaucoup. Au revoir.*
– *Au revoir, M. Perronne.*
7 – *Allô.*
– *C'est Angélique?*
– *Oui, c'est moi.*
– *Salut, c'est Mélanie. Ecoute, tu veux sortir demain soir?*
– *Désolée, je ne peux pas. Je fais du baby-sitting.*
– *Alors, dimanche soir?*
– *Je ne peux pas sortir le dimanche soir. Mais tu pourrais venir chez moi. On pourrait écouter de la musique …*
– *D'accord. Je vais apporter des CD.*
– *Tu viens à quelle heure?*
– *A huit heures, ça va?*

> – Ça va. A bientôt.
> – Au revoir.

3

To help them learn the dialogues, pupils could begin by reading them through. They then place a rubber or pencil over the dialogues at an angle, covering parts. Little by little, they cover up more and more, until they are saying the dialogues completely from memory.

4

Get pupils to suggest alternative invitations before they change the dialogues in pairs.

5

Answer
◆ B

COUNTER

> – Allô.
> – Salut, Isabelle. C'est Fatima.
> – Salut, Fatima! Mais … tu n'es pas sortie avec tes amis du Quick?
> – Euh … non.
> – Mais pourquoi?
> – Oh, je ne sais pas … Ils sont assez sympas, mais ils sont un peu ennuyeux.
> – Ennuyeux?
> – Oui. En fait, je … je préfère sortir avec toi et Delphine … Euh … tu veux sortir cet après-midi?
> – Oui, je veux bien!
> – On va au bowling?
> – D'accord! Bonne idée!
> – Super!

6

Answers
1 Look it up in the Yellow Pages.
2 Look it up using *Minitel* service 3611.

Get pupils to think about the similarities and differences between the system in their country and the one in France, e.g. *Pages Jaunes* / Yellow Pages, but *liste rouge* / ex-directory.

G Es-tu rap ou techno?

pp 134–135

Objectives
Reading for interest: music

So many teenagers are interested in music, but their tastes vary dramatically. Here is an article with something for most people: a survey and comparison of different types of rock and pop music. They can read about a subject which interests them, and perhaps learn something new in the process.

Here, as elsewhere, the wording has not been simplified. Point this out to pupils: it is doubly motivating to read an interesting article as it was written for an audience of French teenagers. Remind pupils that they do not need to understand every word to follow the gist. They might also be surprised as they read to find how much they can follow thanks to cognates and their own knowledge of the subject.

1

After pupils have browsed through the article and noted down their own favourite families and family members, you could talk to them about which, if any, of the types of music mentioned you used to listen to at their age, what you liked and hated, and what you like listening to now. While the fact that you actually once were their age may come as a surprise to some pupils, they will probably be fascinated to find out your musical tastes. What's more, with revivals of music from previous decades and many new bands openly acknowledging the influence of much older bands, you might even find that your tastes overlap with some of your pupils'…

2

After pupils have browsed through the article and noted down their own favourite families and family members, you could talk to them about which, if any, of the types of music mentioned you used to listen to at their age, what you liked and hated, and what you like listening to now. While the fact that you actually once were their age may come as a surprise to some pupils, they will probably be fascinated to find out your musical tastes. What's more, with revivals of music from previous decades and many new bands openly acknowledging the influence of much older bands, you might even find that your tastes overlap with some of your pupils'…

Pupils could work in groups: each group concentrates on a family member and works together to produce a rough translation. Pupils could then comment on any statements they disagree with.

Able pupils could simplify or paraphrase the descriptions in French.

As ever, pupils can use their dictionary or refer to the vocabulary list at the back of the book if necessary. Some words will not be found in the dictionary. This could lead to discussion about the limitations of a dictionary, e.g. size (pocket?); slang; technical words.

Ask your pupils how many words and phrases they can find which have been borrowed from English or American English (e.g. *riff de guitare, samplé*). Can they comment on that? (i.e. it arises from the predominance and influence of music from the USA and, to a lesser extent, the UK. This partly reflects the music's origins in Black American gospel music and then blues.)

3

Differentiation
An easier option would be for pupils to choose their favourite 'family member', copy the text, but substitute their own suggestions for people to listen to (with magazine photos).

Pupils might also be interested to hear that France has legislation regulating the amount of non-French music played on French radio music programmes. This was passed in order to help preserve and encourage the development of French music and culture which, it was felt by some, was at risk of losing its character and status. What do pupils think about this sort of legislation? (*C'est une bonne idée? C'est nécessaire? C'est ridicule?*) Would it be a good idea to do the same to preserve and promote Scottish/Welsh/Irish music and culture?

If you are lucky enough to have a foreign language assistant, you could invite him or her to talk to pupils about some French groups and singers, with extracts of songs to listen to.

Taking the 'family' idea further, pupils could make a 'family' display on sports, films or TV programmes. This could be very simple, for example with names of types, *famille sports d'équipe* or *famille athlétisme* – pupils use a dictionary to research the names of athletics disciplines. They could add names of famous athletes, current record holders etc.

H Grammaire

pp 136–137

Grammar
ce, cette, cet, ces
aller + infinitive

Pronunciation
-ation; -ition; -assion

Resources
Cassette for Pronunciation

---

ce, cette, cet, ces (this, these)

1 You could display the mini conversation on the board or OHP, and ask pupils to find the phrases before looking at page 136. That way, you could invite them to try to work out the pattern for themselves. Give them other phrases to test their hypotheses against, e.g.
J'aime bien ce pull-over.
Je ne sors pas cette semaine.
Ils sont à qui, ces crayons?
J'ai trouvé cet argent.

2 This activity is designed to encourage pupils to transfer the grammar point to a different situation. Having seen *ce* etc. with time phrases, pupils use it with clothes.

Having worked in pairs, pupils could write up the questions afterwards.

There is further practice of *ce, cette, cet, ces* on *Feuille 11*.

le futur proche (aller + infinitive)

This is revised from **Camarades 2.**

3 Pupils practise this construction in the third person. They could go on to read their partner's list or interview him/her, then write a description of what their partner is going to do, e.g.
Samedi matin, il va jouer au foot.

For more practice, pupils play the chain game, e.g.
Scott: *Ce week-end, je vais regarder la télé. Et toi, Becky (qu'est-ce que tu vas faire)?*
Becky: *Ce week-end, Scott va regarder la télé. Moi, je vais aller en ville. Et toi, Adam?*
Adam: *Ce week-end, Scott va regarder la télé et Becky va aller en ville. Moi, je vais faire du velo. Et toi, Emma?*
and so on.

Prononciation

In Exercice B, pupils could say how they think **all** these words should be pronounced in French.
In Exercise C, pupils could make up a rap of their own about themselves. They could then adapt their partner's rap, putting it into the third person.

I Les grandes vacances

pp 138–139

Objectives
Discussing plans for the summer holidays

Resources
Presentation sheet 24
Cassette for Exercises 1 and 2

Key language
stage de …, colonie de vacances, louer, rester, maison, vacances, sortir, famille, partir, voir, copains, faire, sport, camping (and activities from earlier units)

Grammar
Perfect tense
aller + infinitive

Strategies
Writing: writing a letter
Reading and Writing: recognising tenses and using them appropriately

Ways in
You can use Presentation sheet 24 to introduce and practise key phrases.

1

Answers
a
1 *Olivier, Isabelle, Alexandre, Marc*
2 *Fatima, Delphine*
3 *Isabelle, Alexandre, Delphine, Marc*
4 *Fatima, Delphine*
b *Oui*

COUNTER

You could ask additional questions, e.g.
Qui va travailler?
Qui va faire du sport?
Qui va passer ses vacances au bord de la mer?

2

The grid is reproduced on *Feuille 17*.

Answers
1 *–; en colonie; tir à l'arc, planche à voile; sortir avec copains*
2 *magasin des parents; –; –; peinture, voir ses amies*
3 *–; camping à la campagne; vélo et karting; stage de théâtre*
4 *–; deux semaines chez les grands-parents en Belgique; –; pique-niques et barbecues*
5 *supermarché; –; –; discothèque ou bowling*
6 *–; colonie de vacances; –; sa cousine va venir*
7 *–; chez son correspondant anglais à Liverpool; randonnées à la montagne, VTT; visiter la ville*
8 *–; –; –; magazines, baladeur, lettres, aller chez une copine*

COUNTER

1 – *Qu'est-ce que tu vas faire pendant les grandes vacances, Tidiane?*
– *Eh bien, je vais partir en colonie de vacances.*
– *Tu y vas tout seul?*
– *Non, j'y vais avec mon frère cadet. Je vais faire du tir à l'arc et de la planche à voile.*
– *Tu vas faire autre chose pendant les grandes vacances?*
– *Oui, je vais voir mes copains. On va sortir ensemble.*
2 – *Tu vas partir en vacances cet été, Aude?*
– *Non, moi, je vais gagner de l'argent.*
– *Comment?*
– *Je vais aider dans le magasin de mes parents.*
– *Tous les jours?*
– *Oui, le matin.*

– *Et l'après-midi, qu'est-ce que tu vas faire?*
– *Eh bien, je vais probablement faire de la peinture, et voir mes amies.*
3 – *Sylvain, tu vas partir pendant les grandes vacances?*
– *Oui, je vais faire du camping à la campagne avec mes cousins.*
– *Et après ça?*
– *Je vais faire un stage de théâtre. Ça va être génial.*
– *Tu vas voir tes amis?*
– *Oui, on va faire du vélo et du karting ensemble.*
4 – *Julie, qu'est-ce que tu vas faire pendant les grandes vacances?*
– *Je vais passer deux semaines chez mes grands-parents, qui habitent en Belgique.*
– *Et après ça?*
– *Après ça, je vais rester à la maison. Je vais sortir avec ma famille.*
– *Qu'est-ce que vous allez faire?*
– *On va faire des pique-niques et des barbecues.*
5 – *Pascal, tu vas partir en vacances cet été?*
– *Non, je vais rester à la maison. J'ai un petit job au supermarché.*
– *Mais tu vas sortir, quand-même?*
– *Oui, le week-end, je vais voir mes copains. On ira probablement en discothèque ou au bowling.*
6 – *Et toi, Natacha, qu'est-ce que tu vas faire?*
– *Ben, moi, je vais aller en colonie de vacances pendant trois semaines, en août.*
– *Et en juillet?*
– *Ma cousine va venir chez moi. On va sortir ensemble. Ça va être amusant!*
7 – *Moi, je vais rendre visite à mon correspondant anglais.*
– *Il habite où?*
– *Il habite à Liverpool, et il va me faire visiter la ville: le port et les musées.*
– *Ça va être intéressant!*
– *Oui. Et en plus, on va aller au pays de Galles. On va faire des randonnées à la montagne. Ce n'est pas très loin de Liverpool. On pourra faire du VTT aussi.*
8 – *Qu'est-ce que tu vas faire pendant les grandes vacances, Sylvie?*
– *Ça dépend du temps. S'il fait beau, je vais me détendre dans le jardin. Je lirai des magazines et j'écouterai mon baladeur.*

> – *Et s'il fait mauvais?*
> – *Je ferai quelque chose à l'intérieur. J'écrirai des lettres, par exemple, ou j'irai chez une copine.*

Do lots of oral practice round the class, focusing on pupils' plans for this year, perhaps using pictures from Presentation sheet 24 as prompts.

Then get the class to do a *mêlée* activity. Armed with the question *Qu'est-ce que tu vas faire pendant les grandes vacances?*, pupils have to go round interviewing their classmates. Give them the following task:

Trouve dans la classe quelqu'un qui va …
* *rester à la maison*
* *partir en vacances*
* *travailler*
* *voir ses amis*
* *faire des activités sportives*
* *faire des activités non-sportives.*

Answers
1 Camping in the south of France for three weeks with her parents. For the rest of the time, she'll stay in Rouen and probably go out with her friends.
2 They're going to a camp in the country.
♣ She's pleased.
3 The family rented a caravan in Bordeaux. It was miserable and boring.
♣ The weather was rotten and there was nothing at all to do.

Discuss Isabelle's plans and previous holiday in the third person, e.g.
Qu'est-ce qu'elle va faire cet été?
➩ *Elle va partir avec ses parents.*

4

As preparation, display pictures from Presentation sheet 24. Say sentences, using either *aller* + infinitive or the perfect tense. Pupils have to say whether you are talking about *cette année* or *l'année dernière*. Remind pupils that *rester* is one of the verbs which takes *être*.

Go on to do more practice round the class, asking pupils about
* their plans for this year,
* what they did last year,
* then both, mixed up.

Before pupils write their letter, discuss with them ways of using Isabelle's letter as a model for support, but avoiding straightforward copying and substitution. For example, what key phrases do they think they could use or adapt?

Remind them also of strategies they have met previously, e.g.
* writing in paragraphs,
* time phrases (including *après ça, ensuite*),
* drafting, checking, revising,
* starting and ending a letter (page 29).

Pupils should refer to at least five things they did last year and five things they plan to do this year.

5

Pupils could play this in groups. Those not directly involved in an interview could take notes, then listen out for mistakes when the interviewer repeats the details from memory.

Feuilles 3 and *4* and *5* and *6* provide further listening and speaking work.

J Atelier

pp 140–141

Objectives
Making friends on holiday

Resources
Cassette for Exercise 1

Key language
Asking for and giving information about family and hobbies; commenting on weather; suggesting activities

1

Answers
1 a c d **2** b c d **3** a d b **4** e **5** d b c **6** c d

1 – Il fait beau, n'est-ce pas?
– Oui, il fait très beau. C'est idéal pour nager dans la mer.
– Tu aimes la natation?
– Oui, beaucoup. Je vais à la piscine deux fois par semaine. Tu aimes ça aussi?
– Oui, mais je préfère le volleyball. Je suis membre de l'équipe scolaire.
– Ecoute, je vais jouer au volley sur la plage cet après-midi, avec ma sœur et ses copains. Tu veux jouer avec nous?
– Oui, je veux bien. A quelle heure?
– Oh, vers deux heures.
2 – Tu es en vacances avec ta famille?
– Oui.
– Tu as des frères et des sœurs?
– J'ai deux frères cadets, qui s'appellent Nicolas et Etienne. Mais ils m'énervent vraiment. Et toi?
– Moi, non, je suis fille unique. Qu'est-ce que tu aimes comme musique?
– J'aime le techno et le rap. Tu aimes MC Solaar?
– Oui, je l'adore! J'ai apporté beaucoup de cassettes. Tu veux venir les écouter?
– Oui, bonne idée. Moi aussi, j'ai des cassettes. Je vais les apporter.
3 – Il fait froid, aujourd'hui, n'est-ce pas?
– Oui, trop froid pour aller à la plage.
– Tu veux jouer au tennis de table?
– Euh, non, pas vraiment. Je n'aime pas le sport. Je suis nul en sport!
– Alors, quels sont tes passe-temps?
– Eh bien, j'aime la musique. Je joue de la guitare.
– Tu es dans un groupe?
– Euh non, pas exactement. Et toi, tu aimes la musique?
– Oui, mais je ne joue pas d'un instrument. J'aime écouter de la musique, aller aux concerts.
4 – Hé, écoutez, comment fait-on entrer un éléphant dans une cabine téléphonique?
– Je ne sais pas. Comment on fait entrer un éléphant dans une cabine téléphonique?

– On ouvre la porte! ... En voilà une autre. Comment fait-on entrer une girafe dans une cabine téléphonique?
– On ouvre la porte?
– On ouvre la porte et on demande à l'éléphant de sortir!
5 – Tu veux venir en ville avec mon frère et moi ce matin?
– Oui, je veux bien. Vous allez où?
– Au centre commercial, pour faire les magasins et acheter des cartes postales.
– D'accord. Tu as combien de frères et sœurs?
– Eh bien, j'ai mon frère, Simon, et j'ai deux sœurs, aussi.
– Elles sont en vacances avec vous?
– Non, non, elles sont plus âgées que moi. Elles sont mariées.
– Qu'est-ce que tu fais ici, normalement, le matin?
– Ça dépend, parfois je fais du sport avec mon frère, parfois je lis un livre et j'écoute mon baladeur.
6 – J'aime bien tes baskets. Elles sont cool.
– Merci. C'est moi qui les ai achetées. J'ai un petit job, le samedi.
– Tu gagnes beaucoup, alors?
– Oui, c'est assez bien payé.
– Tu travailles où?
– Dans un supermarché. Et toi, tu travailles?
– Moi, non, je n'ai pas le temps!
– Pourquoi? Qu'est-ce que tu fais le week-end?
– Je suis membre d'un club de randonnées. Je vais à la campagne tous les week-ends. C'est génial! Dis, tu veux faire une randonnée demain?
– Euh non ... désolé ... je ne peux pas.

2

Pupils could work in groups or in pairs.

3

Refer back to the questions from Exercise 2. How many came in useful?

Possible answers
A *Tu as des frères ou des sœurs?*
B *Tu veux aller à la piscine / faire de la natation?*
C *Il fait froid, n'est-ce pas?*
D *Tu aimes le sport? / Quels sont tes passe-temps?*
E *Tu aimes les randonnées?*
F *Tu veux* (+ sporting activity)?

G *Comment s'appelle ta sœur / ton amie?*

H *Quelle est ta chanteuse préférée?*

I *Qu'est-ce que tu fais normalement (le week-end etc.)?*

J *Qu'est-ce que tu vas faire (demain, cet après-midi etc.)?*

Pupils could act out some exchanges.

Pupils could perform their sketches in front of others, who say how good they were at making conversation. They might also have fun inventing sketches in which one person is trying to chat another one up – the other person could either show interest, or be cool towards the first.

K Révision

Objectives
Talking about food, sport, activities

This board game provides revision of food, sport, ailments, hobbies, past and future, in a novel context.

To make the three packs of cards for this game for each group, photocopy the pictures on Presentation sheets 16–20 and the parts of the body phrases from Sheet 15. Alternatively, pupils could make cards showing people with different ailments. The packs should then be placed face down on the desk.

The rules of the game, and the language which pupils need to use to play the game, are explained on page 142, and pupils are encouraged to draw on their own knowledge of board games to establish how the game works. Go through the instructions and speech bubbles with your pupils, encouraging them to work them out and ensuring that everyone has understood.

You could add to the key language for 'managing' the game. For example, where pupils can move backwards and forwards, depending on their answers, the other players can act as judges – shouting *tricheur/tricheuse* if someone answers untruthfully. (The player can then attempt to justify his/her answer!)

Before pupils start the game, do some practice round the class, to elicit possible things to say for each of the squares with instructions.

Pupils could go on to invent a similar board game, with questions on certain squares or question cards, which players have to answer on landing on particular squares.

A – Epreuve d'écoute

Exercice 1

This exercise tests elements of performance at **Level 3**. Pupils note in French the main details heard in a short message spoken over the telephone. They first hear a similar message as an example.
Total 5 marks.

Award 1 mark for each detail. Do not penalise poor French, nor the use of understandable abbreviations in the first task (e.g. *ven*) or figures in Task 2. Do not accept answers in English (though the final task is an English/French cognate). Pupils scoring at least 4 marks are showing some characteristics of performance at **Level 3**.

Answers

vendredi; six heures; gare; centre sportif; (jouer au) badminton

Exercice 1

— *Un message au téléphone. Regarde le bloc-notes et écoute l'exemple.*
  Exemple:
— *Salut! C'est Yves à l'appareil. Veux-tu me rencontrer samedi à dix heures à la poste? Si tu veux, on peut aller au centre commercial pour faire des courses.*
— *Ecoute Catherine et écris les détails.*
— *Salut, mon ami! C'est Catherine. Je te téléphone pour savoir si tu veux me rencontrer vendredi. Vendredi à six heures – ça va? Est-ce que tu peux me rencontrer à la gare, s'il te plaît? Après, on va aller au centre sportif. Là, on peut jouer au badminton, si tu veux.*
— *Ecoute le message encore une fois.*

Exercice 2

In the next exercise, pupils hear a much longer passage in the form of an interview. They listen for details in order to select 'true' or 'false' for each of five statements. The passage is delivered at near normal speed and is repeated. This tests elements of performance at **Level 4**.
Total 5 marks.

Award 1 mark for each correct answer.
Pupils scoring at least 4 marks are showing some characteristics of performance at **Level 4**.

Answers

1 *faux* **2** *vrai* **3** *vrai* **4** *faux* **5** *vrai*

Exercice 2

— *Marcel parle de son job. Regarde les phrases de 1 à 5. Ecoute l'interview de Marcel. Pour chaque phrase, choisis 'vrai' ou 'faux'.*
— *Bonjour, c'est Marcel, n'est-ce pas?*
— *Oui, c'est ça. Je m'appelle Marcel.*
— *Et quel âge as-tu?*
— *J'ai quinze ans.*
— *Et tu as un petit job?*
— *Oui. Je travaille dans un café. Enfin, nous sommes quatre à travailler.*
— *Mais tu ne travailles pas là toute la semaine, non?*
— *Ah non, samedi et dimanche seulement.*
— *Et tu travailles jusqu'à quelle heure?*
— *Eh bien, je travaille de deux heures de l'après-midi jusqu'à huit heures du soir, quelquefois neuf heures.*
— *Et qu'est-ce que tu fais comme travail?*
— *Ça dépend. Je fais beaucoup de choses. Je sers les clients, je fais la vaisselle dans la cuisine, je prépare les consommations.*
— *Et le travail est bien payé?*
— *Non, pas du tout. Je ne reçois que quinze francs l'heure. Mais ça ne fait rien parce que j'aime beaucoup le travail, même si ce n'est pas bien payé.*
— *Merci bien, Marcel.*
— *Ecoute l'interview encore une fois.*

Exercice 3

This exercise contains material based on future events. It is spoken at normal speed. Pupils are asked to listen for specific details and select them from alternatives. The exercise tests elements of performance at **Level 5**.
Total 5 marks.

Award 1 mark for each correct answer. Pupils scoring at least 4 marks are showing some characteristics of performance at **Level 5**.

Answers

1c **2**b **3**c **4**c **5**a

Exercice 3

— *Jean-Paul parle des grandes vacances. Lis les questions de 1 à 5. Ecoute l'interview de Jean-Paul. Pour chaque question, choisis une réponse.*
— *Jean-Paul, qu'est-ce que tu vas faire pendant les grandes vacances?*
— *Eh bien d'abord, je vais partir en vacances à la montagne, dans les Alpes.*
— *Chouette! Et tu vas partir avec tes copains?*
— *Non, malheureusement. Avec mes parents et mon frère.*
— *Et vous allez loger où?*
— *Alors d'habitude, vous savez, on loge dans un hôtel, mais cette année, nous avons décidé de faire du camping. Ça va être moins cher que l'hôtel, mais moins confortable aussi, je pense!*
— *Eh oui, je pense! Et vous allez passer combien de temps là-bas?*
— *Une quinzaine – quinze jours, quoi.*
— *Et après ça?*
— *Ben après ça … euh … je reviens chez moi, je vais voir mes amis au café et je vais travailler un peu pour mon père.*
— *Il travaille où, ton père? Dans un magasin?*
— *Non non, c'est ma mère qui travaille dans un magasin. Mon père, lui, il est garagiste.*
— *Et il va bien te payer, ton père?*

> *– Eh bien, j'espère bien, hein! Mais il faut dire que je ne sais pas encore combien il va me payer. Faudra que je lui demande, hein!*
> *– Ecoute l'interview encore une fois.*

Exercice 4

The final exercise is based on a longish narrative in the perfect tense. Here, pupils are required to write answers in French. The questions aim to use all the main interrogatives. This is fairly typical of a GCSE Foundation and Higher exercise and of performance at **Level 6**.

In marking this exercise, teachers must bear in mind that the standard of written French is not being assessed. Answers need not be in full sentences and they can contain errors. However, they must be comprehensible to a speaker of French with no knowledge of English. Answers in English are not, therefore, to be accepted, although cognates can be credited.

Total 10 marks.

Award one mark for each correct answer. Award ½ mark if the answer is partially correct or if there is some doubt as to meaning.

Pupils scoring at least 7½ marks are showing some characteristics of performance at **Level 6**.

Sample correct answers

(These minimal answers would all score 1 mark.)
1 *dimanche*
2 *trois*
3 *10 heures*
4 *beau avec un peu de vent* (½ mark for each aspect)
5 *alimentation/magasin/épicerie*
6 *jambon et fromage* (½ mark for each)
7 *Marc*
8 *fatigué(es)*
9 *tombé du vélo* (accept infinitive *tomber*)
10 *non*

Exercice 4

> *– Une promenade à vélo. Lis les questions. Ecoute Sylvie. Réponds aux questions.*
> *– Je vais te parler du week-end dernier. Samedi, comme d'habitude, je suis allée en ville avec ma mère faire des courses. Et puis le lendemain, j'ai décidé de faire une promenade à vélo avec mes copains. On était quatre.*
> *Tout le monde est arrivé chez moi à neuf heures et demie puis, une demi-heure plus tard on est parti, tous les quatre. Il faisait beau, mais il y avait aussi un peu de vent. Après quatre kilomètres, vers onze heures, nous nous sommes arrêtés dans un magasin d'alimentation pour acheter des provisions pour le pique-nique. Moi, j'ai acheté des fruits – des pommes et des bananes. Guy a acheté du jambon et du fromage. Véronique a acheté à boire – de l'eau minérale et du coca – et Marc est allé à la boulangerie d'à côté pour acheter le pain.*

> *Ensuite on a continué à faire du vélo dans la campagne. Nous avons fait environ quinze kilomètres et puis on s'est arrêté près d'un lac. C'était très beau. Là, on a pris le pique-nique. Les garçons ont décidé de nager dans le lac. Véronique et moi, nous avons dormi un peu parce que nous étions fatiguées.*
> *Après, nous avons commencé le voyage de retour. Malheureusement on a eu un petit accident – enfin, Guy est tombé de son vélo. Il s'est fait mal à la jambe, mais ce n'était pas sérieux.*
> *– Ecoute Sylvie encore une fois.*

B – Epreuve orale

Exercice I

Pupils choose one of the *Fiches* and give the following information; age, a detail about a brother or sister, their favourite pastime or a pastime they like and a reason, and an activity they dislike and a reason. Support may be given by the teacher or partner in the form of questions such as *Quel est ton passe-temps préféré?*. Teachers could indeed write out questions on OHT to help pupils prepare. Alternatively, some pupils may treat this as a straightforward presentation. Given that the teacher's input may vary, the bonus system (extra marks out of three) may be awarded (see below). Pupils use visual and verbal cues as support to help them initiate and respond and they use short phrases to express likes, dislikes and feelings. This tests elements of performance at **Level 3**.

Total 8 marks.

Pupils scoring at least 6 marks are showing some characteristics of performance at **Level 3**.

Teachers may prefer to ask pupils to prepare their own *Fiche* based on the model, in which case they will show the ability to adapt and substitute single words and phrases. This would then test some elements of performance at **Level 4**. At **Level 4** pronunciation is generally accurate and pupils show some consistency in intonation.

Exercice 2

Pupils work in pairs or with the teacher and take part in simple structured conversations of five exchanges on the subject of part time work which is supported by visual and verbal cues. This tests some elements of performance at **Level 4**.

Total 5 marks.

Pupils scoring at least 4 marks are showing some characteristics of performance at **Level 4**.

An example of a **Level 4** response would be:
Je fais du baby-sitting, Je travaille le samedi (soir) de 6h à 11 heures. Je gagne 100 francs. J'aime mon job – c'est intéressant – j'aime les enfants.

Messages should be clear and, provided that they are so, inaccuracies can be tolerated.

Exercice 3

Pupils use a spider diagram as a basis for ideas about future holiday plans. Pupils should give one item of information for each leg of the diagram and are free to choose from any of the visual cues. Short verbal cues are also given. The test is intended to elicit characteristics of performance at **Level 5** and **Level 6**. Total 6 marks.

At **Level 5** pupils may make an attempt to communicate details in the correct time reference and make themselves clear, but not always very accurately. Pupils scoring at least five points are showing some characteristics of performance at **Level 5**. An example of **Level 5** language would be:
Je vais aller/partir en avion avec ma famille. Je vais à la montagne pour huit jours. Je rester dans une tente. Je nage et je vais promenader.

Such language is not always accurate but the messages are communicated. Pupils who do not perform at this level and only manage to communicate three or four messages are more likely to be performing at **Level 4**.

At **Level 6**, all the messages are clearly and usually accurately communicated. The time references should be clear and pupils can make themselves understood with little or no difficulty. They may improve and paraphrase and add extra detail. An example of **Level 6** language would be:
Moi, je vais partir en vacances en avion. Je vais aller avec ma famille et on va aller à la plage, en Espagne, pour deux semaines. On va rester dans un hôtel moderne, près de la plage et je vais nager dans la piscine et aller au restaurant.

Teachers may wish to add bonus marks as below. These enable the amount of help or support needed from the teacher to be taken into account. Some pupils may be able to treat the exercise as a presentation and proceed unaided, whereas others may need extra support from the teacher in the form of questions. These marks also give the teacher the opportunity to reward the degree of accuracy shown by pupils.

1 mark – pupil manages to communicate the basic messages; language is often inaccurate but the meaning of most of the messages is there. Substantial help is needed from the teacher.

2 marks – pupil communicates nearly all the messages, despite inaccuracies, in short simple responses. Some help from the teacher.

3 marks – pupil communicates messages well; language is often very accurate. Little help is needed.

Exercice 4

As in Exercice 3 the outcome of this exercise may be assessed at several different levels. Pupils should prepare a presentation using the cue card as the basis of their ideas. These details are the minimum to be communicated and they can be told to add extra details as they wish. References to time are in the past. Total 10 marks.

Pupils who can attempt to communicate five points and who make themselves understood, despite inaccuracy, are showing some characteristics of performance at **Level 5**. An example of **Level 5** performance would be:
Le weekend dernier j'ai allé à la campagne à vélo, à 9 heures. J'ai nagé dans un lac et à midi et demi j'ai mange une pique-nique. Il fait soleil. C'était chouette.
Pupils failing to reach this level and who can communicate three or four points just using the present tense may be producing work more typical of **Level 4**.

At **Level 6** the time references should be clear and accurate and extra detail may be added. For example:
J'ai passé un très bon week-end! A 10h je suis parti(e) en ville en bus avec des copains. J'ai fait les magasins et à une heure moins le quart je suis allée chez McDo. J'ai pris un hamburger et après, j'ai acheté un pantalon rouge et à 4h je suis allé au cinéma. Le film, c'était génial. La journée ... c'était super!

At **Level 6**, pupils may be hesitant at times. Pupils who can relate at least five of the set points accurately and who can communicate as above are showing some characteristics of performance at **Level 6**.

C – Epreuve de lecture

Exercice 1

Pupils show understanding of four short texts based on work. They note likes, dislikes and main points. This tests elements of performance at **Level 3**. Total 9 marks.
Pupils scoring at least 7 marks are showing some characteristics of performance at **Level 3**.

Answers

Julien   **a**
Didier   **d**
Sandra   **c**
1 *vrai* **2** *faux* **3** *vrai* **4** *vrai* **5** *faux* **6** *vrai*

Exercice 2

Pupils show understanding of a factual text. They show understanding of both main points and details by choosing the appropriate word from the list. Accept incorrect spellings of the word, as long as the word is recognisable as being the correct one, as this is a test of reading comprehension, not writing skills. This tests elements of performance at **Level 4**. Total 5 marks.
Award ½ mark per correct word.
Pupils scoring at least 4 marks are showing some characteristics of performance at **Level 4**.

Answers

   2 *carte*
   3 *équipement*
   4 *confortables*
   5 *dos*
   6 *secours*
   7 *pique-nique*
   8 *boîte*
   9 *fruit*
  10 *bouteilles*
  11 *l'argent*

Exercice 3

Pupils show understanding of a handwritten letter to a friend which includes different time references. The exercise requires them to identify and note main points and specific details. This tests elements of performance at **Level 5**. Total 5 marks.
Pupils scoring at least 4 marks are showing some characteristics of performance at **Level 5**.

Answers

1a   **2**c   **3**b   **4**c   **5**a

Exercice 4

Pupils show understanding of an authentic source about a gymnast which includes different time references. They identify and note main points, specific detail and points of view. This necessitates some inference. Some unfamiliar language is also included in the text which requires deductive skills. Pupils have to correct incorrect statements which necessitates some writing in French. This tests elements of performance at **Level 6**.
Total 6 marks.
Pupils scoring at least 4 marks are showing some characteristics of performance at **Level 6**.

Answers

1 *faux* – accept either *Elle est venue habiter en France en 1993*, or *Elle a fait un stage en France en 1992*.
2 *faux* – *Elle habite au centre d'entraînement/à Marseille*. Acccept also *Ses parents habitent à la Réunion*.
3 *vrai*
4 *vrai*
5 *faux* – *Elle a participé aux Jeux d'Atlanta*.
6 *vrai*

D – Epreuve écrite

Exercice I

Here, pupils write five sentences on the topic area of pains in parts of the body, using a picture stimulus and one verbal stimulus (the example provided). They are therefore writing short phrases from memory, and the exercise therefore tests elements of performance at **Level 3**.
Total 5 marks.
Award 1 mark for each sentence. Do not penalise spelling errors as long as the French is 'readily understandable'. Award ½ mark if a sentence is only partially completed or if there is some doubt as to meaning.
Pupils scoring at least 3½ marks are showing some characteristics of performance at **Level 3**.

Exercice 2

In this exercise pupils are given a guided outline for writing five sentences and thereby composing a brief letter. It is based on future plans using the *aller +* infinitive construction. This tests performance at **Level 4** or **Level 5**, depending on the outcome provided by pupils.
Award 2 marks for each of the five stages of the letter. Spelling need not be perfect but should be readily understandable. Use an impression mark for each stage.
Total 10 marks.
Teachers should use their own judgements, but the following criteria are suggested:
2 marks – all elements pictured are included, using verb(s) in the correct tense and with a good standard of accuracy. An opinion or reaction is included for stages 2 and 5.
1½ marks – all elements are attempted, though there is a little doubt as to the meaning of some words.
1 mark – only some elements are attempted and/or there is doubt as to the meaning of some of the

French. Future tense is not attempted.
½ mark – there is only very partial success in rendering any of the elements of each stage. The verbs are not in the correct form. There is no reaction or opinion in stages 2 and 5.
Pupils scoring at least 7½ marks are showing some characteristics of performance at **Level 5**. A lower mark of 5 to 7 marks may indicate characteristics of performance at **Level 4**.

Exercice 3

Another letter, but in this case, although the five tasks are clearly laid out, pupils are free to express them as they wish. Support is provided, however, in the form of visual examples. This is an example of an informal letter requiring a range of tenses and giving pupils the opportunity to use their imagination, to include opinions etc.
Pupils need to be given separate paper to write their answers on.
This tests elements of performance at **Level 6** writing, but again the outcome will dictate the level it represents.
Total 10 marks.
Award up to 2 marks for each of the five tasks. The following criteria are suggested:
2 marks – the task is clearly and fully accomplished, with appropriate tenses and to a good standard of accuracy (tolerate minor errors).
1½ marks – the task is generally well accomplished, though with some errors which cast some doubt on meaning.
1 mark – the task is fairly well accomplished, though with a generally poor level of accuracy, impeding successful comprehension.
½ mark – limited success in accomplishing the task. Only a few correct items of vocabulary. Verbs confused.
In assessing the separate tasks, teachers may need to take into consideration the degree to which they are linked into a coherent letter.
Pupils scoring at least 7½ marks are showing some characteristics of performance at **Level 6**. A mark of 5 to 7 marks may indicate characteristics of performance at **Level 5**.

A – Epreuve d'écoute

Exercice 1

This exercise uses a fairly long passage spoken with a little hesitation and at near normal speed. Pupils pick out the words describing the characteristics of the members of a family. This is typical of performance at **Level 4**.

Total 4 marks.

Award ½ mark for each correctly selected letter. There are eight letters to select.

Pupils scoring at least 3 marks are showing some characteristics of performance at **Level 4**.

Answers

1 d; h; k   **2** i; a   **3** e; g; j

Note: the letters within each group can be written in any order.

COUNTER

> *Exercice 1*
> – *Yvette parle de sa famille. Lis les descriptions. Ecoute Yvette. Choisis les bonnes lettres.*
> *Exemple:*
> – *Alors ma famille … euh … mon frère, Luc, il a seize ans et il est grand. Il a les cheveux blonds et … euh … en général il est gentil.*
> – *Continue.*
> *Numéro un.*
> – *Et puis, euh, ma mère – oui, ma mère Marianne. Elle a quarante ans et elle est très petite. Elle a de beaux yeux bleus, ma mère, et elle est sympa – oui, très sympa.*
> – *Numéro deux.*
> – *Et mon frère, mon frère Bernard. Faut dire que je ne l'aime pas trop, mon frère, parce qu'il m'énerve. Il est très grand, aussi.*
> – *Numéro trois.*
> – *Mon père s'appelle Robert. Il a … quarante-sept ans, je crois. Il a les cheveux bruns et les yeux verts. Il est marrant, mon père – il raconte souvent des histoires stupides!*
> – *Ecoute Yvette encore une fois.*

Exercice 2

Here pupils write brief details in French about a young person's job. They first follow an example. Spelling of the French words should not be assessed, provided the meaning is clear enough to a French reader. It again has elements of performance at **Level 4**.

Total 6 marks.

Award 1 mark for each detail. Award ½ mark if the answer is not clear (i.e. impedes comprehension). Pupils scoring at least 4½ marks are showing some characteristics of performance at **Level 4**.

Answers

restaurant; vendredi et samedi; 7 heures; minuit; vaisselle; pas mal / assez bien

COUNTER

> *Exercice 2*
> – *Deux jeunes parlent de leur petit job. Ecoute Claude et regarde la grille.*
> – *Claude, tu as un petit job?*

> – *Oui oui. Je travaille dans un café – un grand café au centre-ville.*
> – *Et tu travailles quand?*
> – *Je travaille après l'école le lundi, le mardi et le mercredi.*
> – *Tu travailles après l'école, tu dis?*
> – *Oui, c'est ça. Je commence le travail à six heures et je finis à dix heures.*
> – *Ouf! Ca doit être dur, ça! Et on te paie bien?*
> – *Eh ben, pas mal – je reçois 25 francs de l'heure.*
> – *Et que penses-tu de ton petit job?*
> – *C'est formidable! Je l'aime bien!*
> – *Ecoute maintenant Fatima. Ecris les détails dans la grille.*
> – *Et Fatima. Tu travailles, toi aussi?*
> – *Oui. Je travaille au 'Petit Canard', un restaurant qui se trouve dans la banlieue de ma ville.*
> – *Tu travailles quels jours?*
> – *Le week-end – vendredi et samedi, quoi.*
> – *Et tu travailles de quelle heure à quelle heure?*
> – *Le soir, de sept heures jusqu'à minuit.*
> – *Et tu fais quelle sorte de travail? Tu sers les clients?*
> – *Non, malheureusement. Non, moi, je fais la vaisselle!*
> – *C'est pas très intéressant, ça! Qu'est-ce que tu en penses, toi?*
> – *C'est pas mal – assez bien, quoi!*
> – *Ecoute l'interview de Fatima encore une fois.*

Exercice 3

The text in the next exercise is now quite dense. It includes several topic areas and past, present and future events. Pupils identify specific details. This is typical of performance at **Level 5**.

Total 6 marks.

Award 1 mark for each correct answer.

Pupils scoring at least 5 marks are showing some characteristics of performance at **Level 5**.

Answers

1a   **2**b   **3**b   **4**a   **5**c   **6**a

COUNTER

> *Exercice 3*
> – *Un message de ton correspondant. Lis les questions. Ecoute ce message de Christophe, un correspondant français. Pour chaque question, choisis une réponse – a, b ou c.*
> – *Salut! C'est Christophe, ton correspondant français, qui te parle! J'espère que tu vas bien, et ta famille aussi. Le temps ici est mauvais – il pleut. Quel temps fait-il en Angleterre? Le week-end dernier, je suis allé à Paris avec mes parents. C'était formidable! Nous avons visité Notre Dame et Montmartre. Nous sommes montés aussi à la Tour Eiffel. C'était superbe, mais la vue n'était pas très bonne parce qu'il y avait un peu de brouillard.*
> *Aujourd'hui, je suis chez moi. Je ne vais pas à l'école parce que je suis un peu malade.*

Hier, j'avais mal à l'estomac et maintenant, j'ai mal à la tête. Je lis un peu, je joue sur l'ordinateur et je fais ce message pour toi. Pendant les vacances d'été, je vais aller en vacances en Espagne avec un groupe de mon école. Nous irons au bord de la mer sur la Costa Brava. Il va faire très chaud, j'espère! Je ne vais pas travailler du tout – je vais m'amuser!
Je dois terminer ce message maintenant. Maman a préparé le déjeuner et il faut que je mange quelque chose. Ciao!
– *Ecoute le message de Christophe encore une fois.*

Exercice 4

In this exercise there is a variety of short extracts including some unfamiliar language. It is a gist comprehension exercise in which pupils match what each speaker says with a particular problem. The language is spoken at normal speed, with natural hesitation and rephrasing. This exercise is typical of performance at **Level 6**.
Total 7 marks.
Award 1 mark for each correct answer.
Pupils scoring at least 5 marks show some characteristics of performance at **Level 6**.

Answers
1f **2**a **3**h **4**c **5**k **6**d **7**g

Exercice 4
– *Les problèmes des jeunes. Lis la liste des problèmes de **a** à **k**. Ecoute les jeunes. Pour chacun, choisis un des problèmes.*
Exemple:
– *Oh là là! Je souffre! J'ai la grippe depuis trois jours maintenant. Ça a commencé lundi, à l'école. Lundi soir je tremblais et j'avais mal à la gorge. Donc mardi, je ne suis pas allé à l'école et je suis resté au lit. Et ça continue! Je n'aime pas avoir la grippe!*
– *Continue.*
Numéro un.
– *Il y a plusieurs cours que je déteste. Les maths, par exemple, c'est trop dur, et je trouve l'histoire très ennuyeux. Il y a des profs qui sont sympas, mais il y en a d'autres qui ne s'intéressent pas du tout aux élèves. Et il faut en plus se lever si tôt le matin! Et tous ces devoirs! Ça ne me plaît pas du tout!*
– **Numéro deux.**
– *Avec mon frère ça va assez bien, quoi – on se marre bien ensemble. Et avec ma sœur – enfin, on se dispute de temps en temps mais en général ça va. Mais je ne me débrouille pas très bien avec mon père qui est très … distant, quoi. Et ma mère – eh bien elle, elle me traite comme un petit enfant de huit ans.*
– **Numéro trois.**
– *J'ai cherché partout. Je lis les petites annonces dans le journal et je téléphone, mais c'est toujours la même histoire – «Désolé mademoiselle, cette place a été prise.» Et j'ai écrit je ne sais pas combien de lettres!*

J'ai eu deux interviews, une dans un café et l'autre dans un magasin, mais je n'ai pas réussi. Tant pis – je trouverai peut-être quelque chose un de ces jours, mais pour l'instant, je n'ai rien.
– **Numéro quatre.**
– *Ça s'est passé hier, en route pour l'école. Je suis descendu du bus et je suis tombé – c'est bête, mais je suis tombé. Les autres ont ri de moi, j'ai essayé de ne pas faire attention, mais le problème, c'est que maintenant je trouve difficile de marcher. Aïe! J'ai vraiment de la peine à marcher, tu sais!*
– **Numéro cinq.**
– *D'habitude on va au bord de la mer. C'est bien d'y aller mais je commence à en avoir assez, quoi. J'aimerais mieux aller ailleurs – à la montagne, peut-être? Ou bien peut-être à l'étranger? J'ai jamais été en Angleterre et on dit que c'est bien là-bas. Enfin on verra – on n'a pas encore décidé.*
– **Numéro six.**
– *Je suis à Paris depuis trois mois maintenant et il faut dire que je ne suis pas très heureux parce que … enfin, quand j'habitais en Normandie j'avais beaucoup de copains, beaucoup de bons camarades, hein. Et puis on a dû déménager, à cause du travail de mon père, vous voyez … et … on est donc venu ici à Paris et … enfin, j'ai l'impression que personne ne s'intéresse à moi. Vraiment, je trouve les gens ici très froids, quoi.*
– **Numéro sept.**
– *Le problème, c'est qu'il n'y a rien à faire. Pas de clubs des jeunes, pas de disco. Deux ou trois cafés, mais ils sont moches. Et tout est si sale – c'est vraiment déprimant. Si seulement j'habitais … je ne sais pas, moi, Lyon, Nice, quelque part comme ça!*
– *Ecoute les jeunes encore une fois.*

Exercice 5

The final exercise, in which some questions are to be answered in French and some require the ticking of a box, uses a fairly complex passage spoken at normal speed in which two young people talk about future plans. Some of the language may be unfamiliar to the pupils. The exercise is typical of performance at **Level 7**.
Total 7 marks.
Award 1 mark for each answer. Complete sentences are not required and errors of French should not be penalised. As long as the meaning is clear (and is expressed in French) the mark should be given. Give ½ mark if there is some doubt as to the meaning or if the answer is only partly correct.
Pupils scoring at least 5 marks are showing some characteristics of performance at **Level 7**.

Sample correct answers
1 *se bronzer*
2 *Elle va avec ses parents*
3 c
4 *Elle part avec sa cousine.*
5 d
6 *Ils partent en vacances.*
7 *C'est bien / Ça lui plaît;*
or: *C'est fatigant.*

COUNTER

Exercice 5

- *Projets de vacances. Lis les questions. Ecoute l'interview de Joëlle et Luc. Réponds aux questions en français ou coche les bonnes cases.*
- *Eh bien, mes amis, c'est bientôt les grandes vacances, les vacances d'été, n'est-ce pas, et je voudrais savoir ce que vous avez l'intention de faire.*

Joëlle

Toi, Joëlle, pour commencer. Que vas-tu faire?
- *Eh bien moi, je vais partir en vacances en Provence – Nice – comme d'habitude.*
- *C'est bien, ça!*
- *Oui et non. Ce qui est bien, c'est qu'il fait généralement chaud là-bas à Nice, et j'aime bien me bronzer sur la plage – donc, de ce point de vue-là, c'est bien.*
- *Et qu'est-ce qui n'est pas bien, alors?*
- *Ben, ce qui n'est pas si bien, c'est que je dois partir avec mes parents.*
- *Donc tu n'aimes pas tes parents?*
- *Si, si – enfin, ça va pas mal, mes parents et moi, quoi. Mais c'est que j'aimerais mieux être avec mes copains. On part toujours au même endroit en vacances, mes parents et moi, et je dois les accompagner partout et tout le temps, vous voyez, donc ... euh ... ça devient un peu ennuyeux à la fin, quoi.*
- *Oui, d'accord. Je comprends.*
- *Mais remarquez, cette année, ça va être un peu différent peut-être.*
- *Ah bon! Pourquoi ça?*
- *Eh bien, cette année il y a aussi ma cousine Delphine qui va nous accompagner. Je m'entends bien avec Delphine, donc on va peut-être s'amuser ensemble.*
- *C'est bien. Merci, Joëlle.*

Luc

Luc, si je peux m'adresser à toi maintenant. Alors ... où vas-tu passer les grandes vacances? Tu pars au bord de la mer comme Joëlle?
- *Non. Je ne pars pas. Je reste chez moi.*
- *Ah bon. C'est dommage, ça. Tes parents n'ont pas assez d'argent pour aller en vacances, peut-être?*
- *Non, non. C'est pas ça. C'est qu'on préfère rester à la maison – enfin, on est obligé d'y rester. Nous avons un petit restaurant, vous voyez, qui est très populaire pendant les vacances d'été – il y a beaucoup de touristes – de vacanciers, qui viennent manger dans notre restaurant, donc ... euh ... on ne prend pas de vacances en été.*
- *Ah bon. Vous partez quand, alors?*
- *A Pâques en général.*
- *Et le travail de restaurant – ça te plaît ou non?*
- *Oui oui – enfin, c'est fatigant, bien sûr, mais oui – la plupart du temps, ça me plaît, le travail de restaurant.*
- *Ecoute l'interview encore une fois.*

B – Epreuve orale

Exercice 1

Pupils working in pairs choose one of the two *Fiches* and describe a friend, Corinne or Lionel. They relate information on the following points: age, (1 mark), description of hair (colour, length – 1 mark) and characteristic (cool, sporty – 1 mark), name and age (1 mark each) of brother/sister, favourite pastimes of friend (2 marks).
Total 7 marks.
This tests some characteristics of performance at both **Level 2** and **Level 3**.
At **Level 2**, short simple phrases to describe people are expected. At **Level 3**, more details can be given, including likes/dislikes and these may be cued with visual or verbal support as on the *Fiche*.
Pupils scoring at least 5 marks, including a mark for the favourite sport, are showing some characteristics of performance at **Level 3**. Pupils could be encouraged to substitute details about their own brother/sister. If they can adapt and substitute single words and phrases and if pronunciation is generally accurate they may be showing characteristics of performance at **Level 4**.

Exercice 2

Pupils work in pairs and choose one of the three places to go to. Only partner B is assessed (1 mark per task). The roles are then reversed and the new partner B is then assessed (on a different destination).
Total 4 marks.
This is a test intended to elicit some characteristics of performance at **Level 4** (pupils take part in simple structured conversations of at least three or four exchanges supported by visual or other cues).
Responses such as *On pourrait aller au bal-disco; Ça commence à 8 heures; Ça finit à 11h 30; Ça coûte 50 francs*, are examples of performance at **Level 4**.
Pupils gaining at least 3 marks and whose pronunciation is accurate and consistent are showing some characteristics of performance at **Level 4**.
It would also be possible to ask pupils to devise their own cue cards containing similar information. This would then test their ability to adapt and substitute words and phrases (also a characteristic of **Level 4** performance).
Pupils who give briefer answers *(11h30)* or who need prompting may be showing characteristics of performance more typical of **Level 3**.

Exercice 3

Pupils use a spider diagram as a stimulus for a mini presentation on pastimes. If preferred pupils can produce their own, provided that the verbal cues of *D'habitude, Le week-end dernier, Le week-end prochain* are retained, together with *où?, quand?* and *avec qui?*. This test is intended to elicit characteristics of performance at **Level 5** and **Level 6**.
Total 8 marks.
At **Level 5** pupils make an attempt to communicate details 'referring to recent experience, future plans as well as everyday activities and interests', but not always very accurately.
Pupils scoring at least 6 marks (1 mark per clear message) are showing some characteristics of performance at **Level 5**. An example of **Level 5** language would be:

D'habitude, je lis et je fais équitation. J'aime écouter la music. Le week-end dernier j'ai allé au bowling samedi matin et j'ai fait de vélo avec mes amis. Le week-end prochain je vais nager et le soir je vais danse.

There are mistakes, but the messages are communicated. An attempt is made to use tense correctly.

At **Level 6**, at least six items of information are clearly, and usually accurately, communicated. The time references should be clear and pupils can make themselves understood with little difficulty. They may improvise and paraphrase and add extra detail. An example of **Level 6** language would be:

Comme passetemps, moi, j'aime aller à la patinoire et faire de l'équitation à la campagne avec mes amis. J'aime aussi écouter de la musique chez moi. Le week-end dernier j'ai fait des achats en ville et samedi soir je suis allée au bowling avec mes copains. Dimanche je me suis bien amusée – j'ai fait du vélo, c'était chouette. Le week-end prochain je vais nager et samedi soir je vais aller à la discothèque.

Exercice 4

Pupils make a presentation about where they live based on 4 cues which ask them to describe where they live (2 marks), to describe the sporting possibilities and attractions – or lack of them – (2 marks), to give an opinion and justification of this opinion about where they live (2 marks) and to outline a change they would make (1 mark). Preparation time could be given either in class or at home. This is a test intended to elicit characteristics of performance at **Level 7**.

At **Level 7** pupils should be able to 'give and justify opinions when discussing matters of personal or topical interest'. At this level, pronunciation and intonation should be good and the language should be accurate. An example of **Level 7** language would be:

J'habite une assez grande ville dans le nord de l'Angleterre. (1) *C'est une vieille ville avec une belle cathédrale et beaucoup de monuments touristiques.* (1) *Il y a un grand centre commercial et beaucoup de magasins.* (2 marks already scored on point 1, but at this level pupils will often add detail.) *Il y a beaucoup de possibilités sportives. On peut aller à la piscine, jouer au tennis et faire du bowling.* (1) *Pour les jeunes il y a des cinémas et des discothèques.* (1) *Moi j'adore habiter ici, c'est chouette.* (1) *C'est une vieille et belle ville mais le centre-ville est moderne* (1) *avec des magasins intéressants et j'adore faire du shopping.* (1) *Mais je n'aime pas la circulation – moi, je propose moins de circulation et moins de voitures dans le centre-ville.* (1)

Pupils scoring at least 6 marks and who are able to give and justify opinions are showing some characteristics of performance at **Level 7**. Pupils not able to give and justify opinions but who can otherwise communicate details on the above points may be showing characteristics of performance more typical of **Level 6**.

Exercice 5

Pupils prepare responses to the four cues on the topic of part time jobs. Ideally, the teacher should ask the questions as this enables the extent to which the pupil can cope with the unpredictable element in the question on the second cue, which is a characteristic

of performance at **Level 8**, to be ascertained. If this is impractical in terms of organisation, the teacher could copy the questions below on to OHT and pupils could then work in pairs. If working in pairs partner B should ask the questions and should start the conversation.

1 *Que fais-tu comme travail?*
2 *Tu gagnes combien d'argent?*
3 *Quand as-tu commencé à faire ce travail?*
4 *Bon … et que penses-tu de ton travail?*

This tests some characteristics of performance at **Level 8**.

Total 4 marks.

At this level, the language should be accurate and pupils should speak confidently with good pronunciation and intonation. They should be able to cope with unpredictable elements (Task 2) and use time references correctly (e.g. a perfect tense in Task 3). On tasks which have two elements, both should be completed for the mark to be awarded.

Pupils scoring at least 3 marks, including response to the upredictable element, are showing some characteristics of performance at **Level 8**.

Again, the teacher should use his/her judgement to assess performance if pupils do not rise to this level. Pupils communicating accurately and using a perfect tense may be showing more characteristics of performance at **Level 6** or **Level 7**.

C – Epreuve de lecture

Exercice I

Pupils show understanding of sentences which build up to complete a short text on the subject of everyday activities. Pupils identify and note main points by re-ordering the letters so as to make a correct and logical sequence. Two letters (f and g) are given as examples to provide extra help.

Total 6 marks.

Award 1 mark for a letter in the correct box.

Pupils scoring at least 5 marks are showing some characteristics of performance at **Level 3**.

Answers

(Exemple: f) d b a (Exemple: g) c h e

Exercice 2

Pupils show understanding of a factual text on the topic of how young people spend money. They show understanding of both main points and details by choosing the appropriate word from the list. Accept incorrect spellings of the word as long as the word is recognisable as being the correct one, as this is a test of reading comprehension, not writing skills. This tests elements of performance at **Level 4**.

Total 5 marks.

Award 1/2 mark per correct word.

Pupils scoring at least 3 marks are showing some characteristics of performance at **Level 4**.

Answers

2	*poche*	7	*vêtements*
3	*confiserie*	8	*parents*
4	*achètent*	9	*enfants*
5	*musique*	10	*jouets*
6	*plus*		

Exercice 3

Pupils show understanding of a handwritten letter to a friend which includes different time references. They identify and note main points, specific detail and opinion. This tests elements of performance at **Level 5**.
Total 6 marks.
Pupils scoring at least 4 marks are showing some characteristics of performance at **Level 5**.

Answers

1c 2b 3b 4c 5b 6a

Exercice 4

Pupils show understanding of an authentic article about a young *raï* singer, which includes familiar language in an unfamiliar context. They identify and note main points and specific detail, including points of view. This necessitates some inference. This tests elements of performance at Level 6.
Total 6 marks.
Pupils tick the *vrai/faux* box as appropriate and correct the false statements. If a statement is false it must be corrected to gain the mark. Full sentences are not required. Inaccuracies should be tolerated provided that the message is clear.
Pupils scoring at least 4 marks are showing some characteristics of performance at **Level 6**.

Answers

1   *Faux. Il parle de l'amour.*
2   *Vrai.*
3   *Faux. Il a entendu le raï à la télévision/par des cassettes*
4   *Vrai.*
5   *Faux. On travaille beaucoup.*
6   *Faux. Il rêve d'être un grand chanteur.* Accept also: *Il a déjà une grande famille.*

Exercice 5

Pupils show understanding of different viewpoints on the subject of being the eldest child in a family, taken from an authentic source. Some complete sentences and unfamiliar vocabulary feature in the four texts (typical features of **Level 7**). Pupils also recognise attitudes and emotions (typical features of **Level 8**) and need to make use of skills such as inference and reformulation or use of synonyms in order to answer the questions. The topic, however, is familiar (**Level 7**). A similar type of exercise, testing similar skills, using similar language and questions but also including one or two extracts on unfamiliar topics would raise the level of difficulty to **Level 8**. This therefore is a test of characteristics more typical of performance at **Level 7**.
Total 7 marks.
Pupils scoring at least 6 marks are showing some characteristics of performance at **Level 7**.

Answers

1	*Laura*	5	*Laura*
2	*Edouard*	6	*Julie*
3	*Amélie*	7	*Edouard*
4	*Julie*		

D – Epreuve écrite

Exercice I

Here, pupils use visual cues to construct six sentences on opinions about places in the town. This is typical of performance at **Level 3**.
Total 6 marks.
Award 1 mark for each sentence. Spelling should be 'readily recognisable'. Award ½ mark for partial completion of a sentence or if there is some doubt as to meaning.
Pupils scoring at least 4 marks are showing some characteristics of performance at **Level 3**.

Exercice 2

In the next exercise, pupils are again required to construct sentences based on visual stimuli, though the stimuli are more varied than in the previous exercise. Topics include activities, time, family, transport and rooms in the house. It is again typical of performance at **Level 3**, moving towards **Level 4**.
Pupils may use a dictionary for this exercise.
Total 6 marks.
Award 1 mark for each sentence. Accept approximate spellings. Award ½ mark for partial completion or unclear meaning as above.
Pupils scoring at least 4 marks are again showing some characteristics of performance at **Level 3**, though a high standard of writing could be considered to be typical of **Level 4** performance.

Sample correct answers

1   *Je joue au basket avec mes amis.*
2   *Je regarde la télévision à neuf heures.*
3   *Je prends (mange) le dîner avec ma famille.*
4   *Je vais aux magasins en autobus.*
5   *Je fais mes devoirs dans ma chambre.*
6   *Je me couche à dix heures et demie.*

Exercice 3

This exercise gives pupils the opportunity to show characteristics of performance at **Level 5** or **Level 6**. They may make use of dictionaries.
Pupils need to be given separate paper to write their answers on.
Total 6 marks.
It is suggested that teachers assess pupils' performance in bands as follows:
5/6 marks – full account, using appropriate tenses and including opinions, to a generally good standard of accuracy which does not impede meaning.
3/4 marks – fairly full account, verbs generally recognisable as being in the past tense. Opinions may have been omitted. There are certain errors which make the meaning unclear.
1/2 marks – little attempt to convey the material; verbs poor; mistakes impede comprehension.
Pupils scoring 5/6 marks are showing some characteristics of performance at **Level 6**.
Those scoring 3/4 marks demonstrate some characteristics of performance at **Level 5**.

Exercice 4

Pupils write a reply to a letter containing a number of questions. The letter is in an informal style and requires use of present, past and future tenses. This is typical of performance at **Level 6** or **Level 7** (depending on outcome). Pupils may use dictionaries. Pupils need to be given separate paper to write their answers on.

The scheme suggested for Exercice 3 can again be followed, though including pupils' success in answering four or five of the questions (for 5/6 marks), two or three of the questions (for 3/4 marks) or only one question (for 1/2 marks).
Pupils scoring 5/6 marks are showing some characteristics of performance at **Level 7**. Those scoring 3/4 marks demonstrate performance at **Level 6**.

Exercice 5
The final exercise gives pupils the opportunity to write at length imaginatively on an imaginary subject. The way in which pupils deal with the subject will determine the level of performance. They may make use of dictionaries.
Pupils need to be given separate paper to write their answers on.
Total 6 marks.
Again pupils should be assessed in bands.
5/6 marks – the most able pupils will write at length imaginatively and to a good standard of accuracy. They will include their opinion as requested.
3/4 marks – a fair attempt to cover the details about the school but with only limited expression of opinions and with a certain amount of inaccuracy.
1/2 marks – very limited success in conveying the details and a poor standard of accuracy.
Pupils scoring 5/6 marks are showing some characteristics of performance at **Level 7**. Those scoring 3/4 marks show some characteristics of performance at **Level 6**.